BODY LANGUAGE
A GUIDE for PROFESSIONALS

3 REVISED EDITION

Thank you for choosing a SAGE product! If you have any comment, observation or feedback, I would like to personally hear from you. Please write to me at contactceo@sagepub.in

—Vivek Mehra, Managing Director and CEO,
SAGE Publications India Pvt Ltd, New Delhi

Bulk Sales

SAGE India offers special discounts for purchase of books in bulk. We also make available special imprints and excerpts from our books on demand.

For orders and enquiries, write to us at

Marketing Department
SAGE Publications India Pvt Ltd
B1/I-1, Mohan Cooperative Industrial Area
Mathura Road, Post Bag 7
New Delhi 110044, India
E-mail us at marketing@sagepub.in

Get to know more about SAGE, be invited to SAGE events, get on our mailing list. Write today to marketing@sagepub.in

This book is also available as an e-book.

BODY LANGUAGE
A GUIDE for PROFESSIONALS

3 REVISED EDITION

HEDWIG LEWIS

$SAGE | Response Business Books

www.sagepublications.com

Los Angeles • London • New Delhi • Singapore • Washington DC • Boston

First published in 1998
Second edition published in 2000
This third edition published in 2012 by

SAGE Response
B1/I-1 Mohan Cooperative Industrial Area
Mathura Road, New Delhi 110 044, India

SAGE Publications Inc
2455 Teller Road
Thousand Oaks, California 91320, USA

SAGE Publications Ltd
1 Oliver's Yard, 55 City Road
London EC1Y 1SP, United Kingdom

SAGE Publications Asia-Pacific Pte Ltd
3 Church Street
#10-04 Samsung Hub
Singapore 049483

Published by Vivek Mehra for SAGE Publications India Pvt Ltd, typeset in 10/13pt Palatino Linotype by Star Compugraphics Private Limited, Delhi and printed at Chaman Enterprises, New Delhi.

Second Printing 2015

Library of Congress Cataloging-in-Publication Data Available

ISBN: 978-81-321-0720-0 (PB)

The SAGE Team: Rudra Narayan, Anupam Choudhury, Rajib Chatterjee, and Rajinder Kaur
Illustrations: Nishith Mehta

Contents

Preface to the Third Edition

Body language is a by-word in the world of today. It is the X-factor or the USP (Unique Selling Proposition) that completes the personalities of professionals, performers on screen and field, of politicians, celebrities and talk-show hosts, of models on the ramp or on the road, in public speaking and presentations. The list goes on.

One shows no surprise when a new book on body language appears on a publisher's list or a shop window. One only hopes to find in it new insights and updated references to expand ones body language 'vocabulary', fluency, and expertise.

Given this general consciousness in the language of the body, and the thumping success of the previous edition, the publishers felt it was time to upgrade *Body Language: A Guide for Professionals*. The author has painstakingly combed through the existing text in order to append new insights in several areas of the book, especially with more practical hints on some topics. It provides what in technical terms would be called 'soft skills' in communication.

Since the last edition of this book a decade ago, the internet and media have brought renewed interest to non-verbal communication, particularly to Body Language. Institutes of management, business, and human resources have included the study and practice of body language as a 'Soft Skill' in their syllabi and training programmes. The traditional topics dealing with the different parts of the body remain, but they have been more widely discussed and made easily accessible through the internet.

The author has surfed the internet to his heart's content and has embellished the present volume with his discoveries. The structure of this new edition has been changed a great deal; each chapter is replenished with details that make for depth, clarity, and greater comprehensiveness. There are several new dimensions added to a topic, with the inclusion of modern-day observations of human behaviour and body-talk. Care has been taken to include typical Indian gestures where relevant. Each chapter has a set of wide-ranging insights. Perhaps the only 'new' inclusion is 'Body Language in Sleep', research findings of which have become popular after the previous edition of this book was published.

All in all, this edition has been expanded so as to make the theories more experiential—and popular.

Preface to the Second Edition

It would not be too much of an exaggeration to declare that today 'body language' is a household word. The media: print (newspapers, magazines), visual (movies, TV), and electronic (internet), draw attention to body language every now and then, be it with respect to sportspersons, film stars, fashion models, or politicians. The postures, gestures, physical movements of 'these public personalities', the media demonstrates, expose much more than their words do, and often betray their deeper intentions and real motives.

In the recent past, the study of body language has gained in importance and popularity. One assuring evidence of this is the overwhelming response to the first edition of this book; it was demanding enough to justify an updated version. And hence this volume.

Readers of the first edition will notice significant additions to the present volume. Various definitions have been elaborated and technical terms have been updated or further clarified. Finer points regarding facial expressions and 'time' as a factor in non-verbal communication have been dealt with.

There are a few novel entries on sartorial fashions and ornamental accessories which, given our repeated successes at global fashion contests, are making a louder 'statement' than ever before, on the body as an ambassador of one's inner self. There are special blocks of information and illustrations on body language in business, including corporate etiquette, sales interactions, and spatial arrangements. There is a new section on 'Personology': the scientific reading of the faces based on genetics, as also on body types. The bibliographical list has been expanded. The illustrations have been entirely revised and redone, and the format also changed.

I do hope readers will find the revised and updated edition even more useful and appealing.

Preface to the First Edition

When we encounter people, we usually look first at their face to see if their expression reflects what they are saying. Then we listen to the tone of their voice to check if there are any indications of the emotions involved. Finally, we actually listen to the spoken words. Even if these are cynical or sarcastic, we will accept them as a joke if the speaker's face is jovial and happy.

Practically all the judgements we make—about people being merry or moody, nice or nasty, amicable or hostile, frank or secretive, secure or shy, and so on—are generally based on the cues we have received from their non-verbal and visual rather than verbal communication. According to a pioneer in the field of non-verbal communication, Professor Ray Birdwhistell, 'More human communication took place by the use of *gestures, postures, position* and *distance* than by any other way.'

Body language is powerful and indispensable in communication. Our verbal descriptions would fall flat without non-verbal accompaniments. Further, they would be shallow, unexciting, and inaccurate, too. As someone put it, 'No matter where we look, non-verbal communication is at the heart of every message conveyed or received whether in face-to-face encounters, or over the telephone.'

In other words, we can exude relaxation, confidence, and warmth in any situation, with appropriate and powerful non-verbal communication. Moreover, by extending our arms, raising our eyebrows, or nodding our heads, we can make our points even more succinct and dramatic as we communicate with those we can see or those we cannot (telephone conversation).

This book contains a sufficient amount of theory to understand a concept, with illustrations that provide the necessary cues for visual representation. We begin with an overview. The first chapter consists of a set of important background material necessary for obtaining a complete picture of body language. The rest of the chapters deal sequentially in individual gestures and gesture clusters, zones and spaces, traits and attitudes, and the role of body language in job interviews. The book concludes with a general practice session.

The book is so structured that its contents can be accessed expediently. The topics are presented systematically; hence particular gestures can be located and referred to easily and efficiently. The 'professional' who uses this book will find it handy to both check and confirm the meaning and interpretation of a gesture or gesture cluster.

The objectives of the work are clear. It will serve as a working manual in our personal encounters with people—individuals as well as groups. It will be a useful tool in the hands of managers and subordinates in an office set-up, marketing executives on their rounds, teachers, parents, and especially those who are in the 'helping professions'—nurses, counsellors, social workers, and so on.

In fact, the book should appeal to *everyone*, since we are all social beings whose primary focus in life is on interaction with others at various levels. We all spend much of our working life in face-to-face encounters with others. The book will sharpen our perception in several ways to make relationships and interactions more fruitful.

This book is the outcome of research, personal observation, and seminars. I am particularly indebted to the core group of Advance-'*PROBE'RS* (Personal Resources and Organizational Behaviour Effectiveness Programme) at St. Xavier's College, Ahmedabad, for their involvement in the course on body language. I am grateful to Frs V. Ishanand, J. A. Arroyo, V. Braganza, Devasia M., and Ms Mrinalini Sarabhai for providing relevant resource material, and especially to Fr Robert Arokiasamy who so graciously video-taped the 'models' and computerized the illustrations (for the first edition), to Fr M. A. Kulandairaj who did the computer setting, and to Mr Pratap Kumar for his valuable suggestions. Special thanks to the 'models': Vinita Bhansali, Hem Gandhi, Leo John, Ruchi Mishra, Sonal Ramrakhiani, Namita Shekhawat, Dina Thomas, Kamakshya Trivedi, and Vincent Varghese.

Preliminary Tests

TEST ONE

This is a simple test. Look at each of the following figures carefully and tick one of the statements below it, which, according to you, is the correct interpretation of it.

1.

(a) Where is the book?

(b) Can you get me *that* file?

2.

(a) My fingers are sticky.

(b) It is only this small.

3.

(a) My fingers are itching.

(b) I need some cash.

4.

(a) Are you up or down?

(b) May I use your telephone?

5.

(a) You are a loser.

(b) Look at the people behind me.

6.

(a) Where is my pen?

(b) Come closer.

7.

(a) There are two of them.

(b) We have won!

8.

(a) You are a frog.
(b) The jar is quite big.

9.

(a) Don't hold it tight.
(b) Please give me a few minutes more.

TEST TWO

What finger/hand movements do you do when you want to communicate something to somebody without using words? Answer the following in a sentence:

1. What time do you have on your watch?
2. Can you give me four marbles please?
3. Where are you going?
4. It's OK. You've done a fine job.
5. Namaste!
6. I will punch you in the face.
7. Come here quickly.
8. Stop!
9. That boy is very tall.

TEST THREE

Presented below are a set of 'faces'. Identify the emotions listed below to match the expressions in order.

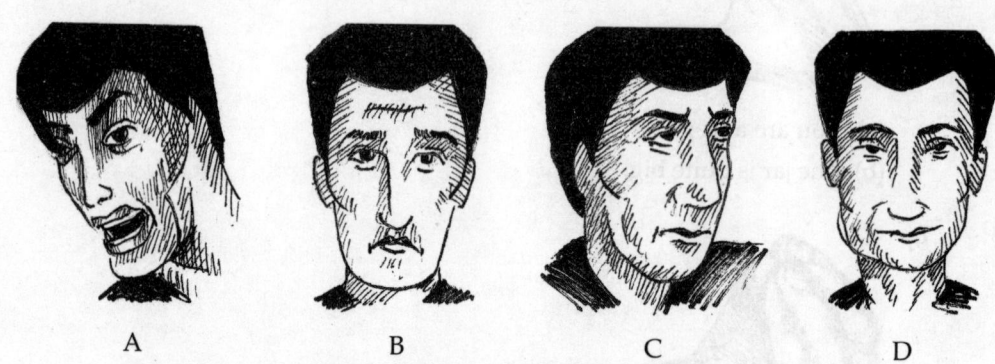

A   B   C   D

Surprise—Anger—Guilt—Happiness—Sadness—Disgust.

TEST FOUR

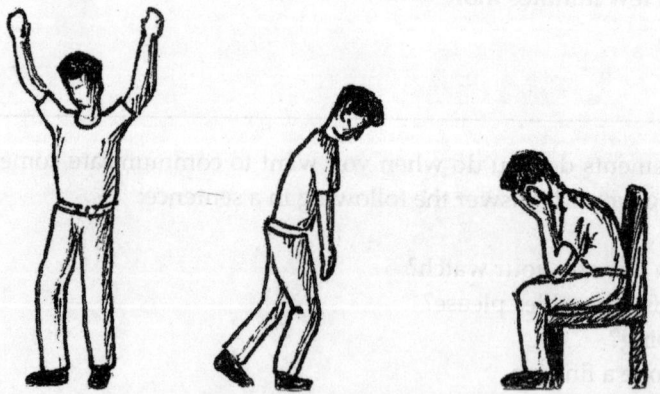

What feelings do the above postures suggest?

ANSWERS

Test One

The statement (b) in all figures is the right interpretation.

Test Two

Possible finger/hand movements:

1. What time do you have on your watch?
   Tapping your wrist with your index finger.
2. Can you give me four marbles please?
   Holding up four fingers.
3. Where are you going?
   Twisting your upturned wrist.
4. It's OK. You've done a fine job.
   Touching the tip of your thumb and index finger to form an *O*.
5. Namaste!
   Placing your palms together and holding them in front of your body.
6. I will punch you in the face.
   Making a fist and thrusting it forward.
7. Come here quickly.
   Stretching out your hand and moving your fingers in quick movements inward to your palms.
8. Stop!
   Raising the flat palm of your hands outward.
9. That boy is very tall.
   Stretching out your hand (palms open and facing down) and raising it at some level from the floor to indicate height.

Test Three

A. Anger; B. Sadness; C. Guilt; D. Happiness.

Test Four

Joy, Tired, Depressed.

If you have got most of them correct, you can pat your back. You are quite observant of body language. You may now realize that there is no great mystery or mystique about body language. All humans use it and have a 'built-in' ability to recognize and read it. Unfortunately, since we have become increasingly better at 'verbal' communication, our ability to consciously recognize body language has been taken for granted.

If you have got many incorrect answers, you are poor in reading body language.

This book will help you sharpen your skills at reading body language.

Body language is instinctively interpreted by us all to a limited degree, but the subject is potentially immensely complex. Perhaps infinitely so, given that the human body is said to be capable of producing 700,000 different movements (Hartland and Tosh, 2001).

OBJECTIVES OF THIS BOOK

To demonstrate the extent to which people communicate non-verbally.

To identify the major sources of non-verbal messages.

To discuss facts related to an accurate decoding of non-verbal messages.

Objectives for Studying Non-verbal Communication

1. *To gain an insight and awareness* of the various non-verbal signals used in our communication with others, so that we can modify our behaviour so that it has a positive impact.
2. *To master the skills* of non-verbal communication so as to easily 'read' the body language of others and respond to it appropriately or adequately.
3. *To apply the skills* of non-verbal communication so as to make the total communication process more functional, since we speak two 'languages' concurrently: the verbal and non-verbal. Our speech is generally accompanied by gestures, facial expressions, and body movements, which change from moment to moment. We can thus respond at both levels.
4. *To comprehend the impact of non-verbal messages*, which far exceeds that of any given vocal transaction, dialogue, or conversation between persons, so as to make communication more effective.
5. *To become aware of and monitor our own non-verbal behaviour* so that we send out the right 'signals' and decode the signals we receive from others more accurately. Non-verbal communication tools can be used to transmit our own ideas, feelings, and desires in such a manner that people will understand us and respond in a way we intend them to. Besides, we can prevent misunderstanding by accurate decoding, by being more objectively perceptive, and by being able to distinguish a signal from a mannerism.
6. *To establish rapport with others* by perceiving their body language to know what pleases or offends them. We can anticipate the reactions of others to specific situations, break through their defences, and influence their decisions in a positive manner. By being aware of our own body language, we can check the impact of our own intervention—as to whether we are inadvertently precipitating in the reactions by others.
7. *To bring out into the open, to the conscious level*, our subconscious motivations and to understand them more concretely. This will also help us to become more deeply empathic towards others.

Chapter 1

The Characteristics of Body Language

WHAT IS BODY LANGUAGE?

Introduction

Body language is the communication of personal feelings, emotions, attitudes, and thoughts through body movements—gestures, postures, positions, and distance, either consciously or involuntarily, more often subconsciously, and accompanied or unaccompanied by the spoken language.

Simply put, body language is the way in which we 'express' ourselves through the different parts of our body. It can be compared to the ordinary language we speak, known as 'verbal language', where we express our ideas and needs through words. Body language is communication without words; it is 'non-verbal' and expresses itself through the movements and gestures of our head, face, eyes, hands, legs, and so on. It is 'language' in the sense that just as verbal language is guided by 'grammar' and 'styles', that is, rules and patterns of speaking and writing which are universally accepted, so does body language. There are 'universal' or common body movements, signs, and gestures that are understood by everybody anywhere in the world. For instance, pressing the upward-pointing index finger to your tightly shut lips to order people to be quiet, for silence.

Everything is body language: tone of voice, clearing our throats, rubbing our eyes, touching our nose—everything except the words we say. Eye contact, or lack of it, pauses, crossed legs, open hands, aroma, and in particular, our appearance, hairstyle, type of eye glasses, accessories, tattoos, and over-all choice of attire, communicate.

In other words, body language is the way people unconsciously telegraph their private thoughts and emotions through body movements—the manner in which they fold their arms, cross their legs, sit, stand, walk, use their hips, eyes, and even in the subtle way they move their lips. Certain gestures like touching the nose, rubbing the eye, clearing the throat, pausing while speaking, even the clothes and scent one wears 'speak louder' than words.

Body language is indispensable for sportsmen, entertainers, models, and people in the public eye. However, body language is not limited to celebrities and public personalities. It is part and parcel of everyday life. It is necessary for healthy relations among family and friends; for teachers, in order to make their classes livelier; for students, to be more active

1

mentally and physically in class and at study; for superiors and subjects, managers and employees. In fact, body language affects life at all levels.

Most of us 'pick up' body language just as we do the language we speak, subconsciously, from infancy. We learn both these 'languages' in an unstructured way—without knowing the rules. Only later, through our parents at home and our teachers in school are we taught the elements of verbal language and its correct usage.

We do read body language by default, as it were. We know through the gestures and postures of a person's body whether the person is excited, worried, or calling for help. We have 'learnt' to read these physical 'signs' or 'signals' through observation and experience, through trial and error. Much research has been done by experts in the field of non-verbal communication. We can now study their findings and learn to interpret body language more correctly and accurately. This will help us to understand what our own body is 'telling' us about our moods, attitudes, as well as help us in relating more smoothly with others, by using behaviours that can help instead of hurt in certain circumstances from the 'non-verbal messages' we receive.

The key to using effective body language is understanding how your expressions, gestures, eye contact, use of space, postures, and all the other aspects of non-verbal communication will *most likely* be interpreted by others—and how those interpretations will *most likely* effect the observers' behaviour.

Understanding Body Language

We 'talk' with our bodies all the time, even more than we do when we speak with words. Often, without our being conscious of it, the different parts of our body, like our hands, legs, eyes, lips, and so on, send out messages through the movements they make. Thus, they reveal our thoughts and emotions.

When someone speaks, you listen not only to the words but also observe the speaker's 'body movements', because you know that these matter a great deal. You interpret the words according to the clues the body provided. Different people may say the same things but their words take on varied meanings depending on the movements of the different parts of their body. Others do the same when *you* speak; they observe your body movements, which inadvertently provide cues to the real meanings of your words.

Through body language you can almost read a person's mind, and the person reads your mind, almost! When those who are conversant with body language realize that their body movements are being read by someone, they may try and control their body so as to physically emphasize through actions what they are communicating through words: for example, people bang the table with their fist while shouting 'silence'. Or, they may intentionally fake their body movements to send out signals that are contrary to what they are thinking. They may do this either to hide their true intentions and feelings or to mislead the other person.

Mehrabian (1971), one of the foremost experts in non-verbal communication, conducted a study on the relationships among the three main elements of communication: the verbal, the vocal, and the visual. The verbal refers to the words that are spoken, the message. The vocal refers to the intonation, projection, and resonance of the voice through which the message is conveyed. The visual depicts the non-verbal behaviour while speaking.

Mehrabian's research findings, in fact, focused on communications with a strong emotional or 'feelings' element. His equation:

Total Liking = 7% Verbal Liking (words) + 38% Vocal Liking (tone of voice, inflection) + 55% Facial Liking (non-verbal physical behaviour)

Mehrabian cautions: 'This and other equations regarding relative importance of verbal and nonverbal messages were derived from experiments dealing with communications of feelings and attitudes (like–dislike). Unless a communicator is talking about their feelings or attitudes, these equations are not applicable.' Care must, therefore, be exercised when stating specific figures relating to percentages of meaning conveyed or in making any firm claims in relation to body language and non-verbal communications.

What Mehrabian is saying in effect is that words are only part of a message, but they are a vital part. We also communicate through body language and tone of voice. Non-verbals support the words by conveying the speaker's feelings. When speaking about feelings and attitudes, and there is a mismatch between the words and the body language, we tend to put more trust in the non-verbals. If we have only words, it is possible to misunderstand the emotion behind the words.

It is safe to say that body language represents a very significant proportion of meaning that is conveyed and interpreted between people. Many body language experts and sources seem to agree that that between 50 and 80 per cent of all human communications are non-verbal. So while body language statistics vary according to situation, it is generally accepted that non-verbal communications are very important in how we understand each other (or fail to), especially in face-to-face and one-to-one communications, and most definitely when the communications involve an emotional or attitudinal element (see Businessballs, 2011).

The visual is the most controllable and yet perhaps the most unconscious element of the message from sender to receiver. If the message is consistent, all three elements combine effectively. There is excitement and enthusiasm in the voice, correlated with an energetic, lively face, and body that exudes confidence and the conviction of the message.

How Does Body Language Function?

Words are used for conveying information and our body language communicates the strength and credibility of those words. Body language reveals a person's emotional attitude and/or condition.

In reality, we speak volumes even before we open our mouth. Our facial features, actions, attire, and other non-verbal cues give receivers an impression often more powerful than words alone can create. A striking example of this is when two people meet for the first time. Their initial reaction is to size up each other by observing appearance, attire, facial expression, handshake, and posture. This initial preoccupation, according to Honey (1988) creates an 'information overload'. They are so busy mentally processing all the visual behaviours and non-verbal cues that each is 'radiating' that they fail to register each other's names.

The Five Primary Functions of Non-verbal Behaviour Are

1. *Expression of Emotion*: Emotions are expressed mainly through the face, body, and voice.
2. *Communication of Interpersonal Attitudes*: The establishment and maintenance of relationships if often done through non-verbal signals (tone of voice, gaze, touch, and so on).
3. *Accompany and Support Speech*: Vocalization and non-verbal behaviours are synchronized with speech in conversation (nodding one's head or using phrases like 'uh-huh' when another is talking).
4. *Self-presentation*: Presenting oneself to another through non-verbal attributes like appearance.
5. *Rituals*: The use of greetings, handshakes, or other rituals (Argyle, 1988).

Non-verbal Messages Can

- *Emphasize*: We say 'Yes' and nod our head at the same time to project a strong affirmative.
- *Regulate, Manage, and Control*: Through our actions the communication event.
- *Contradict* verbal messages: A 'wink' may contradict a stated positive message.
- *Complements* what is said verbally: A nod reinforces a positive message.
- *Repeat*: We point in a direction while stating directions.
- *Substitute*: Without speaking, we may use a gesture alone to transmit a message. For example, put a finger to lips to indicate need for quiet, nod instead of a yes.
- *Indicate status relationships*.

- *Accentuate*: They may accentuate or underline a verbal message. Pounding the table, for example, can underline a message. Verbal tone indicates the actual meaning of the specific words.

We are constantly transmitting non-verbal signals. 'You cannot not communicate even if you try ... Sometimes you'll see people let a gesture slip out that contradicts what they're saying' (Walton, 1989). At other times, gestures help the verbal message.

VERBAL AND NON-VERBAL COMMUNICATION

What Is Non-verbal Communication?

Communication is generally defined as having both a verbal and a non-verbal component. Whereas verbal communication often refers to the words we use in communication, non-verbal communication refers to communication that is produced by some means other than words (eye contact, body language, or vocal cues, for example) (Knapp and Hall, 2002).

Non-verbal refers to all stimuli (except meaningful words) generated by the individuals in a communicative set-up. These non-verbal messages may be intentional or unintentional. All cultures have their own system for understanding body movements, so there will be differences across cultures.

Anderson (1997) summarizes 'intercultural differences' under the following headings: Time; Space; Gestures and Facial Expressions; Touch; Dress, Grooming, Adornments, Uniforms, Head Coverings; Eye Contact, Blinks, Movement, Pupil Dilation; Vocal inflections—'Paralanguage'; Music, Singing, Dancing; Smells.

Non-verbal communication is often referred to under several technical terms. 'Proxemics' deals with the use of space in communication. Space falls into four categories: intimate, personal, social, and public. There are many factors that define the use of space: age, gender, cultural and ethical backgrounds, personality, physical characteristics, attitudes, emotions of people, interpersonal dynamics. 'Oculesics' has to do with eye contact and behaviour, 'haptics' with the use of touch, 'vocalics' with tonal quality of the voice, 'kinesics' with body movements, and 'objectics' with the use of objects in communication.

Conventional Dimensions of Non-verbal Communication

The following dimensions will be discussed within the course of this book.

- Physical Appearance
- Territory and Personal Space (Proxemics)

- Facial Expressions
- Gestures and Posture
- Touch (Tactile Communication)
- Eye Contact

BODY LANGUAGE AS 'LANGUAGE'

Similarities between Body Language and Verbal Language

Body language, as the term suggests, has several properties of ordinary verbal language. Verbal language consists of words, sentences, and punctuation. Similarly, body language consists of individual gestures ('words') that can be grouped together into a logical cluster ('sentence') to give meaning to particular behaviour of body movements, where individual gestures and posture may 'punctuate' others by vocalizations or pauses while one speaks.

Birdwhistell (1952) discovered a number of 'kinesic markers' that supplement the linguistic markers. When a person asks a question, for instance, 'What is it?', his head comes up on 'it'. Just as the voice rises at the end of a question, similarly the head also moves up. The hand tends to move with the rise in pitch, in a meaningless gesture; the eyelids open wider with the last note of the question. When a speaker intends to continue his statement, his voice will hold the same pitch, and his head will remain straight, and the position of his hands unchanged. Posture is not only a means of punctuating a conversation but it is also a way in which people relate to each other when they are together.

Like the written or spoken word, each gesture may have several meanings. Only when gestures are fitted together in a cluster (like words in a sentence) can we get the complete meaning and learn about the speaker's attitudes and feelings.

As for vocabulary, verbal languages have a large vocabulary of words with commonly understood meanings. Non-verbal communication has a relatively limited vocabulary: a few facial expressions and body gestures. While verbal vocabulary consists of discreet symbols, non-verbal contains 'signals' (that is, behaviours which comprise a single unit of meaning and call for some response) that are continuous, such as proximity, gaze, and volume of voice.

Body Language and Paralanguage

The meaning of what we say is contained, in part, in the words we express, but *how* we say things also contains powerful messages. The word 'Yes', for example, can mean completely different things (even in the exact same sentence) depending on *how* it is said. The 'how' something is said is referred to as paralanguage, which includes intonation, emphasis, word and syllable stress, and so on. Paralanguage is your voice minus the words you speak.

Paralanguage is the technical term for 'voice cues' which are not body language or something you see. But they are non-verbal, and they certainly change the meaning that's derived from your words (Walton, 1989). Paralanguage, in brief, is a non-verbal code for the way we say something rather than what we say. It is usually considered as having three parts, each of which conveys meaning. These parts are: voice pitch; vocalizations, such as groans or sighs; and vocal segregates, such as pauses, fillers, and other hesitation sounds. Silence is also an aspect of paralanguage that conveys meaning. The range of vocal behaviour includes: laughing, crying, groaning, yawning, and intonation, voice quality, and emphasis, which are commonly used to reinforce verbal meaning.

Some experts extend this list to include such speech mannerisms as 'by the way', 'incidentally', 'honest', 'before I forget', 'believe me', 'curiously enough', and so on. There are also feedback signals such as 'good' and 'really'. Besides, there are non-verbal cues such as a change in the rate of speech, a loudness or gruffness, a tightness, a hesitation, which reveal the genuineness of sincerity, enthusiasm, and so on, of the speaker. Like gestures, these cues at times slip out unconsciously; they can put alert listeners on guard while they interpret what is being said.

Whistling could fall within this category; it indicates a variety of feelings. There is the normal whistling of melodies for pleasure, or whistling to draw somebody's attention. But here we are concerned with unconscious whistling. When a person finds himself in a really tight spot, he may resort to whistling as his displacement of sound for comfort. A person may 'warble' when he is frightened or apprehensive and is trying to build up his or her courage or confidence.

Paralanguage, therefore, consists of 'non-lexical' vocal communications. It may be considered a type of non-verbal communication, in its broadest sense, as it can suggest many emotional nuances. This category includes a number of subcategories:

- Inflection (rising, falling, flat)
- Pacing (rapid, slow, measured, changing)
- Intensity (loud, soft, breathy)
- Tone (nasal, operatic, growling, wheedling, whining)
- Pitch (high, medium, low, changes)
- Pauses (meaningful, disorganized, shy, hesitant)

Relation between Body Language and Paralinguistics

Paralinguistics takes into consideration certain 'expressions' that accompany speech, which are not actual words—for example, *'um'*, *'ah'*; a splutter, giggle. Some of these signals, however, do have clear meanings: 'um', for instance, is usually a sign of agreement and can be a highly useful reinforcement. Other signals seem to be ambiguous; for example, hesitation.

More specifically, vocalizations such as 'uh-huh' and similar grunts serve as listening signals. The 'tsk' sound is usually made to communicate astonishment or disgust when things are not in good order. The cluck sound is made by the tongue being raised to the roof of the mouth and then released to drop quickly. This sound is usually associated with self-satisfaction. At times, it is accompanied by the snapping of the fingers.

The sound 'whew' is often used as an air-expelling gesture. This expressive sound is used when people wish to communicate relief after some task is done or obstacle overcome, or to signal the termination or easing of a somewhat difficult situation. It could be an entirely unconscious sound.

Some gestures combine movement with sound effects: for instance, taking short breaths and expelling the air through the nostrils in spurts similar to snorting. In a state of sorrow, highly emotional people take deep breaths and expel the air slowly, making long sighing sounds. Breathing also plays a prominent part in the communication of frustration and disgust: people often take a deep breath before issuing a threat or warning.

Vocal Qualifiers

The non-technical term, tone of voice, means the same thing as vocal qualifiers. Vocal qualifiers refer to the manner in which a verbal statement is presented, for example, its rhythm, breathiness, hoarseness, and loudness. It reflects psychological arousal, emotion, and mood. It may also carry social information, as in a sarcastic, superior, or submissive manner of speaking.

The voice is an extraordinary human instrument. Our voice reveals our gender, age, geographical background, level of education, native birth, emotional state, and our relationship to the person spoken to. All these clues (and many more) are contained in even small fragments of speech, and other people can read our voice with remarkable accuracy—whether it is standard or non-standard speech, it contains regional or national accents and reflects emotion and true feelings.

Voice quality reveals the emotional state; for example, depressed people speak in a low, slow voice, with falling pitch. It can also indicate the attitude towards the other—friendly or hostile, dominant or submissive. Besides, accent shows social class and regional origins. All this information can be obtained from a single, short utterance. People with deeper voices communicate more authority; what they say appears truer or more important.

Tone of Voice

Tone of voice is the manner in which a verbal statement is presented, including its rhythm, breathiness, hoarseness, or loudness. It reflects psychological arousal, emotion, and mood. It may also carry social information, as in a sarcastic, superior, or submissive manner of speaking. Our vocalizations, both while speaking and apart from speech, reflect three basic sound modes, as in using a low-pitched, low and loud, or high-pitched voice to argue a discussion point (Givens, 1999).

Tone of voice is an important means of emotional expression. According to Argyle (1992), the pattern of the pitch of an utterance 'frames' it as suspicious and hostile, funny, sarcastic, serious, and so on; a clear example is the rise in pitch at the end of a question. Stress can be placed on particular words to emphasize them or to indicate which of several possible meanings is intended; for instance, 'I am selected to the football team' will change in meaning depending on which word the emphasis is put on.

A significant number of voice qualities are universal across all human cultures, though they are also subject to cultural modification and shaping. Across the globe, adults use higher pitched voices to speak to infants and young children. The softer pitch is innately 'friendly' and suggests a non-aggressive, non-hostile pose. With each other, men and women use higher pitched voices in greetings, to show harmlessness and to invite physical closeness. In almost every language, speakers use a rising intonation to ask a question. The higher register appeases the request for information and is often accompanied by diffident palm-up gestures and by submissive shoulder-shrugs (Givens, 1999).

There are various things that can vary and that affect our perception of tone of voice:

- Increasing loudness or softness (of a syllable, word phrase or sentence).
- Raised or lowered pitch can convey things like fear, anxiety, or tenseness, or designate a question.
- Raspiness due to muscular tensions in the larynx when someone speaks. Tenseness will result in a more raspy type of utterance, for example, a kind of choked sound.
- Drawling or clipping which is associated somewhat with accent and whether the speaker is drawing out individual syllables or clipping them.
- Tempo can be increased or decreased. Speaking quickly tends to communicate urgency or a high emotional state. Slow tempos give the impression of uncertainty.

Vocal Differentiators

This category of paralanguage refers to another way that how one says something can be influenced by how it is said.

Examples of vocal differentiators are crying, laughing, and breaking, where breaking refers to speaking in a broken or halting manner. Clearly, a phrase uttered by a crying person will mean something different than once said by a laughing person.

Vocal identifiers

These refer to the small sounds we make that are not necessarily words per se, but have meaning. For example, *ah-hah*, *un-huh*, and *huh-uh*.

Verbal associates

There are audible signals which are not technically regarded as part of body language or non-verbal communications. But they are quite different from the spoken words, and they can all convey more and/or different meaning compared to the spoken words themselves. Chapman (2010) provides the following examples:

- pitch (the constant musical note of the voice)
- pace (speed or rate of talking)
- volume—from whispering to shouting
- volume variation (how volume changes in phrases or longer passages of speech)
- intonation and 'musicality' (how the pitch changes according to what is being said)
- timbre (quality or sound of the voice, and how this changes)
- emphasis (of syllables, words, or phrases)
- projection (where the voice is being projected to—for example, lots of projection, as if talking to a big group, or none, as if mumbling)
- uses, silences, and hesitation
- *rm*'s and *erh*'s
- gasps, tuts, and other intakes and exhalations of breath
- habits, such as 'I think ...', 'You know ...', 'Like ...'
- laughing and giggling (which can be interspersed within speech, or separate signals, such as nervous laughter) and all sorts of other audible/vocal effects, including:

  o accents and dialects
  o accent affectations ('received' or conditioned, false or exaggerated—permanent or temporary, for example, social climbers, and ordinary people who have a 'telephone voice', or a voice for talking to authority figures)
  o mistakes (spoonerisms, malapropisms, mispronunciation)
  o drying up, being lost for words, stuttering (as distinct from a stammer)
  o over-talking (feeling the need to fill a silence)

- interrupting
- holding back (someone has something to say but is not saying it)
- coughs and grunts (some types of coughing suggest something other than a tickly throat)
- belching and burping
- whistling
- tongue clicking, teeth-sucking

Vocal Cues that Accompany Speech (Paralanguage)

Vocal cues include intonation, voice quality, and vocal emphasis, and that can enhance verbal meaning. Laughing and crying are also considered vocal cues. These cues may reveal an emotional state, attitudes towards others, social class, or origin. Individuals may exercise dominance with a loud projecting voice and indicate submission by using a lower, softer pitch. When communicating verbally, it is important to ensure that the paralanguage aligns with the verbal messages it accompanies.

We can communicate with our voice through changes in rate, volume, quality, resonance, pitch, pauses, and hesitations. These changes indicate our mood. How something is heard and vocalized varies and holds different meanings in different cultures. There are three categories of vocalizations:

1. Vocal characterizers (laughing, crying, yelling, moaning, belching, whining, yawning). These send different messages in different cultures. In India, belching indicates satisfaction.
2. Vocal qualifiers (volume, pitch, rhythm, tone, tempo).
3. Vocal segregates (uh huh, shh, oooh, mmmh, humm, eh, mah, lah). Segregates indicate formality, acceptance, assent, uncertainty.

Time (Chronemics)

Chronemics refers to the value we attach to and the way we use time. It can provide useful information about people. For instance, we can observe how different people behave depending on their psychological orientations towards the present and future. We can see how people are controlled by their biological clocks or how people in different cultures handle time.

Hall and Hall (1990) describe *monochronic* and *polychronic* time orientations. *M*-time is practiced largely by Northern European and North American cultures and is characterized by a segmented orientation towards time that emphasizes schedules, promptness, and 'doing'. *P*-time is practiced by African, Native American, and Mexican cultures. It is characterized by an emphasis on people rather than schedules and a perception of time as holistic and less tangible.

Proxemics (Space)

Proxemics is the way we use space. We all operate under certain zones in our day-to-day interactions with people. At times we are in the 'intimate zone', at times in the 'personal' or 'public' zone.

Use of space in interpersonal situations and home/office arrangement communicates. If a supervisor's office furniture is arranged so that people must sit at a distance to talk, it may indicate that this supervisor is a distant person. Responses to violations of personal space are based on individual and cultural factors. Space between couples and space between individuals in public settings vary culturally. Seating and furniture arrangements are also influenced by culture and can reflect status, roles, and interpersonal norms.

Silence

Silence sends non-verbal cues during a communication situation. Meaning assigned to silence is contingent on such factors as duration, appropriateness, preceding behaviour or activity, and relationship between participants. Like other non-verbal behaviours, our use of and reaction to silence is culturally determined. Many Eastern cultures use silence as a common and preferred form of communication. Some Western cultures see silence as non-functional and prefer continuous verbalization during interaction.

THE MAIN ASPECTS OF BODY LANGUAGE

Gestures

A gesture is the verbal or non-verbal body movement used to express or emphasize an idea, an emotion, or a state of mind.

Gesture is defined as 'visible bodily action by which meaning is represented' (Kendon, 1983). This includes manual gestures, movements of the whole body (shoulder-shrug), head movements (nodding) and facial expressions (smiling), postures (spatial distance), and 'clothing cues' (neckwear) (Givens, 1999).

Gesticulation is a form of non-verbal communication. Gestures convey messages. They are voluntary—often even involuntary—movements we make with the fingers, hands, arms, legs, head, indeed every part of the body—with the intention to communicate. They usually serve one of the following purposes. They can be used to emphasize, clarify, or amplify a verbal message, such as when we point to a chair while offering someone a seat. They can regulate and control human interaction, such as a nod of agreement while someone else is speaking. They can also display effect or emotion: like making a fist with one hand and hammering the open palm of the other to prove insistence (see Sussman and Deep, 1989).

Gestures are often used in conjunction with verbal messages. They are often simultaneous with the words they illustrate or come slightly before them.

Gesture clusters refer to 'the myriads of attitudes expressed by not one gesture but a series of related ones ... called gesture-clusters' (Nierenberg and Calero, 1975). Gesture clusters, which are groups of non-verbal communications, are related to different attitudes. We have a cluster when a person talks with his fists clenched, shakes his index finger, and is blushing either due to heat or anger. A person who is preoccupied will cross his arms or legs, bend his head, close his eyes; he may also have his hand in his hand. The gestures that combine to make a cluster can occur simultaneously, as crossing the arms, locking the ankles, and making a fist, or can follow one after the other.

Each gesture is like a word in a language. To understand any language, we need to structure the words into units or sentences to obtain their complete meaning. If we isolate the various gestures in a cluster, we will not find it easy to understand the attitude expressed. Likewise, if we jump to conclusions on our interpretation of an isolated gesture, we could find ourselves making a mistake, because it is very important to understand the 'congruence' of gestures, that is, the harmony of gesture, one with another. We should look for attitudinal gestures that are so similar that they not only endorse one another but serve to make a cluster as well. Gestures cannot be separated from their 'context' either.

Body Movements

Birdwhistell (1952) was the first to use the term 'Kinesics' for interpreting non-verbal behaviour related to movement, either of any part of the body such as facial expressions and gestures or the body as a whole.

Drawing heavily on descriptive linguistics, Birdwhistell argued that all movements of the body have meaning (that is, are not accidental), and that these non-verbal forms of language (or paralanguage) have a grammar that can be analyzed in similar terms to spoken language. Thus, a 'kineme' is similar to a phoneme because it consists of a group of movements which are not identical but which may be used interchangeably without affecting social meaning (Knapp, 1972: 94–95).

As many movements are carried out at a subconscious or at least a low-awareness level, kinesic movements carry a significant risk of being misinterpreted in an intercultural communications situation. In one current application, kinesics are used as signs of deception by interviewers. Interviewers look for clusters of movements to determine the veracity of the statement being uttered.

We can distinguish five main kinds of gesticulations or body movements: emblem, illustrator, regulator, self-touching, and adaptors.

1. *Emblems* are non-verbal acts that have direct verbal translation and can substitute for words, the meanings of which are well understood by a particular group, class, or culture. They originate in learning, most of which is culture specific, and may be shown in any area of the body and tend more often to substitute for a verbal equivalent; it consists of symbolic gestures which replace words. Examples of emblems are thumbs up (or down)—the hitch-hike sign, head-nods, beckoning, pointing, a wave to a friend in the distance, and certain rude gestures like the upward extended index (or middle) finger. Emblems are not used much during conversations.

    There are a number of reasons why using emblems can be faster than speech; they are silent (and can therefore be used for private comments), they have more impact than words, and they can be received at a greater distance.

2. *Illustrators* are non-verbal movements, mainly of the hands, that are directly related to speech; they serve to illustrate what is verbalized; for example, pointing to oneself, making a shape with the hands (like describing a spiral staircase), defining objects, movements, and relationships, pointing, and as 'batons' to mark new points. They are more closely linked to speech than emblems and serve to clarify what is being said. They add considerably to the amount of information conveyed by speech, especially about shapes, physical objects, and spatial relationships. Gestures and speech are a joint production. Illustrators are a supplement rather than a substitute for speech. They are socially learned, usually through imitation by a child or a person of someone he wishes to emulate.

3. *Regulators* are subtle indicators, which are non-verbal acts that serve to regulate the flow of conversation between people. Regulators are non-verbal cues that monitor or control the speaking of another individual. When speaking, one nods one's head to show understanding or agreement, or when listening, one looks away or yawns to indicate that one is bored with the speaker. A frown shows that one either disbelieves or cannot comprehend what the speaker is saying. Regulators are culture-specific. Examples of regulators are the head-nod, eye contact, and shift in body position. Because they are subtle, they often tend to lead to miscommunication and inappropriate responses among people of different cultures and ethnic backgrounds.

    Argyle (1988) lists the signals used for the synchronization of utterances, to show how regularly these regulators are used:

    To 'take the floor', a listener can actually interrupt; there may be a brief battle, volume being the principal weapon to show impatience, using rapid head-nods, often accompanied by verbal signals such as 'yes', 'but', or 'well'.

To '*keep the floor*', a speaker can raise the volume when the other interrupts and keep the volume raised if the other continues to try to interrupt by keeping a hand in mid-gesture at the end of sentences.

To '*yield the floor*', a speaker can come to the end of a sentence; or, end by trailing off, or end with something open-ended like 'you know'. He could also drawl the final syllable, end on a prolonged rising or falling pitch, come to the end of some of the hand movements accompanying speech, or gaze at the other.

To '*decline an offer of the floor*', a listener can grunt or make 'uh-huh' noises, complete the sentence, briefly request clarification, or briefly restate what the speaker said.

4. *Self-touching* is a body-focused movement. Touching the face can indicate shame or other negative attitudes about oneself. Self-touching is associated with hostility and suspicion. It occurs more often under certain conditions, for instance, during informal and formal interviews, when in subordinate roles (like being interviewed), and when with the opposite sex.

5. Adaptors are unnoticed gestures or movements we use to calm ourselves in moments of stress. For instance, leaning back and moving forward in ones seat during a conference, twitching or moving ones eyes, or changing ones breathing rate.

   Some typical self-touching gestures are the hand-to-nose (fear) gesture, fingers on the lips (shame), and making a fist (anger). Other gestures include covering the eyes, ears, or mouth; movements connected with eating and excretion, grooming, and picking the nose, ears or teeth. These gestures are mainly used in private or in intimate relationships and are inhibited in public, where the people present usually ignore them. Fidgeting is an activity that often involves self-touching.

Emotions

One of the major aspects of body language is the expression of emotions. Emotions refer to such states as happiness, depression, anxiety, and milder 'moods' such as feelings of pleasure and displeasure, different degrees of excitement or drowsiness, and the arousal and satisfaction of hunger, sex, and other drives. According to social psychologists, there are three components in each case: a physiological state, a subjective experience, and a pattern of non-verbal signals—in face, voice, and other areas. It includes feelings of agreement, anger, certainty, control, disagreement, disgust, disliking, embarrassment, fear, happiness, hate, interest, liking, love, sadness, shame, surprise, and uncertainty, as expressed non-verbally apart from words.

Though our fingers, hands, and arms show feelings as well, the study of emotion has focused mainly on facial expression. From research on the face, six basic emotions—surprise, happiness, fear, anger, disgust, and sadness—have been proposed (Ekman, 1984, cited in Givens, 1999).

An 'emotional cue' is 'a facial expression, body movement, or tone of voice indicative of emotion'. Some obvious emotional cues are making a fist when angry, dropping your jaw when surprised, or clearing your throat when you are not sure of something. Though there is a 'rich vocabulary' in verbal language regarding emotions, 'words are often less trustworthy than nonverbal signs'. The words we used to describe emotions are conventional and cannot really capture the emotions which are spontaneous—'usually unintentional, involuntary, and unconscious' (Givens, 1999).

The face is the most informative channel for expressing emotions. Gestures, postures, and bodily movements are the second channel for emotion; they are, however, less informative than the face.

People do not always display the emotional expression that corresponds to their emotional state. There are 'display rules' governing which emotion may be expressed, and there are often very good reasons for not showing what one is feeling. In general, however, it is quite difficult to control emotional expression, even impossible to control some aspects of it, like pupil dilation and perspiration.

Emotions are recognized from a whole pattern of non-verbal signals, which are usually consistent with each other and also with the expectations created by the context. They provide information about intensity and about the tense versus the relaxed dimension. A tense person sits or stands rigidly, upright or leaning forward, and often with hands clasped together, legs together, muscles tense. In such a case, the hands and feet display emotions that the face tries to conceal.

Those who have observed infants will have realised that they, too, have their own 'language' to express their emotions and moods. One can tell that they are happy through their gestures such as bright eyes, bulging (smiling) cheeks, giggles, squeaks and belly laughs accompanied by joyful sounds (monosyllabic). Whereas, when they are sad, their mouth will be twisted into a grimace, cheek will droop, and they will utter grunts and growls.

Schutz (1958) suggests that psychological attitudes affect body posture and functioning. He cites Dr Ida Rolf's speculation that emotions harden the body into set patterns. For instance, a person who is constantly unhappy develops a frown as a set part of his physical make-up, while an aggressive one who thrusts his head forward, develops this as a set posture. In such cases, the emotions, according to Dr Rolf, cause the posture or expression to freeze into a given position. In turn, this posture pulls the emotion into line. For example, if we have a face 'frozen' in a permanent smile, this will affect our personality by causing us to smile mentally.

There is a relation of body function to emotion. For instance, a person with a flexible back cannot have a strong ego, as would a person with a straight back; but then, the latter, in turn, may not be flexible enough. Retracted shoulders represent suppressed anger; raised shoulders are related to fear; square shoulders indicate the bearing of responsibility, bowed shoulders the carrying of a burden.

Behaviour

Behaviour refers, quite simply, to everything we do which is overt or observable. It therefore embraces an enormous range—the whole gamut of verbal and non-verbal actions and reactions which we are capable of. Body language is a particular group of non-verbal behaviour—such as facial expressions, hand gestures, and body postures—that are always directly observable.

One of the reasons that our behaviour is important is that it is so immediately visible to others. The people we interact with can see our facial expressions and hear our words. The conclusions they reach about us are primarily based on this visible behaviour. Similarly, the conclusions we reach about them are based, quite naturally, on our observations of their behaviour. In a sense, our behaviour is all we have got going for us in our face-to-face dealings with people.

Behaviour is central to human relationships. It reveals our attitudes towards others and their attitudes towards us in a given context. An awareness of the variety of transactions that take place beyond the words that are spoken leads to better and more effective relationships. We can preclude misunderstandings and avoid being manipulated. In turn, we can ourselves stop 'playing games' and deal in an open, explicit, unambiguous manner with others.

McGraine (1999) has a 'rule' for gestural reconstruction: change your 'gestero-type' and you change the response of those affected by your gestural patterns. When your positive gestures have a positive influence, you develop self-confidence and learn to use favourable gestures.

Further examples of emotion related behaviour are:

- *Extreme inhibition:* Withdrawal movements, stereotyped movements, hair gestures, general motor unrest, unnecessary movements;
- *Depression:* Movements are slow, few, hesitating, non-empathic, using of hiding gestures;
- *Elation:* Movements are fast, expansive, rhythmical, spontaneous, emphatic, self-assertive, affected;
- *Anxiety:* Gestures involving the hair, hiding the face, wringing and interlocking of hands, opening and closing fists, plucking eyebrows, scratching the face, pulling the hair, aimless fidgeting;
- *Horror:* Touching of the lips with both hands;
- *Negative feelings:* Constricting of facial muscles, frowning;
- *Pleasant feelings and moods:* Relaxed facial muscles, raised eyebrows, laughs; in some cases, intense joy also brings tears to the eyes;

- *Pain:* Narrowed or closed eye, raised cheeks, lowered eyebrows, with wrinkling on the bridge of the nose, or raised upper lip with wrinkling at the side of the nose (Givens, 1999);
- *Sadness:* Bent body, lowered gaze, pouted lips, slumped shoulders. Sadness shows most clearly in the eye area (Ekman, Friesan, and Tomkins, 1971).

Schutz (1958) who has wide experience with 'encounter groups', a technique for preserving a person's identity in the pressures of present-day society, shows how much feeling and behaviour are expressed in body language. He cites a number of interesting 'phrases' that describe behaviour and emotional states in body terms: shoulder a burden, face up, chin up, grit your teeth, a stiff upper lip, bare your teeth, catch your eye, and so on. While each of these body language phrases express an emotion, it also express a physical body act that signals the same emotion.

Vibrations

The terms 'vibration' or 'vibes' for short is commonly used in relationships, at the individual and group levels, in friendships, workshops, seminars. Vibes are feelings that one person arouses in another by supposedly unobservable means, that is, by non-verbal communications. According to popular understanding, one person sends vibes and the other receives them. According to Beier (1974), the term is a metaphor for the communication of emotions.

Vibes have their source in certain kinds of non-verbal communications. When positive attitudes are communicated—like well-being, security, affection—they lead to good vibe; negative communication—hostility, insecurity, anxiety—on the other hand can lead to bad vibes.

Through a study of the interaction of couples, it was found that happy couples would settle down together, have frequent mutual gazes, and touch their partner more often than themselves. In fact, they create for each other a comfortable and supportive body environment. According to Beier, couples who experience negative relationships or conflicts send out more distant vibrations. They display a tendency to cross their arms and legs, have less eye contact, and touch themselves more frequently than they do their partner.

Moods

Beier (1974) has also found that people 'can, and do, communicate by means of moods'. When received, these moods are more than bits of information. No matter how perceptive or cool-headed a person may be, he is still liable to be influenced by the other person's emotional expression. Most of us are probably aware that 'our own moods somehow bounce off and make demands of those around us, especially people who are very close to us'.

According to Beier, communication by moods can be a simple matter: such as, the laughter of one person sets off laughter in everyone. Paradoxically, communication by moods can also be rather complex and of much significance in the nature of human relationships. When we send out listening or caring cues that allow people to feel deeply understood, then people respond quite differently from how they would if we had sent out cues that are seen to be controlling. It is by the use of such cues, which could be presented consciously or unconsciously, that we can influence to a great degree the human world around us. In fact, we are more responsible for the reactions we obtain from other people than we dare realize.

Predictive

Some gestures are predictive: they show what someone is about to do next. Imagine a situation where a young man and woman are talking to each other on a park bench, and the woman decides that it is time for her to leave. She does not just get to her feet, announce that she is leaving, and then disappear. Instead, she does things by stages. To ensure that she does not upset the man, she starts by producing a series of 'intention movements' to show him that she's thinking of leaving. These may consist of tiny adjustments to her gaze or the way she arranges her arms and legs. The important point about these intention displays is that they are not necessarily conscious, and the woman may not even be aware that she is producing them. Although the woman's signals are very subtle, the man is likely to pick them up and to alter his own posture accordingly. By responding to her displays and producing his own, he is able to show that he has understood her intentions. He may be unaware of the effect that her signals are having on him and how he is responding—in fact, the entire dialogue of body language may be played out without either of them being conscious of what is happening. Our ability to read other people's intention movements is highly developed. We do not need to think about it—it happens automatically, very quickly, and usually with remarkable accuracy (Collett, 2003).

DIMENSIONS OF BODY LANGUAGE

Evolution

The awareness of body language as an important tool of communication is several millennia old. The earliest surviving essay ever discovered, written in c. 3000 BC consists of advice on how to speak effectively. This essay was inscribed on a fragment of parchment addressed to Kagemni, the oldest son of Pharaoh Huni. Similarly, the oldest known book, *Precepts*, composed in Egypt in c. 2678 BC by Ptah-Hotep, is a treatise on effective communication.

In the ancient civilizations, and during the classical and medieval times, 'rhetoric' held pride of place as a medium of communications. As expected, several 'handbooks' laid emphasis on the non-verbal behaviour of the orator or public speaker. Some works described several forms of gestures and provided instructions on how they could be used strategically during a speech to elicit the desired effects on the audience.

In the seventeenth century, Francis Bacon suggested in one of his essays (published in 1605) that 'as the tongue speaketh to the ear, so the hand speaketh to the eye', thereby recognizing the value of gestures as a medium of communication. Inspired by this, several studies were made in the field of chirology—the language of the hands—to examine its value both as a rhetorical and natural language form (see J. Bulwer's *Chirology*, 1644 [2003]).

In the eighteenth and nineteenth centuries, scholars debated and established that the natural languages of emotional expressions and gestures most definitely enhanced the more refined and artificial verbal symbolic communication. Hence, body movement as communication has been a subject of wide and enduring interest on account of its resemblance to verbal language.

With regard to the technical study of body language, the most influential pre-twentieth century work is Charles Darwin's *The Expressions of the Emotions in Man and Animals*, published in 1872. It was this work that gave rise to the modern studies of facial expressions and body language. Many of Darwin's ideas and observations have been validated by modern researchers around the world.

Inborn, Inherited, Learned

Eibl-Eibesfeldt (1973) observes that children born deaf and blind do smile, which implies that smiling is an inborn gesture. Other researchers (like Ekman and Friesen) on studying the facial expressions of people from widely different cultures found that each culture used the same basic facial gesture to show emotion, thus leading to the conclusion that these gestures are inborn (Pease, 1993). According to Givens (1999), the patterns used from ancient times are reflected in our faces today. For instance, infants react to a bitter taste by lowering their eyebrows, narrowing their eyes, and sticking their tongue out.

An infant interacts with its mother or caretaker before it is able to speak. In face, right from birth, a child is pre-adapted to social interactions in a number of ways. It is able to send social signals—like gazes, vocalizations, and smiles—and is receptive to similar signals from others, and can interact with simple exchanges.

In most cultures, the head-nod gesture is used to indicate 'yes' or the affirmative. It has been found that those born deaf, dumb, or blind use this gesture without being taught to do so. It is the same for the head-shake which signals 'no' or the negative. It can be observed that the infant uses this gesture while being breast-fed to express that it has had its fill. The growing child uses the same gesture of shaking the head from side to side to indicate that it has had enough to eat and would like to stop being fed. The gesture is later adapted by the child who wants to indicate disagreement or a negative attitude.

We usually cross our arms in the way we find most comfortable, and we keep the same pattern repeatedly. Researches suggest that this gesture could be genetic, inborn.

Some gestures have been inherited. Studies have shown that the brains of all men are programmed to express the various emotions through non-verbal behaviour, such as, happiness by turning up the corners of the mouth and unhappiness by turn them down.

We 'inherit' several gestures and behavioural traits from members of our family or people under whose influence we come. We tend to copy their gestures and eventually personalize them. In a word, our body language is in part due to our instincts and in part the fruit of our own initiative.

It is interesting to note that babies less than a year old develop a true language that includes sounds and gestures, which parents (and those close to them) understand. For instance, they begin pointing and touching: first with their fingertips, then with fully opened hands. They also understand the 'pointing' gesture of others.

A baby has its own 'welcome' signals. For instance, when a parent returns home in the evening, the baby's face lights up with a big smile, it stretches out its arms, even waves, and lunges forward as if inviting interaction.

Babies everywhere express their moods in similar ways. When happy, a baby's face displays bright eyes, upraised facial muscles, and bulging, smiling cheeks. It utters such sounds as giggles, squeals, belly laughs, and bounces its whole body. When sad, the baby's mouth appears twisted into a grimace, the facial muscles droop, and it utters grunts and growls.

Universality

Most of the common gestures are recognized universally and their interpretations are the same all over the world. For instance, the smile, the frown, the head-nod for affirmation ('yes'), and headshakes for negation ('no'); the shoulder-shrug to indicate that a person is not following what is being said; the spread-out hands to say 'I don't know'; hunched shoulders combined with the raising of eyebrows to indicate doubt; palms facing the listener to mean 'no'; a pointing finger to indicate what we want.

Some gestures, as is the case with other body cues, are more obvious and less ambiguous than others. The gesture used to call people, for instance, is universal and well understood, even though there are 'palm-up' and 'palm-down' variations across regions. Raising a finger during an interaction may indicate one of several things: an attitude of authority, emphasis, accusation, or insult. Cracking the knuckles could betray anxiety, nervousness, boredom, restlessness, and an unresolved state of mind. Click the fingers or clapping the hands could mean calling the attention of someone near or far. It could also convey that some sought-for solution or a brainwave has just flashed. Clapping also indicates applause. Punching a clenched fist into the palm could mean emphasis or determination. Tapping the finger tips of both hands could signal involved thought or scheming.

Pease (1993) points out that the shoulder-shrug is a universal gesture. It indicates that the person does not know about or understands what is being said. He forms a cluster with the palms exposed, shoulders hunched, and eyebrows raised.

Argyle (1975) lists the gestures that are very common or universal: point, shrug, nod, the head, clap, beckon, wave, halt sign, pat on the back, thumbs down, outline female body, tilt the head with flat palm (sleep), indicate height of a child with flat hand.

Although greetings vary a lot across cultures, there are a number of features which are common: close proximity, direct orientation, eyebrow flash, smiling, mutual gaze, body contacts, presenting the palm—either visibly or for shaking, head toss (or head-nod, bow).

Regarding emotion cues, however, there is an ongoing debate about whether they are universal. Darwin (1965) held that 'the different races of men express their emotions and sensations with remarkable uniformity throughout the world'. Birdwhistell (1971), on the other hand, was of the opinion that 'there are probably no universal symbols of emotional states'.

Ekman and Friesen (1969) observe that emotions mobilize the facial muscles in similar ways in all cultures, but the cause of the emotions, and the effects, the 'display rules' with consequent behaviour patterns vary considerably across cultures.

Gestures that express emotions are very similar across cultures: shaking the fist (anger), twisting the hands together (anxiety), touching the face (shame), showing the palm of the hand and lowering the head (submission and appeasement), yawning (boredom).

Cultural Variations

Every culture has its own body language, with gestures that are peculiar to it. The meaning of many of our body movements and gestures are culturally determined, some gestures have different meanings in different cultures.

Brief mention may be made here of some gestures commonly found in South Asia and specifically in India: for instance, touching the feet of an elder or a guru as a sign of respect, namaste for greeting, cracking of knuckles on a loved one's forehead to wish good health (usually done by elderly women), laying the hand(s) on head in blessing, squatting with palms held upward or placed on the knees during meditation, and so on.

Status and Age

Research has shown that high-ranking officials resort to fewer gestures than those lower down on the social/hierarchical scale. The less educated or unskilled person will rely more on gestures than words to communicate. There is a relationship, by and large, between gestures and the command a person has over verbal language. The person with a large vocabulary will gesture less than a person with a limited vocabulary who uses gestures to explain himself.

How quickly some gestures are executed and how obvious they look to others has a direct bearing on the age of the individual. For example, when a child of five tells a lie to an older person, he will deliberately cover his mouth with one hand or both hands immediately. The gesture alerts the other person to the lie. The mouth-covering gesture continues to be used throughout the individual's lifetime; usually it varies only in the speed at which it is done. The teenager telling a lie also brings his hand to the mouth like the five-year-old, but the obvious gesture of slapping the hand over the mouth is substituted by the fingers rubbing lightly around it. In adulthood, this gesture becomes further refined. An adult telling a lie spontaneously takes his hand to his mouth, but at the last moment pulls his hand away from the face and starts rubbing his nose—thus giving the gesture a sophisticated look.

Take some other examples, like the display of anxiety, inner conflicts, and fear. To express any of these, a child sucks its thumb, teenagers bite their nails (or pens, and so on), and adults pick at their cuticles until they are almost sore. This clearly illustrates the fact that with age, many of the gestures become sophisticated and less obvious. No wonder it is often more difficult to read the gestures of an elderly person that those of younger ones.

APPROACHES TO THE INTERPRETATION OF BODY LANGUAGE

Negative Aspects

Interpreting body language is not a simple task; being as complex as the spoken language, it demands serious study for correct and accurate interpretation. This can be difficult or easy depending on our capability of learning 'languages'. But learning it is fun; besides, it is informative and helpful in better integration of ourselves and more meaningful relationships with others.

'No body position or movement, in and of itself, has a precise meaning', cautions Birdwhistell (1971). According to him, body language and spoken language are dependent on each other. The spoken language alone will not give us the full meaning of what a person is saying, nor for that matter body language alone. If we listen only to the words when someone is talking, we may get as much of a distortion (that is, not get the complete message) as we would if we paid attention only to the body language. It is important to observe both.

For an understanding, the impact of our non-verbal behaviour on others must first reflect upon our interpretation of the non-verbal signals of others. We must remember that we use acquired gestures unconsciously, but they mean different things to different people. It follows, therefore, that there are many interpretations of the non-verbal movement we make. These interpretations are based on several things, including culture, economics, religion, politics, geography, and values.

Moreover, to understand body language, those who want to specialize in it often have to take into consideration cultural and environmental differences; otherwise they can misinterpret what they see. Besides, as we have noted above, body movements cannot be viewed in isolation if we want a correct reading. They must be taken in *clusters*. For instance, scratching the head can mean a number of things—dandruff, fleas, sweating, uncertainty, forgetfulness, or lying, depending on the other gestures that occur at the same time.

When dealing with people who are close to us (for example, in a husband–wife relationship) and who generally agree with us, we may feel relaxed enough not to pay close attention to non-verbal signals. Our interpretation may then suffer.

Further, different types of information can be communicated at different levels of understanding. The process of communication goes beyond the written or spoken word. We may inadvertently fail at communication, despite the fact that the arrangement of words and ideas is well ordered. Here the fault may be the receivers', who misinterpret our communication or may not be 'empathic' to it.

In the initial stages, reading individual gestures seems very easy and it is fun. However, a deeper study reveals how each gesture can quickly be countered, amplified, or confused by another. If we are not careful, this can lead to incorrect hasty judgements.

In the beginning of their study, learners of body language may often find it difficult to see gestures objectively. They may tend to focus too much on individual gestures rather than gesture clusters. But as in the learning of any new language, they learn how to interpret gestures correctly. Learning the art of seeing non-verbal communication thoroughly is almost as difficult as acquiring fluency in a foreign language.

Positive Aspects

Though body language has myriads of nuances that require careful interpretation, it is relatively easier to learn than other languages because its 'vocabulary' is rather limited. Moreover, we do not have to make time for its study or sit down with books, as in the case of studying a verbal language. We can study behaviour at odd times, in odd places, without pen and paper in hand. We can even turn it into a pastime activity, for instance, while we wait to catch a train or plane or bus, or as we watch an uninteresting programme on TV. In the latter case we can lower the volume of the TV and observe the actions and interpret them.

Body language is not an esoteric subject. It is just 'another' language. As already noted, while verbal language deals with symbols (words), body language deals with signals (gestures). Ordinary verbal language is written or spoken, body language is 'actioned'—with gestures and other non-verbal components of physical behaviour. Just as we listen to or read words and interpret them, so we can perceive body movements and interpret them. There is a 'design' in both verbal (syntax) and non-verbal (congruence–incongruence) communication which can be learned.

Unlike verbal language where the syntax for a particular language is fixed, gesture clusters in body language are kaleidoscopic—making different 'designs' that are similar and fleeting—which a perceptive eye can interpret correctly.

Just as in the learning of any language, body language too requires motivation and the basic competence to master skills. Beginners will find the going somewhat tough, as happens in most skill-learning (like cycling and typing) situations. By practicing the skill, confidence increases and the task even becomes enjoyable.

Context

'Context' is another area that must be taken into serious consideration while interpreting gestures in order not to misjudge them. Context implies the overall situation of the person—like the surroundings and environment. In different contexts, the same gesture will have different interpretations.

For example, when we see a person sitting in a physician's waiting room with legs tightly crossed and arms folded, and chin lowered, we would obviously conclude that he or she is suffering from fever or nervous tension. Whereas a similar set of gestures before an authority figure, for instance, the boss, could mean that the person is being defensive when reprimanded.

When a student in conversation with a professor holds the older man's eyes a little longer than is ordinarily acceptable, it can either be a sign of respect and affection or a subtle challenge to the professor's authority. The experts look for patterns in context, not in the meaning of isolated gestures.

Again, a person who offers a weak handshake may have a 'weak character'; but it can also indicate that he has arthritis and wants to avoid the pain that comes from a strong handshake. And, it is well established that most artists, musicians, surgeons who generally work with their hands, may prefer not to shake hands, or when compelled to do so, offer a lifeless hand in order to protect it from pain.

When someone covers his mouth with the hand while speaking, the commonest interpretation is that the person is unsure of what he is saying. This, however, could also be a mannerism or a habit that the person has developed, or he might even be suffering from a cold, or from bad breath!

Birdwhistell (1971) points out that a body movement may mean nothing at all in one context and yet be extremely significant in another. For example, the frown we make by creasing the skin between our eyebrows may simply mark a point while we are speaking; in another context, it may be a sign of annoyance; in still another context, of deep concentration. Examining the face alone will not tell us the exact meaning of the frown. We must know what the frowner is thinking.

According to Birdwhistell, the most important thing to realize about body language is that no single motion ever stands alone. It is always part of a pattern.

Environmental setting influences behaviour. One must therefore consider both the physical and the social aspects of the environment in order to interpret non-verbal behaviour. The way in which furniture is arranged in an office can be a major influence on the non-verbal behaviours exhibited. Body movements differ depending on whether a person is sitting behind a desk or in a chair. The proximity and angle of a seating arrangement serves different functions during an interaction and influences such behaviour as eye contact, gazing, and head rotation.

Non-verbal behaviour may take on different meanings in the street and in a classroom. Background noise, for instance, may produce 'exaggerated non-verbal communication' in a particular work setting, for example, in a quiet place like a library. The degree to which our non-verbal behaviour are either suppressed or performed will be determined by how formal a setting is. 'Competitive versus cooperative interaction settings' will give rise to a variety of types, levels, and frequencies of non-verbal behaviour (Rozelle, Druckmann, and Baxter, 1986).

Congruence

When our body language, our words, and the tone of voice all match, then we have congruence. If we are not being congruent, then our listeners will believe our body language, not our words.

While we check for congruence, it is important to observe all related gestures, in their smallest segments, so as not to make rash judgements or label a person's attitude haphazardly in a given situation or speech. Although it is fairly simple to observe and become aware of gestures but it is a rather tricky business to interpret them so as not to make rash judgements or label a person's attitude haphazardly. Indeed, what we should look for are attitudinal gestures that not only endorse one another but serve to make a cluster. By mentally matching the congruent gestures that form clusters, we can understand the attitudes expressed and discover their meaning. Indeed, what we should look for are attitudinal gestures that not only endorse one another but serve to make a cluster.

Sigmund Freud (Pease, 1993) cites an experience of one of his counselling sessions. A client was once verbally expressing happiness with her marriage and at the same time unconsciously slipping her wedding ring on and off her finger. Freud took a note of this gesture. Later in the session the women revealed some deep marriage problems.

When we are perceptive enough to detect congruency of behaviour, then we may feel equipped to monitor our interpretation of a person's attitudes and give his actions meaning. The sensitivity to detect congruency serves as an 'anti-assumption' (Nierenberg and Calero, 1975) control that forces us to observe further rather than jump to a conclusion.

Congruence–incongruence must also be observed in the context of group behaviour. In a group where people copy each others' body positions, it reflects their congruency of attitudes and action. In fact, in such a situation, when one member of the group shifts position, the others eventually follow suit. One may safely conclude that the group members are all in agreement and share the same viewpoints.

Should there be disagreement, the advocates of each viewpoint will take different positions. In such a case, each person will imitate the positions of like-minded members and clusters of congruent positions will ensue. Members who wish to show that they are a cut above the rest of the group may deliberately take a non-congruent position.

When two friends argue, even though their thoughts are at variance, they will adopt congruent positions to indicate that their mental differences have not affected their emotional ties. A husband and wife who are very close will adopt congruent postures that indicate that they are not inimical to each other, even though one is 'attacking' the other in an argument.

Over-congruence

A communication needs to look congruent for its optimum level of acceptance. But to give it a congruent look, at times we go for over-congruence. These situations create conflicting signals between body language and verbal statement. A total match between verbal statement, vocal cues, and non-verbal signals is the only prerequisite to make a communication congruent. Over-congruence gets exposed with overdone facial expressions and physical gestures while speaking. Most of the politicians of the world do this. There are some tips to avoid over congruence in communication (James, 2009). These are:

- *Control your hand gestures*. Keep hand gestures restricted within the zone of congruence. This zone is between shoulders and waist. The higher the hand goes, the less congruent it looks.
- *Ask yourself, who are you?* Am I genuinely a wild and crazy person with full of enthusiasm for my subject? If the answer is 'no' (and it's best to be honest), then tone it down several notches.
- *Practice in front of a mirror*. Look yourself in a full-length mirror and try to observe your body language. Calm down your over-congruent gestures and practice that with your verbal statement to match better.

Remember, the tendency to make too right will end up all wrong. So behave normal during communication with your normal body language.

Inconsistency

Apart from incongruence, there is also the question of *inconsistent cues*. A girl may tell a boy, 'You're an idiot; I don't like you', but her face is aglow with a loving smile and she gives his cheek a gentle slap; the non-verbal signals are inconsistent because they convey a positive signal. In the final analysis, it is the non-verbal signal that has the real impact.

Inconsistent cues could lead to confusion. Take the case of a mother who smiles while telling her child not to touch a glass. Her smile, in fact, contradicts her words. Should the child reach for the glass, the mother would give him a spanking.

A striking example of yet another type of inconsistency is provided by Beier (1974). He says that the question of how people encode and decode emotional signals is extremely complex. For example, we may declare and we really mean it that we want a person to like us, yet we send out contrary non-verbal messages through facial expressions, posture, tone of voice, and many other cues that we do not like that person. It may be that we made a mistake in communication or were misinterpreted by the other person.

According to Beier, there could be a simpler explanation, particularly if such inconsistent behaviour persists. The point is we wanted to communicate two different feelings at the same time and landed up making a compromise. We maintained the image of someone who wants to show liking, but we simultaneously managed to communicate dislike, without taking on the responsibility for it. 'The transmission of discordant cues', says Beier, 'is a way of having our cake and eating it'. Such behaviour is common in intimate relationships.

Faking

A person may fake a gesture by deliberately trying to get other people to draw the wrong conclusion about his thoughts or feelings.

Freud has said: 'If his lips are silent he chatters with his finger-tips, betrayal oozes out of him at every pore.'

Sometimes what a person says with his body gives the lie to what he is saying with his tongue. Thus, a person may appear calm, self-controlled—unaware that his foot is tapping the floor constantly, restlessly. One has to be a real expert to be able to fake body language. But even the experts, it is found, cannot 'fool all of the people all of the time'. For though we may succeed in faking some gestures, other parts of the body may give away the truth through incongruent movements. That is, one will not be able to keep up the lie for long, because the body will eventually emit signals that are independent of the conscious action.

Micro-momentary Signals

There are two situations where we resort to micro-gestures. One, when we deliberately attempt to ensure secrecy; lovers, for instance, may communicate in code, using special words or tiny signs when they are with other people. In this way they can exchange loving signals without anyone else knowing. Two, when we unintentionally reveal our attitudes or feelings. When people are lying, for example, or feeling anxious, the giveaway signs that expose their true feelings are often extremely small and short-lived. Unlike the signs exchanged by lovers, these micro-signs are entirely unintentional.

Psychologists have identified a special group of micro-movements called 'micro-momentary expressions', which are confined to the face (Haggard and Isaacs, 1966). They are very brief and usually appear for no more than one-eighth of a second. When people are describing a painful experience while putting on a brave face, it is not uncommon for them to reveal their discomfort by briefly altering their facial expression. One moment they are smiling, giving the impression that the experience did not bother them at all; the next moment their face is transformed into the briefest of grimaces. Then, before anyone notices anything, the smile is back, and all evidence of discomfort is erased from their face.

In principle, micro-expressions can appear anywhere on the body, but because of the fine-grained nature of the facial muscles, they are most likely to appear on the face. When a micro-tell does appear on our face, it shows that we are in a state of conflict—usually between a positive emotional state that we want other people to see and a negative emotional state that we are trying to conceal. When the negative emotional state momentarily gains the upper hand, our facial control breaks down and the micro-expression appears. Most of the time we are completely unaware of the conflict that is taking place in us and the fact that we are revealing our inner thoughts to the outside world. But even when we are conscious of our conflicting emotions, we still do not realize that our facial micro-expressions are giving us away (Collett, 2003).

TIPS ON INTERPRETATION

There are several considerations with respect to interpreting body language. Here are some important ones:

- There are no precise interpretations for particular gestures.
- Body language is as easy or as difficult to learn as any spoken language. It consists of gesture clusters. It is complex, with a combination of cultural, social, and individual elements. 'No body position, in and of itself has a precise meaning' (Birdwhistell, 1952).
- Each individual is unique; his attitudes and behaviour will have an impact on his non-verbal communication.
- Gestures come in clusters; one must recognize their relationships and draw meaning from a cluster.
- Non-verbal behaviour takes place in a particular context; contexts vary, so we must adapt our interpretation accordingly.
- We use *acquired* gestures unconsciously, but they mean different things to different people. Consequently, there are many interpretations of the non-verbal movements we make. These interpretations are based on many factors, including culture, religion, politics, economics, geography, and values.
- There is danger of our judgements being predominantly 'subjective' rather than objective. We may be inaccurate in our interpretations because of our biases about things and people; for instance, we tend to relax our observation, alertness while conversing with our 'nearest and dearest'.
- Gestures must not be interpreted in isolation but in clusters. We must remember that gesture clusters are kaleidoscopic and change from moment to moment, movement to movement.
- Sometimes gestures do not really mean what they signify, since the person may be making them out of habit or because of acquired mannerisms. Interpretations then take on another colouring.
- One must be aware of the incongruencies and inconsistencies in verbal and non-verbal expressions.
- Sometimes there may be attempts to fake gestures, so one must not be drawn in blindly, taking every gesture at its 'face value', but be alert to giveaway clues.
- We must take cultural variations of gestures into consideration. Over-generalizing about the non-verbal behaviour of a culture leads to the assumption that everybody in the culture behaves in the same way.
- Accurate interpretations come through patient observation, perceptiveness, and experience. To understand what a person is experiencing, one must use ones eyes, ears, and intuition.

ADVANTAGES OF LEARNING BODY LANGUAGE

The key benefit derived from the knowledge of body language 'understanding'—of others and ourselves. Body language sharpens our perception in many ways: for instance, we can gauge what pleases some people, what offends others; and anticipate others' reactions to specific situations and influence their decisions for the better. Thus, such understanding makes relationships smoother and more constructive.

Our attempts at understanding others rebound in our understanding of ourselves. We not only receive the signals others send us, but we become increasingly aware of the signals we ourselves send out. An awareness of the way in which we behave help us transform our negative behaviours into positive ones. We can monitor the signals we send out—through self-transformation—till our 'spontaneous' attitudes and behaviour are sound, relevant, and impactful. We are also able to communicate our messages more accurately, adequately, and effectively.

In addition, we can develop the habit of reading our own gestures and hence be able to check if we are inadvertently precipitating the other person's reactions, or we may realize that the gestures we find undesirable might really be a reaction to the other person's physical idiosyncrasies, like ticks or awkward body movements.

'Learning is acquired by reading books, but the much more necessary learning, the knowledge of the world, is only to be acquired by reading men and studying all the various editions of them', was Lord Chesterfield's advice to his son.

Sigmund Freud said, 'The unconscious of one human being can react upon that of another without passing through the conscious' (Nierenberg and Calero, 1975). Our reactions, in this case, are directly taken as facts, without first being tested, and produce certain reactions. If our subconscious interprets a particular gesture as aggressive, we will unconsciously respond in an aggressive manner. As rational beings, the proper approach would be to make our reactions deliberate, conscious.

Further, through study of body language we can bring to the fore, to the conscious level, our subconscious motivations. This will enable us not only to understand our own and others' gestures more objectively and interpret them more meaningfully, but also to empathize with others more effectively.

The old adage, 'Actions speak louder than words', holds true in this case; it implies that non-verbal behaviours often predominate when it is a matter of influencing people. 'What you are speaks so loudly that I cannot hear what you say' is R. W. Emerson's oft-quoted line.

Studies and research in body language suggest that the visual impact (in a verbal encounter between two parties) is greater than that created by our words. Body language, in addition to sending and receiving messages, if understood and used adroitly, can also serve to break down defences.

You may have observed body language is 'contagious'. Try this 'experiment' in case you do not remember having experienced it. While talking to someone, raise your hand suddenly and deliberately and check the time on your watch. The other person will automatically do the same. Also, you know what happens when someone in a crowd yawns! When you smile at someone, he will most probably smile back. If you look at a group photograph, you will immediately see how many people there are mirroring each others' postures!

SUMMING UP

Body language is the language commonly spoken by infants and adults. It affects our life very 'dramatically'—the way we present ourselves, the way we are perceived by others, and so on. It shapes our relationships, friendships, and negotiations through the impact it makes on others and others make on us.

Body language is a 'universal' language—except for specific cultural variations—used by people everywhere, as well as features that have cultural overtones and are understood by people of the respective cultures. Of course, its study is not similar to that of other languages, like French, or Spanish, or English, because it goes beyond verbal communication. Even if we do not know a foreign language, we can 'communicate' rather well through body language because it is 'read' and interpreted by people the world over. In fact, sometimes not knowing a foreign language has its own advantages; the people in the country we are visiting, seeing that we are foreigners with a language disability, go out of their way to helps us.

Some may claim, and rightly so, that they already *know* and *use* body language, so how will further study help. It is true that we have all been using body language since infancy. But is our knowledge complete and comprehensive? If it is, then this book has hardly anything new or extraordinary to offer. But it could help in another way. It will sharpen our perception by enabling us to 'label' and 'vocalize' what we already know in non-verbal communication and make our observation more deliberate and detailed for greater efficiency and accurate interpretation.

Chapter 2

The Face

PART ONE: FACIAL EXPRESSIONS

OVERVIEW

The human face is the most significant—and the most photographed—part of the body. First of all, its features define a person's identity. The face 'evolves' with the growth of a person from infancy through adolescence, middle, and old age; however, it always retains the features already prominent in childhood—unless altered by plastic surgery! 'A face is every human's visual trademark.' The ability to recognize and recall thousands of faces easily and at a glance is a unique talent of human beings alone (Givens, 1999). Friends and acquaintances recognize one another before a word is spoken.

The face is perhaps the most important human art object. People work on their faces as if it were an art canvas: they use cosmetics, colouring, ornaments, adjust hair length and style to make their faces as attractive as possible.

The face has been called the organ of emotion because it provides vital clues by reacting in fractions of a second, often unconsciously, revealing attitudes, moods, opinions a person would rather keep under wraps. Emotionally, 'the face is mightier than the word' (Givens, 1999).

All five sensory modalities—sight, smell, hearing, taste, and touch—are found on or near the face, and of these, touch is the only modality also to be found elsewhere on the body. But the face is also the most important source of outgoing signals in the form of speech and features of the voice like accent and intonation, as well as myriads of expressions involving the eyes and muscles of the head and face. Some facial expressions, like the startle reflex, are entirely involuntary; others, like the smile, may be a genuine expression of pleasure or a deliberate attempt to create an impression of genuine pleasure. Because the face is partly under conscious control, it is a major weapon in our daily attempts to mislead and deceive each other. In spite of this, the face remains the prime source of information about our emotional states—it is by observing our faces that other people can tell whether we are feeling happy, sad, angry, surprised, or frightened. Looking at our face, they can also tell whether we're feeling dominant or submissive.

33

The face is the site for the major sensory inputs and the major communicative outputs. It is a multi-signal, multi-message response system capable of tremendous flexibility and specificity (Ekman, 1979; Ekman and Friesen, 1975).

Dr Paul Ekman's research (based on the work of Silvan Tomkins) in the study of emotions and their relation to facial expressions took Darwin's work to the next level, proving that facial expressions of emotion are not culturally determined but biological in origin and universal across human cultures. Eckman co-developed the Facial Action Coding System (FACS) with Wallace V. Friesen in 1976. The FACS is a system to taxonomize human facial expressions and is still used today by psychologists, researchers, and animators.

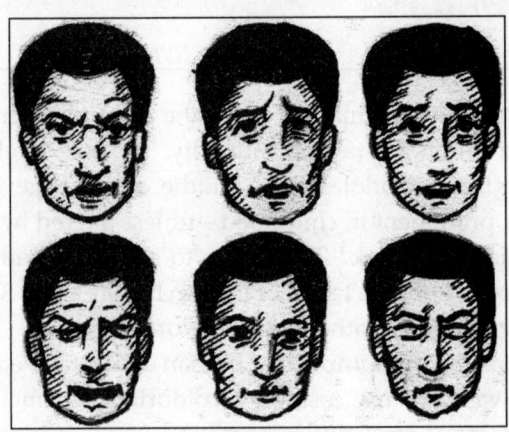

Facial Expressions

The face is the most expressive part of our body. Since it is directly observable, it is the face that first draws our attention in our daily interaction with people. In a normal one-to-one encounter, people look longer at the face than at other parts of the anatomy. Therefore, what we 'read' in the face is of great importance in the communication process.

'Facial expression' refers to recurring configurations of facial muscle movements that communicate some thought, emotion, or behaviour. Not all recurring facial muscle configurations express specific messages. For example, some facial muscle actions that accompany spoken words such as raising one's eyebrows when emphasizing a particular word may modify those words, but are not messages in and of themselves (Ekman, 1982).

The face can express various *thoughts*. By raising the outer corner of an eyebrow, one may convey sophisticated scepticism. When eyebrows are pulled up in the middle, they may convey sympathy. Flashing both eyebrows upward may convey a greeting. Or, lowered eyebrows may convey uncertainty (Eibl-Eibesfeldt, 1989). A wink can convey that one is kidding.

For the most part, facial expressions are learned like language, are displayed under conscious control, and their meanings are culture-specific and rely on the context for proper interpretation (Birdwhistell, 1971).

The face expresses *emotions*. Happiness is expressed by raising lip corners into a smile, sadness by frowning. Facial expression is a basic mode of non-verbal communication. It helps form significant impressions of friendliness, trustworthiness, and status. Researchers have attempted to categorize facial expressions that express emotion and typically agree on seven: happiness, surprise, fear, sadness, anger, disgust, contempt (Ekman, 1982, cited by Argyle, 1988).

Dynamics

A facial expression results from one or more motions or positions of the muscles of the face. These movements convey the emotional state of the individual to observers. A facial expression can be a voluntary action; however, because expressions are closely tied to emotion, they are more often involuntary. It can be almost impossible to avoid expressions for certain emotions, even when propriety demands it. The close link between emotion and expression can also work in reverse; it has been observed that voluntarily assuming an expression can actually cause the associated emotion.

The flashes of facial signals are generally spontaneous reactions, so they are difficult to hide or control. Because they are quick and instinctive, they reflect one's real feelings, whether they are congruent with what one is saying or not. A mismatch is clearly evident when someone is lying, the face is a giveaway, providing a host of clues that negate the words used in self-defence.

Analyzing facial expressions, nevertheless, is a somewhat tricky task, especially because people deliberately control their facial movements so as not to reveal their inner feelings; they manage to keep a straight face, with no giveaways. Professionals like nurses, doctors, counsellors, teachers, air hostesses, entertainers, and so on, are in fact trained to control their expressions as part of the requirements of their job. On the contrary, in movies and TV serials, actors exaggerate and prolong certain gestures so as to make an impression on the audience.

Facial signals are all too fleeting. A micro-expression lasting only one-twenty-fifth to one-fifteenth of a second is difficult to fake. Micro-expressions express the seven universal emotions classified by Ekman.

Besides micro-expressions, there are *subtle* expressions which are not associated with the length of time they appear on the face but rather with the intensity of the emotion that is occurring.

Interpreting Facial Expressions

Some expressions can be accurately interpreted, such as anger and extreme contentment. Others, however, are difficult to interpret even in familiar individuals. For instance, disgust and fear can be tough to tell apart. However, sometimes we can falsely assume a face is expressing some emotion, even though it is neutral, because we confuse it with some other face we have seen containing features in the same proportion and relative position.

Clusters

Facial expression does not occur in isolation. Every part of the face—the mouth, lips, nose, eyes, eyebrow, chin, and so on—each contributes to form an expression. Besides, there are other accompanying features such as head-nodding or head-shaking and change in posture and gestures. However, for better control and coordination of them all, it is necessary to understand the significance of single gestures or expressions, as discussed in other parts of the book.

Characteristics

Since facial expressions are connected with our emotions and our speech, they are highly flexible and changeable. The face can encode a variety of communicative (conscious and intended) and informative (unintended) messages. We tend to alter our facial expressions according to particular situations, like parties, weddings, formal sessions, condolence meetings, and so on.

There are a number of specific features which are evidenced in our face while we communicate: for instance, we furrow our forehead when we are concerned, angry, or frustrated; raise our eyebrows to express astonishment; flare our nostrils while interacting with someone with whom we are very upset, or, in another situation, when we are sexually aroused.

When people chew or bite their lips, they may be giving off messages of uncertainty, hesitancy, attempts to suppress surging emotions, nervousness. When their lips are pursed, clamped, or tightly drawn, and their eyes keep staring into 'nothingness', accompanied by a head movement, it can mean they are in deep thought, or displaying a studied approval or disapproval, and so on. Lip biting, like lip compression, is one of the ways by which people pacify themselves when they are stressed. It helps to relieve tension that may be minor and transitory.

People express their displeasure or confusion by frowning, their envy or disbelief may be displayed by a raised eyebrow, and antagonism may be shown through the tightening of the jaw muscles or by squinting of the eyes. A child may indicate defiance by thrusting out his chin.

People turn up their nose to show dislike, rejection, or contempt. It has been observed that even babies instinctively turn up their noses as a reaction to food they do not like.

To show disgust, we wrinkle up our noses and raise our top lip. It is the same all over the world, though the things which actually disgust are very different.

Emotions

The face is the most reliable indicator of a wide range of emotions. The face seems to be capable of surfacing any emotion that wells up deep inside us. Most of us rely largely on our reading of facial expression to judge how a person feels about a particular matter.

Facial expressions of emotion are involuntary and are produced almost immediately when an emotion occurs. Yet we can, to a large extent, interrupt or suppress expressions if we concentrate on doing so. We can also deliberately put on expressions of certain emotions when we do not feel them. This is hard to do for fear and sadness, because most people do not have voluntary control over the specific facial muscles that are deployed in those expressions. False expressions of enjoyment, anger, disgust, and surprise are easy to make, although careful measurement of the speed, symmetry, and specific muscular activity suggests that it is possible to distinguish the spontaneous from the false expressions of even these emotions (Ekman, 2010).

In the mid-1900s, as the result of the pioneering work of Paul Ekman (Ekman and Friesen, 1969; 1971), at least six pan-cultural basic emotions with facial expressions were reliably recognized as cross-cultural. These emotions are: happiness, sadness, anger, fear, disgust, and surprise. Ekman, Friesen, and Tomkins (1971) later discovered one other emotion: contempt. Even children who have been blind and deaf from birth display them.

Happiness: The corners of the mouth lift in a smile. As the eyelids tighten, the cheeks rise and the outside corners of the brows pull down.

Sadness: The eyelids droop as the inner corners of the brows rise and, in extreme sadness, draw together. The corners of the lips pull down, and the lower lip may push up in a pout.

Anger: Both the lower and upper eyelids tighten as the brows lower and draw together. Intense anger raises the upper eyelids as well. The jaw thrusts forward, the lips press together, and the lower lip may push up a little.

Fear: The eyes widen and the upper lids rise, as in surprise, but the brows draw together. The lips stretch horizontally.

Disgust: The nose wrinkles and the upper lip rises while the lower lip protrudes.

Surprise: The upper eyelids and brows rise, and the jaw drops open.

Contempt: This is the only expression that appears on just one side of the face: one half of the upper lip tightens upward.

However, in the 1990s, Ekman expanded his list of basic emotions, including a range of positive and negative emotions, not all of which are encoded in facial muscles. The newly included emotions are: amusement, contempt, contentment, embarrassment, excitement, guilt, pride in achievement, relief, satisfaction, sensory pleasure, and shame.

Bhavas

Shweder (1993) has written about the *Natya Shastra,* an Indian treaty on emotion from the second century AD, which offers an alternative list of eight 'basic' emotions.

The sixth chapter of the *Natya Shastra* (Masson and Patwardhan, 1970) offers a detailed taxonomy of the eight emotions (bhava) portrayed by actors and the corresponding meta-emotions (rasa) experienced by the audience at a play or by reading poetry or literature.

From the descriptions of the bhavas given in the *Nayta Shastra,* there appears to be a reasonably close match between the two lists on four of the items (anger—*krodha,* fear—*bhaya,* sadness—*soka,* and disgust—*jugupsa*). However, the *Natya Shastra* adds four items (*rati*—love [romantic], *hasya*—amusement, *utsaha*—enthusiasm, and *vismaya*—awe/wonder) that are not on Ekman's list—and it lacks three items that are on Ekman's list (Haidt and Keltner, 1999).

In Orissa, India, the Oriya language contains a single word *'lajya'* to cover a large area of emotion-face that in English includes the words shame, embarrassment, shyness, and modesty. Yet, even this one-to-many translation is misleading, for shyness and a liability to shame appear to be experienced as a moral virtue in Orissa, and as a defect in the confidence-valuing West (Menon and Shweder, 1994).

Aspects

Universal

The muscles that contract to produce the facial expressions of anger, fear, sadness, disgust, and enjoyment are the same the world over, regardless of sex or culture. Three kinds of research have established this. When people from various cultures have been asked to identify the emotions represented by photographs of different expressions, they have, by and large, given the same answer. Love and hate—which probably don't have unique facial expressions—involve strong feelings, but those feelings endure much longer than the emotions which can last only seconds or at most minutes. Love and hate may be better thought of as affective attitudes rather than momentary emotions. There may be facial expressions for other emotions such as shame or awe, but these have yet to be identified (Ekman, 2010).

Cultural Variations

Not everything about facial expressions of emotion is universal. All people learn, in the course of growing up, to manage their facial expressions. Polite and proper behaviour requires that we employ what have been termed display rules that dictate who can show which emotions to whom, and when. For example, in many societies, people who lose in a public contest try to inhibit any sign of their disappointment. Although we know what we should do, that does not always mean that a display rule is actually followed. There are cultural differences in display rules. Misunderstandings in cross-cultural communication occur when people do not realize that it is a difference of display rule that makes for a different expression, not the underlying emotion (Ekman, 2010). The same emotion from a specific facial expression may be recognized by a culture, but the same intensity of emotion may not be perceived.

Recognizing Emotions

The face radiates a large variety of emotions: joy and happiness; fear, annoyance, surprise, anger, sadness, disgust, fatigue, pain, sexual excitement, religious feeling, contempt, interest, concern, embarrassment, despair, pity, boredom, quiet pleasure, complacency, adoration, and a host of others.

A given emotion can find different expressions depending on the degree of intensity. For instance, if we smile very intensely, we will open our mouth wide and display our teeth. Similarly, we may express surprise in several ways: questioning, amazed, dazed.

Specific emotional states, such as happiness or sadness, are expressed through a smile or a frown, respectively.

The face may sometimes show a 'blend' of emotions, expressing different emotions in different parts of it. A 'pleasant surprise', for example, may produce a blend of happiness and surprise—an open smile plus raised eyebrows—while bad and frightening news could produce a blend of sadness and fear.

When shocked or greatly surprised, a person will open his mouth wide; this happens because his jaw muscles relax on account of the emotion and the chin drops. The open-mouth gesture can also occur when a person is concentrating very intensely on a particular task because then all the facial muscles below the eyes are completely relaxed. Sometimes the tongue may protrude from the mouth.

Signs

Following are some emotions with their corresponding facial signals:

Anxiety   Eyes damp; eyebrows slightly pushed together; trembling lower lip; chin possibly wrinkled; head slightly tilted down.

Fear   Eyes wide, closed, or pointing down; raised eyebrows; mouth open or corners turned down; chin pulled in; head down, white face.

Anger   Eyes wide and staring; eyebrows pulled down (especially in middle); wrinkled forehead; flared nostrils; mouth flattened or clenched teeth bared; jutting chin, red face.

Happiness   Mouth smiling (open or closed); possible laughter; crows feet wrinkles at sides of sparkling eyes; slightly raised eyebrows; head level.

Sadness   Eyes cast down and possibly damp or tearful; head down; lips pinched; head down or to the side.

Envy   Eyes staring; mouth corners turned down; nose turned in sneer; chin jutting.

Desire   Eyes wide open with dilated pupils; slightly raised eyebrows; lips slightly parted or puckered or smiling; head tilted forward.

Interest   Steady gaze of eyes at item of interest (may be squinting); slightly raised eyebrows; lips slightly pressed together; head erect or pushed forward.

Boredom   Eyes looking away; face generally immobile; corners of mouth turned down or lips pulled to the side; head propped up with hand.

Surprise   Eyes wide open; eyebrows raised high; mouth dropped wide open with consequent lowered chin; head held back or tilted to side.

Relief   Eyebrows tilted outwards (lowered outer edges); mouth either tilted down or smiling; head tilted.

Disgust   Eyes and head turned away; nostrils flared; nose twisted in sneer; mouth closed, possibly with tongue protruding; chin jutting.

Shame Eyes and head turned down; eyebrows held low; skin blushing red.

Pity Eyes in extended gaze and possibly damp; eyebrows slightly pulled together in middle or downwards at edges; mouth turned down at corners; head tilted to side.

Calm Relaxed facial muscles and steady gaze with eyes. Perhaps mouth turned up slightly at sides in gentle smile.

Spontaneous surprise is real and beautiful to watch. The eyes are wide open, eyebrows raised high, and mouth slightly open. This gesture can be faked. However, one can notice the difference in the length of time the gesture is sustained. A faker holds it longer than a person who shows real surprise.

Anxiety and nervousness are the common side effects from lying. Those lying keep their heads down, but some, to cover up their behaviour, may deliberately hold their heads up. But the dampness in their eyes may betray them, or the slight trembling of their lower lip. When people are scared, they become nervous and anxious. This causes there skin to become hotter and get itchy which in turn cause fidgeting, revealing their anxiety.

In a conflict situation, the person who takes an extremely aggressive approach towards another would show it in his face: his eyes will be wide open and staring, his lips tightly closed, the corners of his eyebrows turned down, wrinkles on the forehead, he will have flared nostrils, and he will clench his teeth while he speaks so that his lips barely move. His chin will jut out. In contrast, the non-aggressive person will approach him with droopy eyes, a slight smile, arched eyelids, and an unwrinkled forehead.

Blushing is another facial phenomenon that expresses emotion and is outside conscious control. Blushing is evidenced in people who feel ashamed, or embarrassed, or angry. A shy person becomes red in the face when attention is focused on him in a group. A nervous person or one with low self-confidence blushes when asked to speak in public. The cheeks and neck turn red with embarrassment. When we are blushing, we are fully aware that other people can see our embarrassment and there is nothing we can do about it. Also, the people who witness our embarrassment are fully aware that they are drawing inferences on the basis of our blushing.

Facial expressions of emotions involve configurations of the whole face, though much information is carried by the eyebrows and mouth. This is evident when we examine a photograph of a person's face; we scan the whole face but concentrate primarily on the eyes and mouth. It is highlighted in *emoticons* or *smileys* which suggest an emotion simply by showing the eyes (and/ or eyebrows) and mouth. In email exchanges, for example, :)

or :), the original smiley, means something like 'I'm happy', but can also mean 'what I have just written was tongue-in-cheek' or 'only joking' (Underwood, 2000).

Stereotyping

Studies in facial expressions have led to interesting observations. 'Baby-faces' are seen as less mature. Faces with small, rounded chins, large and rounded eyes, high eyebrows, a large forehead, and smooth skin are perceived as belonging to people who are warm, submissive, dependent, weak, naive, honest, less threatening, and less mature.

Facial symmetry between a face's right and left hand sides is one trait that is considered when assessing the beauty of a person. In a research done on college students who were asked to rate photographs of young adult faces, it was found that faces having vertical and horizontal symmetry were found to be attractive (Givens, 1999).

Facial features can give indications of the personality in several ways. Should a person's face resemble that of someone we know, we may tend to anticipate similarities in personality too. Or, we may label people according to certain typical facial features: high foreheads are thought to contain larger brains; spectacles are associated with reading and intellectual work. We may also use metaphorical associations, for example, people with a coarse skin and dishevelled hair are thought to be coarse and aggressive.

Brown and Levinson (1987) explain how the face can invite or dispel 'politeness'. A positive face is the desire to be liked, appreciated, approved, and so on. A negative face is the desire not to be imposed upon, intruded, or otherwise put upon.

A puppy face or a puppy-dog face is a facial expression that humans make based on canine expressions: the head is tilted down and the eyes looking up. This gesture causes the eyes to appear larger while the user seems to subjectively decrease in height against the recipient. Consequently, the user appears younger or more childlike, which can cause the recipient to foster feelings of protectiveness and kindness for the user and hence achieves the desired goals.

Contrary Views

The idea of innate and universal facial expressions that have links with human emotions was given the status of scientific hypothesis by Darwin (1965). Substantial evidence, old and new, supports his hypothesis.

There has been a controversy over whether attribution (recognition) of emotions from facial expressions is universal (Ekman, 1994; Izard, 1994; Russell, 1994). Most researchers agree on various issues. There exists at least Minimal Universality (people everywhere can infer something about others from their facial behaviour). Anger, sadness, and other semantic categories for emotion are not pan-cultural and are not the precise messages conveyed by facial expressions. Emotions can occur without facial expressions, and facial expressions can occur without emotions. Further evidence is needed to determine the relationship between emotion and facial behaviour, what determines that relationship, how facial behaviour is interpreted, and how much the interpretation varies with culture and language.

Certain facial expressions have been theorized to be easily recognizable signals of specific emotions. If so, these expressions should override situationally based expectations used by a person in attributing an emotion to another. An alternative account is offered in which the face provides information relevant to emotion but does not signal a specific emotion. Therefore, in specified circumstances, situational rather than facial information was predicted to determine the judged emotion. This prediction was supported in three studies—indeed, in each of the 22 cases examined (for example, a person in a frightening situation but displaying a reported 'facial expression of anger' was judged as afraid). Situational information was especially influential when it suggested a non-basic emotion (for example, a person in a painful situation but displaying a 'facial expression of fear' was judged as in pain) (APA, 1996).

SPECIFIC EXPRESSIONS

The Smile

The smile as a facial expression is formed by flexing the muscles near both ends of the mouth. The smile can also be found around the eyes. The smile customarily is an expression denoting pleasure, happiness, or amusement, but can also be an involuntary expression of anxiety, in which case it is known as a grimace. Cross-cultural studies have shown that smiling is a means of communicating emotions throughout the world. But there are large differences between different cultures. A smile can be spontaneous or artificial (when people feel obliged to smile). Happiness is most often the motivating cause of a smile (Wikipedia, http://en.wikipedia.org/wiki/Smile, accessed on 10 January 2011).

At the age of about four weeks, human babies, even blind ones, smile spontaneously at a pleasing stimulus. Like all innate behaviour, babies' smiling is stereotyped, or always the same (Rank, 2011).

The smile is the most universally recognized non-verbal signal. It has enormous power to diffuse tense situations, smoothen customer service, raise the level of teamwork, and communicate friendliness. A genuine smile can communicate pleasant emotions such as happiness, acceptance, and appreciation. The yellow 'smiley face' that we see so often in publications is the universal symbol of happiness. 'Its colour is associated with the brightness of the sun' (Givens, 1999).

Smiling

Smiling indicates pleasure, either that you are generally happy and are enjoying the other person's company or that you are amused by something in particular, such as a joke. A full smile engages the whole face, particularly including the eyes, which crease and 'twinkle'. A genuine smile is often asymmetric and usually larger on the right side of the face. A false smile may be more symmetrical or larger on the left side of the face.

Smiling without opening the mouth, and particularly with lips firmly pressed together, may indicate embarrassment about unsightly teeth. It may also be a suppression of words, which one does, for instance, when one does not understand a joke but refrains from commenting. A half-smile, on one side of the face, may indicate cynicism, sarcasm, or uncertainty when one is in disagreement. Smiling is also a sign of submission as the person effectively pleads for acceptance.

Smile and laughter are not always expressions of pleasant emotions. Psychiatrists (see Marcos, 1973) say that fear, apology, confusion, covering up, despair, disgust, feeling foolish, irony, stupidity, and so on, can also manifest in smiles and laughter.

The Genuine Smile

Genuine smiles are generated by the unconscious brain, so are automatic. When people feel pleasure, signals pass through the part of the brain that processes emotion. As well as making the mouth muscles move, the muscles that raise the cheeks—the *orbicularis oculi* and the *pars orbitalis*—also contract, making the eyes crease up, and the eyebrows dip slightly.

In a genuine smile, several facial muscles come into play, not just the mouth, and the whole face is involved, including the tightening around the eyes. This action around the eyes is extremely difficult to fake and is the main signal for authentic smiling, revealing real feelings. Genuine smiles appear on both sides of the face. A genuine smile indicates honesty and openness to communication.

Givens (1999) describes the 'zygomatic smile' as the 'heartfelt smile' which 'is hard to produce on demand', for it is a smile of genuine happiness or joy. This smile is formed by the corners of the mouth curving inward and the outer corners of the eyes crinkling into crows feet. This is a spontaneous smile, dictated by emotion, and therefore an accurate reflection of the mood of the person.

Fake Smiles

Scientists distinguish between genuine and fake smiles by using a coding system called the FACS, which was devised by Professor Paul Ekman of the University of California and Dr Wallace V. Friesen of the University of Kentucky (BBC).

While the physical variations of some smiles are apparent, there are smiles that are physically similar but mean different things. A smile can be faked, artificial, or the stamp of habit.

Fake smiles can be performed at will, because the brain signals that create them come from the conscious part of the brain and prompt the zygomaticus major muscles in the cheeks to contract. These are the muscles that pull the corners of the mouth outwards. A counterfeit smile sometimes appears more strongly on one side of the face (usually the right side).

Smiling with lips only is often falsehood, where the smiler wants to convey pleasure or approval but is actually feeling something else. This false smile is known as the Duchenne smile, after the scientists who first described it in 1862. False smiles also tend to last for longer. Lowering the jaw to show a *D*-shaped mouth can be a false smile as it is easy to do. It may also be a deliberate signal of amusement and an invitation to laugh. Many people will intuitively notice a faked smile.

People who put on a smile, usually used out of politeness, restrict their smile to the muscles around the mouth. The upper half of their face remains virtually unchanged. Their smile is also less likely to be showing their teeth. This smile could indicate that the person is not telling the whole truth. Or, as often happens, a person feels embarrassed to show his teeth.

Categories of Smiles

A full smile engages the whole face, particularly including the eyes, which crease and 'twinkle'. Nierenberg and Calero (1975) describe three very common smiles: the simple, the upper, and the broad.

(a)   (b)   (c)

Simple smile: This is when the teeth are not exposed (Figure a). We generally wear the simple smile when we are watching something interesting or pleasant but are not physically involved in the action. We smile to ourselves.

Upper smile: This smile exposes the upper set of teeth (Figure b). It is a friendly smile, usually when we greet someone. It is accompanied by eye contact.

Broad smile: This smile exposes both sets of teeth and is usually accompanied by laughter, often without eye contact (Figure c).

Dr Ewan Grant (see Nierenberg and Calero, 1975) presents a list of five smile types:

Oblong smile: The lips are drawn fully back from both the upper and lower teeth, forming the oblong with the lips. Somehow there is no depth to this smile. 'This is the smile or grimace when one is pretending to enjoy a joke or off-the-cuff remark', or for politeness' sake.

How-do-you-do smile: Only the upper teeth are uncovered and the mouth is generally only slightly open (see Upper smile).

Typically nonsense smile: The lips curve back and up but remain together, so there is no dental display. It occurs when one is by oneself and happy (see Simple smile).

Broad smile: The mouth is open, the lips curled right back, and both upper and lower teeth are visible. It occurs 'in situations of pleasurable excitement'.

Lip-in smile: This is much the same as the upper smile except that the lower lip is drawn in between the teeth. It is often seen on the faces of a coy girl. 'It implies that the person feels in some way subordinate to the person she is meeting.'

The Smirk

Another form of smiling is the smirk. The smirk is a facial expression characterized by turning up the corners of the mouth; it usually shows pleasure or amusement. It has been variously described as: smiling in a self-satisfied or foolish manner; a smile expressing scorn, smugness, and so on, rather than pleasure; to smile in an affected, often offensively self-satisfied manner.

A person smirks by keeping his lips pressed together in a controlled laugh. Though there may be no evidence of negativism, there will be overtones of maliciousness at times. The smirk could also be a secret laugh, with cause of the provocation known only to the smirker. Thus, a smirk evokes insolence, scorn, or offensive smugness.

Laughter

Laughing

Laughing goes beyond smiling to expresses greater pleasure and happiness. Whilst smiling may happen over a longer period, laughter is a relatively brief affair, happening for a few seconds.

There are many variants on laughter and we all laugh differently, from the suppressed titter to the loud and uproarious belly laugh. Louder and less suppressed laughter may indicate someone who is less self-conscious. It may also be used by a person who is trying to gain attention.

Laughing and smiling at the misfortune of others is often socially unacceptable, although we often find this funny. In such cases you may see suppressed grins and giggles as the person tries desperately to hide their feeling of amusement. Laughs, for example, may get disguised as coughs and the person may turn away to hide their expression.

Laughter is largely connected with our speech punctuation and can be more controlled than the actual smile. That is, we can consciously control our laughter and even practice and improve it for greater effectiveness in ordinary communication. On the flip side, we may use laughter inappropriately in social settings.

Social Behaviour

Laughter is a social behaviour: it is used in social settings with others. Seldom do we burst out laughing when alone, even when reading a humorous book or watching TV. In normal circumstances, it is the presence of others with whom we can share our humour that we laugh. We use laughter as a non-verbal punctuation to our speech. The laugh is usually produced in response to embarrassment, excitement, or humour. Socially, laughter increases the bonding between friends when confronting strangers or forces beyond their control. In mixed groups, laughter brings together children and adults, women and men. Psychologically, the comic laugh (in response, for example, to funny jokes, puns, and satire) is a recent development linked to the evolution of speech (Givens, 1999).

It is not uncommon for people under stress to laugh too much and too loud, often revealing the nervousness and discomfort they are experiencing. It is their way of telling others to relax and be comfortable with them, to compensate for their emotional stress.

Dynamics

According to Professor Jan Van Hooff, an ethologist, laughter is composed of a broad range of gestures and sounds. One can distinguish a burst of laughter from the average horse laugh which is characterized by an open mouth and exposed teeth. The horse laughter's head remains level, s   ιat he or she can see what the experts call the 'risible source'. The vocalized smile is the softest form of audible laughter. It is characterized by a mouth slightly open, lips moderately retracted, and slight vocal effects, or 'chuckles'. To laugh 'up one's sleeve' is to laugh silently, through a slightly open mouth. The corners of the mouth turn up, and air is ejected in a staccato rhythm from the nose. Psychologists call this 'risible sniffling' (Bacri, 1992).

Children born deaf and blind smile and laugh as we do when they are happy and emit the correct sounds when they do so (Eibl-Eibesfeldt, 1973).

Laughter is a response to embarrassment, excitement, or humour. There are common labels for different forms of laughter: hollow, forced, mocking, bubbling, and so on. There is also a rich vocabulary to denote types of laughter: giggle, titter, chortle, guffaw, cackle, roar, crow, snigger, jeer, and so on.

One can 'read' laughter from the sounds that ensue (*The Secrets of Body Language*, 1997).

'Ha-Ha' is a laughter that is genuine, coming straight from the heart. It expresses pure joy and self-fulfilment.

'He-He' is a mocking laugh, usually issuing from a condescending remark or a joke about a person.

'Hee-Hee' suggests a secret giggle or a snigger that is emitted when a person is being cynical or spiteful.

'Ho-ho' communicates surprise, even disbelief, by a person who is critical, protesting, or challenging.

As with most gestures, laughter must be interpreted within its social context. No laughter in itself has any particular meaning. More than anything else, women want men to make them laugh (Givens, 1999).

Varieties of Laughter

Foot (1986) defines the following varieties of laughter:

Humorous Laughter: This may be regarded as an overt expression of rebellion against social pressure, codes, and institutions, of which all of us are victims. Some people use this socially harmless channel to effectively displace their frustration. Our primary purpose in engaging in humorous laughter is to convey to others that like them we too find social conventions funny and that we too are continually frustrated by social pressures and the social niceties which exert so much control over our lives.

Social Laughter: It is a means of expressing friendship and liking, gaining social approval, and bolstering group cohesiveness. It does not depend upon individuals finding something but is intended to convey an image of good-natured sociability. It is used for controlling conversation and for smooth social interaction. It is a 'polite laughter' when we laugh at what others have said not because we find it funny but out of consideration for the speakers and to gain their attention and appreciation.

Ignorance Laughter: We recognize that a joke has been told but wish to conceal our ignorance or inability to comprehend it. So we laugh with everyone else in the group in order not to be left out or to look stupid.

Evasion Laughter: Like humour, laughter can serve as an emotional mask for our true feelings. If a friend or acquaintance of ours is being attacked or ridiculed by others behind his back, we have the option to defend him, or, out of expediency, go through the motion of joining in the ridicule so as not to appear different. Laughter gives the impression of sharing in the feeling of the group.

Embarrassment Laughter: Like evasion laughter, here too one can mask one's feelings and stall for time. Here we laugh because we are not quite sure what the other person's comments mean, or whether his intentions towards us are amicable or hostile. The very act of laughing may cause us to tilt the head back and avert our gaze, and thereby relieve our embarrassment by momentarily pretending that the remarks were directed at us.

Apologetic Laughter: This is related to evasion laughter and embarrassment laughter. We may laugh prior to beginning some action, the outcome of which we are uncertain about. We sometimes say, 'I've never done this before ...' or 'I can't guarantee what is going to happen ...' when we embark upon a new task. Laughter may either accompany or substitute for the oral statement and its meaning is obvious: we are gearing up for possible failure or for appearing foolish. Through the laugh, we lead others to believe that we are not taking the situation too seriously ourselves.

Defensive Laughter: We may preface breaking bad news with laughter, perhaps partly in an attempt to soften the blow and partly by way of apologizing for being the one to announce it. This laughter acts as an excuse for some action we did not take or our indecision regarding some event that resulted in a tragedy.

Anxiety Laughter: Tension in social encounters stems from anxiety as well as embarrassment. Anxiety laughter is a manifestation of release of tension from a specific anxiety-provoking situation. We may laugh with the feeling of relief when a period of acute tension comes to an end.

Derision Laughter: This is obviously an alternative, or an additive, to the encoding of hostile humour in situations where one individual wishes to express superiority over another. It is particularly prevalent among children when they mock a child who is physically or mentally deformed. Adults use derision laughter as a weapon in more subtle, psychological ways, not so much for deriding the physical abnormalities of their victims (for which the latter cannot be blamed) and more for ridiculing the odd behaviour, mannerisms, attitudes, or incompetence of their victims (for which they can be blamed more readily).

Derision laughter is also used as a form of refusal or exclusion, particularly when aimed at an individual by the members of a group, and at that individual's expense. Such laughter may draw attention to some characteristics of the individual (voice, accent, manner of dress, age, size) which sets him apart from the rest of the group, or it may be based upon the group's desire to exclude that person from joining in their activities.

Joyous Laughter: This is a pure expression of excitement; a spontaneous reaction to pleasurable and exhilarating activities and particularly characteristic of children at play.

Other Facial Expressions

Frown

A frown, also known as a scowl, is a facial expression used to show displeasure, sadness, or disapproval. The emoticon (icon) for a frown is a curve of the lips facing away from the eyes ('down'). Hence, the frown is related to the mouth. However, it also has to do with the wrinkling of the eyebrow.

The frown is often seen in contrast to the smile. While the smile tends to convey the general states of acceptance and agreement, the frown indicates states of rejection and disagreement. The genuine smile usually displays appreciation, agreement, protection, and so on. A frown may suggest the very opposite: confusion, unacceptability, disagreement, and so on.

It most commonly expresses sadness, dissatisfaction, anger, worry, or pain, although it is also a sign of deep concentration.

Sneer

The sneer is a scornful facial expression characterized by a slight raising of one corner of the upper lip. It expresses contempt either with a sound or a statement. It is known also as curling the lip or turning up the nose. Charles Darwin defined a 'sneer' as 'the upper lip being retracted in such a manner that the canine tooth on one side of the face alone is shown' (Darwin, 1965). It is suggested that the sneer is a universal expression of contempt (Izard and Haynes, 1988).

Snarl

A snarl is a facial expression where the upper lip is raised and the nostrils widen, generally indicating hate, anger, or pain. Snarling is often accompanied by threatening vocalizations.

Yawn

Yawning is a sudden, deep inhalation of air accompanied by an open mouth, tightened cheek muscles, eye closure, and tearing. The yawn includes 'closing of the eyes and lowering of the brows' (Brannigan and Humphries, 1972). We do it when we are tired and blood oxygen is low; in a tense setting, adrenaline lowers the blood's oxygen level and yawning speeds re-oxygenation (Hill, 1977).

Yawning is involuntary; it is the result of sleepiness, fatigue, boredom, or emotional conflict. In tense business meetings, for instance, yawning is a sign of mild anxiety, disagreement, or uncertainty. When alert listeners yawn in response to controversial suggestions or ideas, the yawn signals a probing point, that is, an opportunity to explore unverbalized objections or clarify unvoiced concerns.

Yawning is also due to boredom. In our attempt to conceal a yawn, we turn our head or hold the mouth more closed than it actually wants to be.

Yawning is highly contagious, and that when one person yawns, other people nearby are very likely to follow suit. Research has shown that it does not require a complete yawn for one person to copy another—the mere sight of an open mouth, or the sound of a yawn, is often enough to get other people yawning.

Blank Face

The so-called 'blank face' or 'deadpan' face is in some ways related to masking. It is an expressionless, emotionless face that is relaxed. People usually have this 'expression' when they are by themselves, especially when in a relaxed mood, sitting by themselves, and reading or watching TV. Even though devoid of expression, the blank face sends a strong emotional message: Do Not Disturb.

Thus, the blank face is generally used to keep people at a distance. One encounters such faces in crowded places, like streets and shopping centres (see Givens, 1999).

This facial 'non-expression' is used by most of us to keep strangers at a distance. For example, in a crowded elevator, the blank face is probably the only tool we have to maintain our 'private space' unperturbed. The message is pretty clear: do not disturb.

A deadpan face is rarely perceived as neutral. Although this is a perfectly relaxed pose, if you have a naturally down-turned mouth, others might perceive you as 'angry' or 'sad' when, in fact, you are simply relaxing. Studies show that children do not like to see expressionless faces: they become anxious and frustrated, confused, because they are not able to decipher the real feelings of the ones they look at. And this is not solely the case of children. Even adults tend to wonder about the real feelings of the ones that display an emotionless expression.

It is difficult to 'read' a blank face out of a context. While in public places, a blank face is just a 'keep your distance' mask, the 'meeting' blank face cannot be deciphered so easily. There are other factors you should consider and other body signals before concluding that your co-worker tries to send out a 'do not disturb' message.

Masking

The face we present to others is rarely our genuine face. Only in exceptional cases does one display ones real feelings. 'Day after day we cover up this bare human being. We hold ourselves in careful control lest our bodies cry out messages our minds are too careless to hide' (Pease, 1993).

We use the muscles of our face to form a mask, which regulates our social roles just as surely as the Greco-Roman mask did for the actor who wore it (Fridlund, 1994). Masking includes facial gestures and can involve the whole body.

Since childhood we have been disciplined to carefully control our external behaviour in society. One obvious sign of such disciplining is 'the way we manage our personal appearance, the clothes we select and the hairdos we affect' (Goffman, 1969). By and large, we follow the conventional 'expected' behaviour: neat clothes, a clean-shaven face, well-groomed hair, and so on. Social etiquette decides what is proper and what is not in terms of body language. There are cultural variations in the techniques of masking, but the basic fact of masking exists at all levels of society and in all cultural set-ups.

In times of stress or under exhaustion, however, we drop our masks and expose ourselves as we really are. For example, at the end of a hectic day when we are trapped at the end of a long queue to catch a bus, we cover up our frustration by artificial—or social—smiles when we step on someone's toes, literally or idiomatically. The smile, nevertheless, serves as a good masking device.

It is not possible to mask involuntary reactions, like perspiration when we are under tension, or trembling hands and legs when we feel nervous. We may attempt to hide these signs by placing our hands in our pockets or standing behind a piece of furniture.

Fast (1970) observed that children and servants are treated as 'non-persons', and therefore adults do not need to wear masks when dealing with them. This attitude is also related to class consciousness. One class of society will not wear a mask before a class lower than itself. People of a given status will not mask before those of a lower status. The boss may not feel the need of masking in the presence of his employee; the lady of the house will be her natural self with her maid. Parents will be themselves before their wards. The need to mask is so compelling that it becomes second nature to us, whether in public or private.

Several traditional societies in India require women to cover their faces—mask them physically—with a veil. Thus, they conceal their true emotions and even protect themselves from male aggression.

PART TWO: PROMINENT FEATURES

THE MOUTH

The mouth is a very active part of the face. Whether it is moved deliberately or spontaneously, it communicates much non-verbally. When raised, the mouth communicates positive feelings, happiness, and optimism. Kept straight, it conceals emotions; turned down, it expresses sadness, confusion, and dissatisfaction. A person 'pulls a long face' by deliberately lowering the corners of the mouth to indicate something negative; this will generally be accompanied by a shaking of the head.

The mouth faithfully reflects the consensus of our thoughts and our smiles or grimaces. It is one of the most noticeable parts of the face. It gives automatic expression to deeper and more important aspects of our nature. The mouth, when relaxed, tells a great deal about the person. A person may also tense his mouth by tightening and pressing together the lip and jaw muscles, to express anger, frustration, determination, sympathy, threat, or pensiveness. 'A tense mouth precisely marks the onset of a mood shift, novel thought, or sudden change of heart' (Givens, 1999).

Mouth Functions

Speaking

The mouth sends several signals when it is speaking.

Mumbling: If the mouth moves little, perhaps including incoherent mumbling, this may indicate an unwillingness to speak, for example, from shyness or from a fear of betraying themselves.

Incessant talking: A mouth that moves a lot during speech can indicate excitement or dominance as it sends clear signals that 'I am speaking, do not interrupt!'

Articulation: Careful shaping of words can also indicate a person with auditory preferences or a concern for precision and neatness.

Talking fast: Fast speakers are often visual thinkers who are trying to get out what they are seeing. They may also be looking upwards.

Talking slow: Slow speakers may be deep thinkers who are being careful about finding the right words. They may also have an auditory preference as they carefully enunciate each word.

Eating

The mouth is used for eating, and the way people eat can reveal things about them.

Opening: Good manners demand that a person opens his mouth to the minimum while eating, taking into a moderate amount of food. The mouth is kept closed while masticating or chewing what is in it. And consequently refrain from speaking with his mouth full. An ill-mannered person gobbles large mouthfuls and keeps the mouth open while eating. In the same token, burping is acceptable. In some cultures, people consider it a normal practice to make sounds with the food in their mouths to express that they are relishing their morsel. At times the host may even expect the guest to make such noises to rest assured that the food is acceptable and appreciated. Some people eat slowly because their minds are also occupied at the same time chewing on ideas. Such people also tend to slide their jaw sideways when they eat.

Drinking

As with eating, so with drinking. The proper manner for drinking is to sip small amounts and swallow noiselessly. However, people do drink with loud glugging and gulping, and burp, all of which may appear distasteful or acceptable depending on the culture. Generally, one must raise the glass or cup to the lip rather than lower the head while drinking.

Breathing

Sigh: A short, deep, exhaling sigh can indicate sadness, frustration, or boredom.

Sob: Short inhalation, particularly in a sequence, can be like silent sobs and hence be an indicator of deep and suppressed sadness.

Panting: A person who is frightened or angry by the fight or flight reaction may well open his/her mouth to get more oxygen in preparation for combat or running away. This may also involve breathing faster (panting).

Mouth Parts

Teeth

There is not much to say about the non-verbal communication of the teeth. Following are some observations:

Biting: Baring the teeth in a snarl may appear as a threat to bite an opponent, though actual biting is rarely done. Gently biting another person's lip or ear can be a sign of affection.

Smiling: Exposing the teeth in smiling tends to indicate extreme pleasure. People who are self-conscious and particularly if their teeth are not that attractive may try not to show their teeth when smiling.

Sound: Chattering teeth may indicate extreme fear and is usually accompanied by shaking of the body. This may also indicate extreme coldness. Grinding teeth can indicate suppressed anger or frustration as the person tensely tries not to speak. Light tapping of the teeth can be mild frustration or thinking (it is similar in effect to tapping of a finger). As with other repetitive action, teeth noise can also just be habit.

Tapping: Sometimes people tap their teeth with their nails, making a noise that echoes in the mouth. This can signal thinking or boredom. It may also be a deliberate interruption or irritant, although this is less likely.

Tongue

The tongue is related to the spoken language. However, it can also send some important non-verbal signals.

Sticking out: Sticking out ones tongue at someone is the momentary visible protrusion and retraction of the tongue between the lips. It is generally an impolite gesture. It is a rather childish gesture and thus reflects negatively on the one doing it. A haughty person may deliberately stick his tongue out in an amusingly cheeky way. This will be accompanied by an intense face and often followed by a smile or laughter. A person who is straining while doing a job may also stick out his tongue; it will usually be seen sticking out the side of the mouth. The tongue just slightly protruding from the mouth may indicate that the person doe not want to interrupt others.

Tongue showing is a universal symbol to express 'disagreement, disbelief, disliking, displeasure, or uncertainty. It may modify, counteract, or contradict verbal remarks' (Givens, 1999). When a person says he agrees, yet shows his tongue, it in fact suggests that he is not in agreement. During conversation, when someone protrudes and retracts his tongue while listening, the speaker may read it as a cue for lack of clarity, or a pending issue, and would do well to probe so as to help the listener verbalize his thoughts or mood.

A related gesture is the tongue just slightly protruding from the lips for a while. Studies show that a listener in this posture is less likely to be interrupted. In one situation, a salesman at a large store whose tongue was not visible was preferred by customers over another whose tongue was showing (Givens, 1999).

Licking: The tongue licks the lips at the sight of food the person relishes or another person who is desirable.

Biting: The biting of the tongue typically indicates that the biter wants to say something but he somehow feels unable or unwilling to say it. He is perhaps afraid of offending or of breaking social rules.

Hidden: With mouth closed and tongue inside the mouth, the movements of the tongue can sometimes be detected. Pressed against the cheek, it can indicate thinking and uncertainty. Pushed in front of the teeth, pushing out the lips, can also indicate uncertainty.

THE LIPS

When it comes to feelings and emotions, the lips can be invaluable. Lips convey a lot of information that is often ignored or not even observed. Rich with nerves and highly vascular, the lips react to the reality of the moment and communicate accurately our feelings and sentiments to others. So when people receive bad news or witness a horrific event, their lips begin to disappear, becoming very thin as vasoconstriction takes place. Under extreme stress, they disappear completely or are compressed together. Because disappearing or compressed lips are universal behaviours, controlled by the limbic system, these are behaviours that can be relied upon and are authentic (Navarro, 2008).

The lips all too readily reveal our innermost feelings. Even when one does not utter a word, the lips can be eloquent, because silent lips express a wide range of emotions, and moods, from a smile to a frown. 'Like hands, lips are incredibly gifted communicators, and always bear watching' (Givens, 1999).

Types

Tight lips: People with such lips are brief and concise in their speech. They will say volumes in a few words. They will not waste time. Not only do they themselves prefer to be concise, they expect the same of others too. One must therefore be brief, without being curt, in dealing with them. Such people are also efficient.

Full lips: Persons who are full-lipped are generous with time, words, and materials. Those with large, loose lips are talkative and tend to ramble on a subject. Full-lipped individuals are more outgoing and sympathetic. Such people, since they are generally slow to get started and slow to finish, can overcome their limitations if they organize their time and set deadlines for their tasks.

Relaxed: The lips have a position of rest when they are not pulled in any direction. This usually indicates that the person is also feeling relaxed.

Positions

Compressed lips: Lips that are pressed together to form a thin, tight line indicates a person's disagreement, opposition, or refusal. When someone compresses his lips in a friendly discussion, the other can expect criticism or disapproval. A person who compresses his lips suddenly will most likely be about to express anger, dislike, grief, sadness, or uncertainty (Givens, 1999). Compressed lips combined with eyes staring into nothingness and/or head movement can mean deep thought, studied approval, or disapproval. The 'tight lip' communicates that a person has taken a defensive position and will reveal or react as little as possible.

In babies, lip compression and brow lowering (combined in the pucker face) appear when mothers persist in playing or feeding beyond the infant's tolerance. In children, smiles in threatening situations are combined with tightening and compressing the lips (Stern and Bender, 1974).

Lip compression (lips pressed tightly together and rolled inward) often appears in the company of strangers, where it correlates with gaze avoidance, non contact, and distancing between individuals. Biting one's lower lip with one's teeth and shaking one's head from side to side vigorously indicates that one is angry (Morris, 1994). A sudden lip compression may signal the onset of anger, disliking, grief, sadness, or uncertainty.

Pouting lips: Pouting is pushing the lower lip against the upper protruding lip. It is either a protest gesture or a signal that a person wants to test or enjoy a certain situation. The pout of protest may appear as if a person is about to spit out something, thus suggesting disgust with a situation and a desire to remove oneself from it. It indicates sulkiness, disappointment, displeasure, sadness, or uncertainty. The pout for testing resembles lips ready to taste something, with the corners of the mouth slightly upward. If accompanied with a movement of the tongue over the lips, it suggests enjoyment or pleasure. When done with the head moved backward, it suggests that a person is pleased with what he sees.

Pursed lips: Pursing is rounding of the lips. It could be the gesture of someone who has firmly made up his mind about something and will not budge from his viewpoint. It also displays arrogance and self-importance. Apprehension, scheming, or mere disinclination to speak may be betrayed by tightly screwed lips. 'A brief pout or mouth shrug (Morris, 1994) reveals doubt or uncertainty (even as one says, for example, "I am absolutely sure")' (Givens, 1999). The tightening of the jaw muscles and pursing of the lips indicate antagonism.

Puckered: A light puckering of the lips into a kiss shape typically indicates desire. It can also indicate uncertainty, particularly if the lips are touched with the fingers. When one says 'oo', the lips form the kiss shape.

Flattened: Lips which are kept horizontal but squeezed flat are an exaggerated closing of the mouth and hence indicate a repressed desire to speak. This indicates disapproval ('If I spoke I would be very critical, which I do not want to be'). It can also indicate frustration ('I want to speak, but others are speaking and I feel I should wait'). Flattened lips can also indicate a refusal to eat, either because of dislike of offered food or some other motivation.

Turned up: When the corners of the mouth are turned upwards, this can be a grimace of disgust or a smile of pleasure. In a grimace, the teeth are unlikely to be shown (although toothless smiles are also common). Grimaces are often flatter and tenser.

Turned down: Corners of the mouth turned down indicates sadness or displeasure. Some people are so miserable so often, this is the natural state of rest of their mouths (which is perhaps rather sad).

Retracted: When the lips are pulled back, they expose the teeth. This may be in a broad smile or it may be a snarl of aggression. The eyes should tell you which is which. In a snarl, the eyes are either narrowed or staring. In a full smile, the corners of the eyes are creased.

Movements

Moving: Lips which are moving in the shape of words but without making sounds means that the person is thinking of saying the words. This sub-vocalization often happens with very small movement and is often completely subconscious. Up and down movement may indicate chewing. Some people chew the insides of their mouths when they are nervous. Rolling in the lips so they roll across one another can be a preening gesture for women, evening out lipstick. It can also be a sign of uncertainty or disapproval with the accompanying gesture of lowered eyebrows.

Twitching: Small, lightning-fast movements of the mouth betray inner thought. A single twitch of the corner of the mouth indicates cynicism or disbelief. Liars in particular will often give themselves away with very brief grimaces as their conscience expresses disapproval of the conscious lies.

Protruding: When the top lip is over the bottom lip, this may be linked with biting of the bottom lip, a common indicator that the person is feeling guilty about something. The bottom lip extended over the top lip can indicate uncertainty, as if the person is saying 'umm'. The bottom lip jutting out is often a part of a sulky pout, where the person expresses childlike petulance at not getting their own way. Both lips pressed together and pushed out generally indicates doubt. If the finger touches them, it may indicate internal thinking or may say 'I am considering speaking but am not quite ready to talk yet'.

Biting of lips: Biting of lips can send a message of uncertainty, hesitation, nervousness, embarrassment, or attempts to suppress surging emotions. Biting of the lower lip shows doubt or deliberation, or uncertainty, exercise of caution, or contemplation. A person bites his lip to stop it from making rash statements. He may also do so as a reaction when caught unawares in an embarrassing situation and trying hard to think of something to say.

THE NOSE

The nose is the most prominent part of the face and part by which it is easy to recognize someone's features and identity. Its shape and positioning 'reinforces the vertical height of our face and accents the stability of its feature' (Givens, 1999). Men with larger noses seem physically stronger. Women with smaller noses, 'which may be further reduced with make-up to keep it from upstaging the lips and eyes', seem youthful.

Signals from the Nose

Flared: When we breathe deeply, or are emotionally aroused, our nostrils visibly flare. The widening of the nostrils allows more air to be breathed in and out and readies the person for combat. Flared nostrils may also indicate that the person is making an internal judgement about something or is experiencing extreme displeasure.

Wrinkled: The nose can be wrinkled by pushing up from the mouth. This happens when a person senses an unpleasant odour. It can also happen when a person reacts to someone who suggests a distasteful idea. Another variation is when the person is thinking about something but is not satisfied with his own ideas.

Sniffing indicates displeasure or disgust. This may also happen with one nostril, with the mouth twitching up as well. Sniffing is also the result of suffering from a cold.

Touching the nose can indicate that the person has detected a bad smell. It is also common signal from a person who is not telling the truth. When a person lies, blood vessels in their nose may dilate, making the nose swell or appear redder. This also may lead to him touching or scratching the nose. Nose-picking can signify various states of mind, none particularly positive.

Rubbing the finger alongside the nose can indicate disagreement.

Pinching the bridge of the nose can show the person is evaluating something, usually negatively and with some frustration.

Fiddling with the nose or pressing it down can just be a habit when the person is thinking.

THE CHEEKS

Cheeks can speak body language, although admittedly not very much.

Drawn In or Blown Out

Cheeks can be drawn in or blown out. Cheeks that are pulled in, particularly with pursed lips, indicate disapproval. Cheeks sucked in to the extent that the lower lips curl can indicate pensiveness which may be uncomfortable; usually it would be accompanied with a furrowed brow. Cheeks, when blown out, signify uncertainty, especially when reinforced with raised eyebrows and rounded eyes. It may be accompanied by the person actually blowing air from the mouth. Blown out cheeks can also be a sign of exhaustion.

Chewing the inside of the cheek or mouth can be a hidden sign of nervousness and may indicate lying. Pushing the tongue into the cheek can show pensiveness as the person thinks about something and tries to come to a decision.

Colour

Red cheeks, in other circumstances, are a classic sign of embarrassment or anger. Accompanying signs for anger are enlarged and staring eyes. Cheeks appear pale when blood drains from them. This typically happens when a person is frightened as the blood is moved to the muscles in readiness to flee. Pale cheeks can also be a sign of coldness. During exercising, the face becomes red and sweaty.

Touch

People touch their cheeks in surprise or horror. A light touch, along with an open mouth that says 'Oooh', indicates light surprise. Touching both cheeks with the flat of the palm is an exaggeration of this and may indicate horror. The 'Cheek Scratch with an Open Mouth' is a very common expression of disagreement-related anxiety. It is especially common among men.

THE EYEBROWS

Eyebrows are the arch of short hair above the eyes. Being near the eyes, which are the major senders of signals, they are highly visible communicators, although the limited control of muscles around them can limit what they say.

There are four basic postures involving the eyebrows and the eyes:

- Eyebrows in repose and eyes in repose—this is the expression of the face at rest.
- Eyebrows in repose and eyes widened—this is the threatening facial expression of anger, sometimes involving lowering of the brow.

- Eyebrows raised and eyes widened—this is the facial expression associated with the prototypical fear response.
- Eyebrows raised and eyes in repose—the facial expression of submission (Collett, 2003).

When people want to demonstrate that they are not a threat, they frequently raise their eyebrows. This makes them look attentive and impressed. When the eyebrows are pinched together at the centre, they create an impression of concern. Of course the eyebrows can be raised with or without being pinched. When they are raised and pinched, the result is a hybrid gesture that conveys submission and concern.

Raised

When we first see someone we are attracted to, we give them a quick eyebrow flash. If the person of interest is attracted to you, they will return the flash. Watch out for this. This form of interaction is one of the most common in the human species, even more so than the smile.

People raise their eyebrows to express surprise, doubt, disbelief, exasperation, or exaggeration, or unconsciously when giving orders, making demands, or arguing important points. They also raise their eyebrows when they might want to say or clarify something, end the conversation, or have disagreed with something that has been said. A raised brow adds emphasis to staring, pouting, smiling (Givens, 1999). According to Morris (1994), one eyebrow raised is used everywhere to signal scepticism. And the flashing of eyebrows is a universal sign of welcome (Eibl-Eibesfeldt, 1989).

Raising the eyebrows adds intensity to a facial expression. Brow-raising can strengthen a dominant stare, exaggerate a submissive pout, or boost the energy of a smile. When elevated, the eyebrows form prominent, horizontal furrows in the forehead, making almost any gesture look and feel stronger. In tandem with head-tilt-back, raising one or both eyebrows suggests a supercilious air of disdain, haughtiness, or pride. The word 'supercilious' comes from the Latin word for 'eyebrow'. We unconsciously lift our eyebrows to give orders, make demands, and argue important points (Givens, 1999).

Emotions

If you lift your eyebrows when you meet a person for the first time, it will be a sign of friendliness towards that person. If the feeling is mutual: you will get the same up–down motion of eyebrows in response. It looks funny from the side, especially if one of you has bushy eyebrows, it will look as if one cannot see the other clearly through them. But this is one of the oldest ways of winning sympathy.

When both eyebrows are raised for a few split seconds during a greeting, it is a sign of *submissiveness, a* way of saying 'I come in friendliness'; it also expresses openness in that it lets the other person see ones eyes. When people greet someone with a very excited '*Hey!*', they raise their eyebrows rapidly. Eyebrow raised to express *surprise* typically happens as a part of opening the eyes wider, perhaps to see more clearly what is going on. The more the surprise, the higher the eyebrows are raised. Raising the eyebrows can also signal a question. When a question is asked and the eyebrows raised afterwards, this is a clear invitation to answer the question.

Raising a single eyebrow is something that only some people can do and can be a bit more wry in its meaning, for example, finding out whether the other person is sure of what he is saying when he appears to be talking with limited accuracy.

Middle-raised

By pushing together the eyebrows and pulling up the forehead, the eyebrows can be made to slope outwards. This can indicate relief ('Whew!'). It can also indicate anxiety ('Oh no!').

Lowered

People lower their eyebrows to protect their eyes from openings in a kind of 'non-verbal lock-down'. Emotionally, the expression is a response to their 'gut feelings'. Lowered brows show anger (Ekman and Friesen, 1975) or puzzlement when it appears in a cluster of gestures: curving of the mouth downward, lowering of the eyelids, dropping of the jaw, and constriction of the forehead muscles.

'Lowering the eyebrows is a sensitive indicator of disagreement, doubt, or uncertainty. Slightly lowered eyebrows may telegraph unvoiced disagreement among colleagues, as comments are presented at a conference table' (Givens, 1999).

Lowering our eyebrows is what we use to display aggressiveness, dominance, or sadness; they are also lowered to display concern or authority. Lowering the eyebrows conceals the eyes to a certain degree. Particularly with a lowered head, this can thus indicate deception or a desire that eye signals are harder to see. Lowered eyebrows may also indicate annoyance, perhaps effectively saying 'I am so displeased, I do not want to look at you'. Related to this, lowered eyebrows are a sign of a dominant person. People lower or knit their eyebrows when they show disagreement or displeasure, frown or scowl when in a temper, or while viewing something with full concentration.

Middle-lowered

When the middle of the eyebrows are pulled down so that they slope inwards, this often shows that the person is angry or frustrated. It can also indicate intense concentration.

Oscillating

When we see people we know, we often give a quick up–down flash of the eyebrows in recognition and greeting. Rapid and repeated up and down movement may be an exaggerated signal, meaning 'Well how about that then!'

SMALLER PARTS

Chin

The chin, a part of the face, has its own body language:

Pointing: The chin can be used as a subtle pointing device. A slight flick of the head may give a small signal that only people in the know are likely to notice. Pointing at a person briefly with the chin can be a gesture of insult. It is more covert than pointing with a finger and non-threatening.

Jutting: Jutting out the chin towards a person exposes it and says 'Go on, I dare you, try to hit me and see what happens!' This can thus be a signal of defiance, if not towards the other person then instead towards some situation or person in the conversation.

Stroking: Stroking the chin is often a signal that the person is thinking hard. He may well be judging or evaluating something, particularly if the conversation has offered him an option or a decision to make.

Holding: Propping up the head by holding the chin in a cupped hand, particularly when one is tired, prevents the head dropping due to it sheer weight. Particularly when one is bored and feels sleepy, the hand under the chin stops an embarrassing drop of the head. Holding the chin also prevents the head from moving and can signal that the person is in two minds about sending a head signal. For instance, when he emotionally agrees and wants to nod, but intellectually want more information, he holds his head steady so that he can have good reason to say yes. Holding in the chin protects both it and the throat, and hence is a naturally defensive move that people use when they feel threatened. Holding the chin in also lowers the head, which is a submissive gesture. This is distinct from the defensive move as the head tilts down more and the eyes are often largely downcast. This can similarly be a shy or flirting gesture.

Beard: The beard, moustache, or goatee each makes a non-verbal statement. Beards make the lower face appear wider; moustaches, by turning the lip corners down, produce a fiercer look (Givens, 1999). They are sometimes controversial items, particularly in cultures where being clean-shaven is the norm.

A beard may thus be an indicator of a nonconformist. A full beard is more likely to indicate a person who has no vanity needs and is confident and relaxed as he is. When the beard is shaped and neatly clipped, it may indicate a vainer and fussy person who is particular about how he appears and what he does. An unkempt beard that is left to grow wild may indicate an untidy mind or simply that the person is lazy. It may also point to a person for whom external appearance is unimportant, such as a university intellectual. Stroking a beard can be a preening gesture, symbolically making oneself look beautiful and hence sending 'I'm gorgeous' signals.

The presence of facial hair might suggest nonconformity or conformity depending upon the times and the context. Some interpret a thick beard as a sign of aloofness. Well-groomed facial hair might signify meticulousness; in the same way, unkemptness can suggest laxity (Sussman and Deep, 1989).

Throat

Adam's Apple Jump

An observable feature in the throat is the up and down movement of the Adam's apple (prominent in men, less noticeable in women), when a person gulps or swallows. The Adam's apple jump unconsciously signals anxiety, embarrassment, or stress. While two people are in a discussion, the listener's Adam's apple may inadvertently jump should he or she dislike or strongly disagree with a speaker's suggestion, perspective or point of view (Givens, 1999).

The Adam's apple jump is an unconscious sign of emotional anxiety, embarrassment, or stress. At a business meeting, for example, a listener's Adam's apple may inadvertently jump should he or she dislike or strongly disagree with a speaker's suggestion, perspective, or point of view. Anxiety, social discomfort (for example, embarrassment), and fear are often visible in unwitting, vertical movements of the Adam's apple shows, prominently in men, but less noticeably in women.

The Jaw Droop

The jaw droop is a facial expression seen as a sudden and frequently sustained opening of the mouth, with parted lips and dangling jaw. It is a gesture of surprise or uncertainty.

Sometimes when a person is taken by surprise, he suddenly lets his jaw droop, thus leaving his *mouth wide open*. This gesture is also seen in cases of puzzlement or uncertainty. It is sometimes used as a 'nonverbal sign to mock, challenge, or confront a foe' (Givens, 1999). The expression is often seen in adults and children who have lost their way or are walking through unfamiliar, crowded, or potentially threatening places like darkened restaurants or hall. A sudden appearance of slightly parted lips can signal mild surprise, uncertainty, or unvoiced disagreement. In sleep, the chewing muscles relax and the jaw may droop of its own weight.

Throat-clear

The throat-clear in paralanguage is a non-verbal vibration of the vocal cords caused by a sudden, involuntary release of air pressure from the lungs. In a formal gathering or conference, a listener's unwitting throat-clear may suggest disagreement, anxiety, or doubt. While speaking, the throat-clear may reveal uncertainty. If the throat-clearing is acute or abnormal, it may be a sign of deception. An aggressive version of the throat-clear may be used to interrupt, overrule, or challenge a speaker. Consciously, the throat-clear may be used to announce one's physical presence in a room (Givens, 1999).

SUMMING UP

Facial expressions are a vital part of non-verbal communication. They serve as important and necessary cues to those we communicate with. We often favour the company of people who are enthusiastic and lively in their expressions and movements. One reason for this is that people who are lively keep us from becoming bored or inattentive; their body language and non-verbal communication adds visual appeal to the communication process.

Lively people display a variety of enthusiastic expressions and movements in their roles as speaker and listener. They are aware that non-verbal communication acts as a public relations agent for their attitudes and reactions as well as for their verbal messages. In effect, through their non-verbal communication they proclaim that they are actively involved in the conversation, that they care deeply about the subject, and that they want very much their feelings to be understood by others.

It is important to be aware that in different situations we send out different types of messages through our facial expression. For instance, we can:

- indicate our respect for others;
- reflect our interest in someone or something;
- show our curiosity in multifarious subjects;
- indicate our enthusiasm for life;
- transmit our positive attitude about people and things;
- convey our ambition as professionals;
- express our compassion for co-workers, family, friends;
- reveal the kind of personality we possess;
- communicate our ability to respond emotionally.

Chapter 3

The Eyes

INTRODUCTION

Our eyes are a very significant aspect of the non-verbal signals we send to others. To a lesser or greater extent, we all 'read' people's eyes without knowing how or why, and this ability seems to be inborn. Eyes—and especially our highly developed awareness of what we see in other people's eyes—are incredible. For example, we know if we have eye contact with someone at an almost unbelievable distance. Incredibly also, we can see whether another person's eyes are focused on us or not, and we can detect easily the differences between a 'glazed over' blank stare, a piercing look, a moistening eye long before tears come, and an awkward or secret glance. We probably cannot describe these and many other eye signals, but we recognize them when we see them and we know what they mean. When we additionally consider the eyelids, and the flexibility of the eyes to widen and close, and for the pupils to enlarge or contract, it becomes easier to understand how the eyes have developed such potency in human communications (Businessballs, 2011).

The *eyeballs* produce a great emotional impact in the way they affect the areas of the face around the eyes. From the minute variations in the movements of the eyelids, such as squinting, and their effects on the skin and eyes, practically any meaning can be construed. 'The eye can threaten like a loaded and levelled gun; or can insult like hissing and kicking; or in its altered mood by beams of kindness, make the heart dance with joy' (Emerson, 1860).

Not much goes on inside the head that does not get mirrored in the eyes. By careful observation of a person's eyes, one can deduce a lot about the person's character and attitudes. The eyes can convey a large variety of messages, intended as well as unintended ones. They can signal intimacy, concern, naughtiness, joy, surprise, curiosity, need for approval, affection and love, pleading for mercy, attempts to fake, and so on. The eyes can disclose a person's true moods, state of health, personality, and so on.

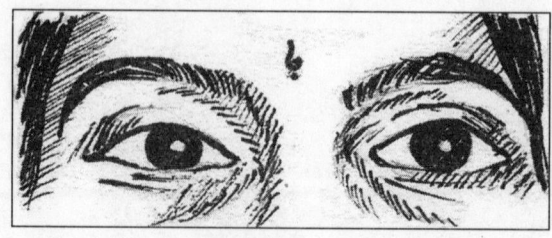

Our eyes are considered to be the most expressive part of the body and they are dead giveaways because they are practically impossible to control. Moreover, they are the most important tool of non-verbal communication since they can communicate even the most subtle nuances of emotions and attitudes.

THE PUPILS

The pupil is the black centre of the eye which opens or closes to let in more or less light. Darkness causes pupils to dilate. So too, for some reason, does seeing something appealing or attractive. Most descriptions regarding the 'look' of one's eyes have to do with the pupils. It is not always possible to get close enough to a person to observe the pupils clearly. Pupils are the only part of the body that are uncontrollable. Unlike any of the other body language gestures that are unconscious but still controllable if someone is aware, pupils will act on their own contracting and dilating based on the light conditions. Pupils also automatically dilate and contract in accordance with the attitudes and changing moods of a person.

When our pupils dilate, we are totally unaware of the information that we are providing about our emotional state. What is equally interesting is that people who see us, and who recognize our heightened state of arousal, do not know how they came to that conclusion—they know there is something attractive about our face, but they cannot identify what it is. In other words, when our pupils dilate, we produce a genuine clue, but we do not know that we are doing it. At the same time, other people react to the clue but they do not know why (Collett, 2003).

In pupillometry, an area of scientific investigation (Sussman and Deep, 1989), changes in pupil configuration as a function of emotional arousal are examined. When registering positive moods in favourable situations, like interest and excitement of some kind, the pupils of the eye can dilate up to four times their size. When registering negative sentiments in unfavourable situations, like anger, boredom, and disinterest, they contract considerably, to what are ordinarily regarded as 'beady little eyes' or 'snake eyes'. The pupils thus reveal actual feelings. So, by observing the pupils—which is not an easy task—when we look at a person 'eye-to-eye' while communicating, we can figure out what is going on inside the person.

Infants and children have larger pupils than adults; their pupils constantly dilate when there are people around, so that they appear as appealing as possible and thus attract attention. Young lovers tend to look deeply into each other's eyes. Unconsciously, they search for reactions in the pupils. When either or one of the partners is excited, the pupils get dilated. Some people wear dark glasses in order not to let their eyes betray their real emotions.

The studies made by Hess (1975) generated a lively interest in 'expressive eyes'. The studies revealed that pupil dilation or constriction was an extremely accurate indicator of the person's response to stimulation. According to his conclusion, the pupils dilate when a person is interested or aroused. For instance, the pupils of a man's eye enlarge to twice their size when he sees a pornographic movie, while the pupils of women dilate to almost three times the normal size when she sees the same. When faced with unpleasant or repulsive stimuli, the pupils constrict. Knowledge of this has led some 'glamour' photographers to enhance their models in the same way and thus increase their attractiveness.

A subtle signal that is sometimes detected only subconsciously and is seldom realized by the sender is where the pupil gets larger (dilates) or contracts. Sexual desire is a common cause of pupil dilation; what is known as 'gazing deep into each others eyes' is an unconscious way of looking for pupil dilation in the other to get excited if we see it. When another person's eyes dilate, we may be attracted further to them and our eyes dilate in return. Likewise, when their pupils are small, ours may well contract also. The reverse of this is that pupils contract when we do not like the other person, resulting in a squint-like narrowing of the eyes.

GAZING

Gazing is the visual connection made between two people. One gazes into the eyes of the other. This visual interaction arouses strong emotions. Such eye contact normally lasts for about three seconds before one or both viewers 'experience a powerful urge to glance away. Breaking eye contact lowers stress levels (as measured, for example, by breathing rate, heart rate, and sweaty palms)' (Givens, 1999).

Gazing, therefore, is the act of looking intently. It is a non-verbal signal which concerns the act, the duration, and the manner of looking. We gaze in order to perceive the expressions of others, especially those of their faces, to gauge whether the person is genuinely interested in us or not. Real communication takes place when the partners gaze at each other 'eye-to-eye'. It is difficult to conceal a gaze as we are particularly adept at identifying exactly where other people are looking.

There are different reactions to gazing. There are people who feel uncomfortable when they are looked at in the eye; they become self-conscious with the feeling of 'being observed' or being looked upon as inanimate objects rather than persons. There are others whose eyes communicate comfort. All these reactions are gathered from the amount of time one person looks at another.

Following are some gazing traits points based on research findings (see Givens, 1999):

- People generally look away as they begin to speak, then turn their gaze back to their listeners.
- While speaking, people alternate between gazing at and gazing away.
- There is more direct gaze when people like each other and cooperate.

- People make less eye contact when they dislike each other or disagree.
- An unwavering gaze can signal dominance and threat.
- Gaze avoidance can be a cue for submission.
- A direct gaze when accompanied by a smile with body thrust forward is a sign of trust between two individuals.
- Gaze direction clearly shows others where our attention lies.

When looking at a person normally, the gaze is usually at eye level or above (see 'Eye Contact' below). The gaze can also be a defocused looking at the general person. Looking up and down at a whole person is usually sizing them up, either as a potential threat or as a sexual partner (notice where the gaze lingers). This can be quite insulting and hence indicate a position of presumed dominance, as the person in effective seems to suggest that he is more powerful than the other, and that the other's feelings are unimportant to him; consequently, the other must submit to his gaze. Looking at their forehead or not at them indicates disinterest. This may also be shown by defocused eyes where the person is 'inside their head' thinking about other things.

Length of Gaze

The duration of eye contact can vary considerably with different individuals and cultures. Argyle (1967) offers some useful statistics based on extensive research. He observes that in a given interaction, a person looks at the other between 30 and 60 per cent of the time. If in a face-to-face encounter people exceed this range, then one may conclude they are more interested in the other person than in the words spoken. This can happen in two extreme cases: lovers gazing adoringly at each other, or two people getting ready for a 'battle'.

According to Pease (1993), if a person gazes at another for more than two-thirds of the time, it can mean either that the person looking finds the one he is looking at very interesting or appealing, in which case the former's pupils will dilate, or he finds him hostile, in which case the pupils contract.

Argyle (1992) makes some interesting observations on eye contact. Speakers look at their listeners quite a lot of the time, about 40 per cent for strangers two metres apart, more than this if they like each other or are further apart. They look in glances of about three seconds, which includes mutual glances of one second.

According to Givens (1999), a gaze arouses strong emotions, so people really gaze at each other for longer than three seconds before either one or both viewers experience a powerful urge to glance away. Breaking eye contact lowers stress levels (as measured in, for example, breathing rate, heart rate, and sweaty palms).

Effective rapport can be established if we gaze at the other person for about 60–70 per cent of the time. A person who is timid and nervous may gaze for less than one-third of the time. Such avoidance may give false signals to the listener, who may read into it doubt or hesitation, while in truth the speaker may be honest and sincere in what he is saying. People who are confident have more frequent eye contact than those who are unsure or evasive, and the duration of the contact is longer. Confidence also causes the eyes to blink less; hence, the person appears to be a better listener. As a rule of thumb, in individual communication, our normal gaze should be between 5 and 15 seconds, and while talking to a group, we should gaze at specific individuals for 4–5 seconds.

Types of Gazes

Natural Gaze   This gaze can last from 5 to 10 seconds. We use it when we talk to another person in an excited, enthusiastic, and confident manner. This is natural in a one-to-one conversation. The five-second period makes listeners feel comfortable.

In studying social interaction, Watson (1970) found cultural variability in the intensity of the gaze. He distinguished between three forms of gaze:

- Sharp: Focusing on the other person's eyes.
- Clear: Focusing on the other person's head and face.
- Peripheral: Having the other person in the field of vision, but not focusing on the ear or face.

Of the groups studied, Watson showed that the sharpest gaze was found amongst Arabs, followed by Latin Americans and South Europeans; the most peripheral gaze was that of the North Europeans, followed by Indians, Pakistanis, and other Asians.

Mutual Gaze   This is the percentage of time that two interactors look at each other in the region of the face. Mutual gaze gives a feeling of intimacy, mutual attraction, and attentiveness. Mutual gaze narrows the physical gap between us like no other facial cue.

When two people are involved in mutual gaze, they are visually 'locked together'. When they are of unequal status, the person who averts gaze or 'unlocks' first tends to be the subordinate. The issue of who 'out-looks' whom can have far-reaching consequences. When two people meet for the first time, the person who 'out-looks' the other is likely to be more talkative and influential when they go on to work together in a group. In a business firm, if the boss and a subordinate happen to look at each other at the same time, it is usually the subordinate who breaks off first. Veiled challenges to the boss can, however, be delivered through the eyes. For example, instead of openly disagreeing with the boss, a subordinate can simply engage him in a subtle bout of 'ocular arm-wrestling', holding his gaze for slightly longer than he would normally do. If carefully timed, this can have the desired effect, without appearing to be disrespectful (Collett, 2003).

In conversations between people of unequal status, dominant individuals usually show 'visual dominance', that is, they spend proportionately more time looking at the other person while they are talking than they do while they are listening. Subordinate people, on the other hand, spend proportionately more time looking while listening than while talking.

Gaze Down   A person may bow or tilt his head forward so that the eyes face the ground or floor. The eyeballs will rotate in their sockets to a downward position. The gaze down gesture may convey a defeated attitude. It may also reflect guilt, shame, or submissiveness, as when distorting the truth or telling a lie. Gazing down while or shortly after stating 'I am innocent', for example, shows that a speaker may not believe his or her own remarks. True statements are normally given with a confident, face-to-face, or level gaze, which may be held longer than three seconds (Pease, 1993).

Head lowered and eyes looking back up at the other person is a coy and suggestive action as it combines the head down of submission with eye contact of attraction. It can also be judgemental, especially when combined with a frown.

The Concentrated Gaze   Eyelids lowered, not to conceal the eyes but to focus them on some interesting object, is often used by artists and lovers.

The Intimate Gaze   The gaze area ascribed to intimacy extends across the eyes and below the chin to other parts of the person's body (Figure a, next page). The triangle of greater intimacy covers the area between the eyes down to the crotch. Those who use this gaze are indicating their interest in each other.

One must distinguish between 'intimacy', 'intimidation', and 'involvement' gazes. The first two are long gazes, of 10 seconds to a minute or more; but these take only 10 per cent of 'looking time'. Involvement gazes take the bulk—90 per cent of our looking time. Identified below are the involvement gazes:

The Social Gaze   To create a social atmosphere, the gaze must drop below the other person's eye level; the triangle is located between the eyes and the mouth (Figure b). This is generally the area people direct their gazes at during social interaction. Greetings (welcoming people) and partings (wishing goodbye) involve complex sequences of non-verbal communication, in which the making and breaking of mutual gaze plays a central role (Pease, 1993).

(a)   (b)   (c)

Business Gaze   Pease (1993) proposes that while discussing business, imagine that there is a triangle on the other person's forehead (Figure c). When we direct our gaze at this area, we have a look of seriousness; hence, the other person realizes that we mean business. As long as we keep to this level of gazing, we will be in control of the interaction.

The Gaze and Emotions

There are varying theories regarding the relationship of the gaze and emotions. Some hold that the gaze varies with the intensity of emotions rather than with different emotions. Others believe that positive moods such as warmth and elation produce high levels of gaze, while negative feelings caused by depression, submission, and anxiety produce low levels of gaze. There are also findings which suggest that surprise evokes the highest level of gaze, followed by excitement, joy, and scorn. Emotions such as embarrassment, sadness, anger, annoyance, and despair are associated with low gazes.

When the object of emotion is outside of themselves, people tend to gaze more than when the self is the object of emotion. Teachers who are accustomed to looking long at their students encourage them to be more responsive, and thus they enhance learning. People who want to be persuasive succeed in being so through long gazes. Those with higher levels of gaze are viewed as credible and trustworthy, though in fact gaze aversion is not a very reliable cue for deception.

Eye contact or the lack of it can tell us much about a person's feelings and disposition. In a face-to-face encounter, the eyes can tell the other person if we are attentive and interested or bored or preoccupied. Anger, authority, fear, timidity, coyness, confidence, diffidence, and so on, can also be read off from one's eyes. Our eye contacts (or avoidance of eye contacts) can encourage, sustain, consummate an interaction, or they can discourage and damage it, depending on how they are used. A constant stare in the eye may embarrass the other person; a total gazing may 'tell' him or her off.

As in other gestures of body language, the cultural factors and the context must be taken into consideration when reading eye movements. For instance, 'juniors' will not look directly into the face of their elders. There are also individuals who for reasons of shyness tend to avoid eye contact or look at the other person as little as possible. Though they may be honest and open persons, their avoidance of eye contact unintentionally gives the impression that they are in doubt or are vacillating.

In social relations, people who like each other gaze longer and oftener. People gaze more if they anticipate positive reactions from another. People look longer, by and large, to see if they can catch positive facial expressions; they avert their gazes if they foresee negative reactions. Individuals look more when they are cooperating than when they are competing with each other.

Gaze Behaviour

Varying gaze behaviour can be observed in varying situations. When two individuals are in a state of conflict, they express themselves in a typical way. Their eyebrows will be lowered, particularly at the inner ends, to produce a frown; simultaneously, their lips will be tight and pushed slightly forward, though their teeth will not be visible; their head, and often their chin, will be thrust forward in a defiance; and their eyes will glare at the opponent in an eye-to-eye confrontation. In situations such as these, individuals rarely lose eye contact with each other, since this would signal defeat or fear of the one who looks away. Instead, the eyes seem to stare hypnotically with intense concentration.

Goffman (1969) categorizes the bigoted gaze, as, for example, that which a white American shows to blacks as a sustained 'hate stare'. Danny Saunders (see O'Sullivan et al., 1994) suggests that the stare—sustained eye contact—displays an aggressive attitude and leads to the depersonalization of the 'victim', who does not stare back in turn.

Dyer (1992) observes how women are at a disadvantage in terms of gazing. A woman confiding to a male friend remarked that one thing she envied about men is 'the right to look'. She illustrated how in public places 'men look freely at women, but women could only glance back surreptitiously'.

When we want to show that we are interested in a person, we will 'give him the eye', even with a brief glance. One way to get the attention of a person is to look him straight in the eye. A direct glance generally means that one is interested, honest, extrovert, friendly, ready for feedback, or in some cases, intending to dominate. People who do not look at the other either while talking or listening can be suspected of being secretive. Generally, a person who avoids eye contact might be perceived as uninterested, confused, introverted, embarrassed, ashamed, sorrowful, sad, submissive, or evasive. Within the bounds of cultural conventions, people who avoid one's gaze may be seen as nervous, tense, evasive, and lacking in confidence, while people who look a lot may tend to be seen as friendly and self-confident (Argyle, 1983). Since those who tend to get lost in their own thought processes are able to integrate incoming data, they tend to have longer eye contact and are less distracted by it than those who think in concrete terms.

As noted earlier, according to Pease (1993), researchers have claimed that on analysis of the receptivity of a certain amount of information relayed on the whole to a person's brain, '87 per cent comes via the eyes, 9 per cent via the ears, and 4 per cent via the other senses'. He explains that when visual aids are used during presentations, there are different kinds of responses. In general, the respondent may absorb as little as 9 per cent of our message if it is not directly related to what he sees. Should the material be related to the visual aid, the amount of absorption will be between 25 and 30 per cent if he looks at the visual aid. However, if used effectively, a pen or a pointer enhances the level of response. For the audience to focus their gaze on the speaker, the speaker must hold the pen or pointer at eye level.

When a person is asked a question that requires much thought, his eyes will consistently move in the same direction—always to the right or always to the left. Rightward eye-movers were observed to be more outgoing, fun-loving, and gregarious, while leftward eye-movers were observed to be just the opposite: quiet, brooding, introspective, with a tendency to suppress extreme emotion, and to be choosy or selfish. Tests have shown that eye movement has nothing to do with being right- or left-handed; rather, it has something to do with increased activity in the right or left frontal lobes of the brain.

WAYS OF LOOKING

By observing the eyes, one can tell the quality of relationship between people. Eye contact, directions, and movements during a conversation can reveal which one is playing the dominant role. Strong personalities make eye contact rather fast and gaze more often and more persistently. Following is a brief overview of various ways of looking:

The Direct Look   is when while conversing, one or both persons look at the other with wide open eyes, directly. This shows undivided attention to, genuine interest in, and sincere respect of the other. Looking at a person can be an act of power and domination.

Looking Up   When a person looks upwards at nothing in particular, he is thinking, visualizing something. In particular, he is probably making pictures in his head and this may well be an indicator of a visual thinker.

A speaker who looks up during his speech is, generally, 'looking up' in his mind for the words he has prepared.

Looking upwards and to the left can indicate recalling a memory. Looking upwards and the right can indicate imaginative construction of a picture.

Looking up may also be a signal of boredom as the person examines the surroundings in search of something more interesting.

Looking Down   Looking down involves not looking at the other person, which hence may be a sign of submission ('I am not a threat, really; please do not hurt me. You are so glorious I would be dazzled if I looked at you.'). Looking down can thus be a signal of submission. It can also indicate that the person is feeling guilty. A notable way that a lower person looks down at a higher person is by tilting their head back. Even taller people may do this.

Looking down and to the left can indicate that they are talking to themselves (look for slight movement of the lips). Looking down and to the right can indicate that they are attending to internal emotions. In many cultures where eye contact is a rude or dominant signal, people will look down when talking with others in order to show respect.

Head lowered and eyes looking back up at the other person is a coy and suggestive action as it combines the head down of submission with eye contact of attraction. It can also be judgemental, especially when combined with a frown.

The Vertical Scan   This is an important body language cue that is not easy to detect unless one is paying close attention. When a person finds someone attractive, he takes a sharp look at the face, then looks down over the body, going from head to foot to check the other out.

The Horizontal Scan   This usually occurs after one has been talking to someone intimately, for example, lovers. There comes a moment when both look deeply into each other's eyes and read into them an invitation to greater intimacy and contact: like kissing.

Lateral Movement   Much of our field of vision is in the horizontal plane, so when a person looks sideways, he is either looking away from what is in front of him or looking towards something that has taken his interest.

A quick glance sideways can just be checking the source of a distraction to assess for threat or interest. It can also be done to show irritation, as when a comment is not appreciated. Looking to the left can indicate a person recalling a sound. Looking to the right can indicate that they are imagining the sound. As with visual and other movements, this can be reversed and may need checking against known truth and fabrication.

Eyes moving from side-to-side can indicate shiftiness and lying, as if the person is looking for an escape route in case they are found out. Lateral movement can also happen when the person is being conspiratorial, as if they are checking that nobody else is listening. Eyes may also move back and forth sideways (and sometimes up and down) when the person is visualizing a big picture and is literally looking it over.

The Sidelong Glance   This is generally referred to as 'the stolen look'. The observer looks furtively sideways, rather than directly, so as not to be caught in the act. He keeps on looking for as long as the subject of his gaze is unaware of being observed. The observer, of course, ensures this by looking only at an angle. However, the moment he is detected and the eyes of both meet, he immediately lets his glance slide away. To steal sidelong glances takes skill!

The sidelong glance is also given deliberately to indicate that one is suspicious, or doubtful, or distrusting of the other person.

The Stare   This is looking fixedly at a person. If we wish to pointedly ignore someone or to treat him with contempt, we can stare at him. If we wish to humiliate a person, we may gaze, and after we have locked glances, continue to stare.

Fast (1970) makes a case out for staring. He says that people stare at art, at sculpture, at scenery, and at animals in the zoo for as long as they want to; they stare even from close quarters. However, to stare at people in this way is a sign of disrespect, so we generally avoid doing do.

The blank stare is an indicator of boredom. The person stares blankly into space, with an unfocused look, though in fact he may have his eyes fixed on the speaker, he is paying no attention to what is being said. An added cue to his disinterestedness is that he does not even blink.

The Sparkle in the eyes can be commonly found in interactions between lovers or when they are questioned about their relationship. It is a very reliable cue to the opposite partner of genuine love. The eyes sparkle when one is in a pleasant or joyous state. Sparkling eyes are also an attribute of those who have 'magnetic' personalities. The physical origin of the eye sparkle continues to remain a mystery. Even after a detailed examination of the pupils, the cornea, and even the white sclera of the eyes, there are no scientific data to show how the sparkle originates. Yet, we all recognize it when we see it.

Eye Dart   This happens when a person is under pressure. His eyes tend to dart in all directions. It becomes obvious that the person is nervous, and this tension is transferred to the listener, who begins to feel uncomfortable.

Eye Shuttle   Submissive people frequently flick their eyes from side to side, often without moving their head. This is designed not only to try and take in everything that is happening around them, but also, instinctively, to search for possible escape routes.

Eye Block   A person who feels superior to the other may combine the eye block gesture with that of tilting the head backwards and giving the other a long look; this is commonly referred to as 'looking down one's nose'.

EYE CONTACT

Eye contact is an essential form of non-verbal communication. Having eye contact with the person you are talking to or having an argument with signals your attention, shows your personal involvement, and may even overcome physical and attitudinal gaps.

Overview

Eye contact is a natural by-product of effective communication, and vice versa. To look someone in the eyes is to invite him to communicate with you. Eye contact indicates degree of attention or interest, influences attitude change or persuasion, regulates interaction, communicates emotion, defines power and status, and has a central role in managing impressions of others. Eye contact is, of course, also one of the greatest ways to build positive and trusting relationships with others. Our eyes betray our true feelings; eye contact creates intimacy and trust. However, if it is not accompanied by words or a smile, it might be interpreted as hostile and lead to confrontation.

Avoidance of eye contact will very likely produce mistrust and suspicion; the other may feel that you want to terminate the conversation or that you are hiding something or your words may seem insincere.

As a rule of thumb, when speaking to someone, match their frequency of eye contact. This will build good rapport, whereas mismatching will take away from the rapport. To avoid being interrupted, break eye contact at the end of each sentence. It is considered rude to interrupt a speaker without eye contact; reversely, if you want to interrupt someone, make eye contact first. If you want to invite someone to speak after you finish your sentence, simply look at them, invitingly.

Variety of Eye Contacts

Direct eye contact: It is generally regarded as a sign of truthfulness when speaking; however, practiced liars know this and will fake the signal. When listening, eyes which stay focused on the speaker's eyes tend to indicate interested attention, which is normally a sign of attraction to the person and/or the subject.

Widening eyes: Widening the eyes generally signals interest in something or someone and often invites positive response. Widened eyes with raised eyebrows can otherwise be due to shock, but aside from this, widening eyes represents an opening and welcoming expression.

Narrowing eyes: People who have narrow eyes, or who narrow their eyes, are seen as dominant. When the eyes are narrowed, they take on the appearance of a visor—it looks as if the person is peering through a slit in their helmet. They also produce other revealing signs of dominance, like the lowering of the eyebrows, the narrow, resolute set of the mouth, and the absence of smiling (Collett, 2003).

Fast (1970) offers several insights into eye contacts:

Polite inattention: When we encounter unfamiliar people, we avoid either staring at them or ignoring them; we glance at them deliberately with 'polite inattention'. That is, we look at a person just long enough to make it obvious that we have seen him, and then we turn our eyes away. We do not 'catch the eye' of the other, neither do we 'lock glances'. Our passing glance is just to let the other know that we are aware of his presence, do not recognize him, and do not want to intrude upon his privacy.

Exchanging glances: When we pass a stranger on the street, we may exchange glances with him when we are about eight feet apart, signal the route we are taking with a brief look in that direction, and then keep looking away till we pass each other. This facilitates the passage; each takes the indicated direction without clashing. Goffman (1969) notes that the passing glance and lowering of the eyes indicate trust and lack of fear. This attitude is emphasized if we look directly at the other's face before looking away.

The look and away technique: This is often used when we face persons of repute or those physically disabled. It is an assurance to them that we respect their privacy and will not intrude upon it by staring. This technique is also used to avoid embarrassing someone who we find odd—with an unconventional hairdo or outlandish clothes, for instance. Conversely, we might sometimes stare at and lock glances with people longer than is acceptably polite to indicate our disapproval.

We may give the 'look and away' gaze when we meet someone's eye by accident in a crowded place and feel awkward. Looking away during a conversation may signal that we are concealing something. However, in class, when a student is answering a question and looks away from the teacher while speaking, it usually means that he is still explaining and does not want to be interrupted. Locking his gaze with the teacher's at any point would be a signal to interrupt when he pauses. If he does not look at his teacher during a pause, it means he has not finished speaking yet.

Bedroom eyes: What Fast (1970) aptly categorizes as 'bedroom eyes' is charmingly labelled by Ortega (1957) as the look which is 'furtively infurtive' in that a person makes no real attempt to conceal the fact that he is looking. The eyelids are almost three-quarters closed, and it appears as if they are hiding themselves, though in fact the lids are only compressing the look. 'It is the look of eyes that are, as it were asleep, but which beyond the cloud of sweet drowsiness are utterly awake' (Fast 1970).

Flashbulb eyes: This is an involuntary and dramatic widening of the eyes, performed in situations of intense emotion, such as anger, surprise, and fear. The eyelids are opened to the maximum to display the roundness and curvature of the eyeballs. Flashbulb eyes are a danger signal 'of imminent verbal aggression or physical attack' by an angry individual (Givens, 1999).

Doe eyes: A softening of the eyes, with relaxing of muscles around the eye, and a slight defocusing as the person tries to take in the whole person is sometimes called doe eyes, as it often indicates sexual desire, particularly if the gaze is prolonged and the pupils are dilated. The eyes may also appear shiny.

Brief Eye Contacts

Glancing: Glancing at something can betray a desire for that thing, for example, glancing at the door can indicate a desire to leave. Glancing at a person can indicate a desire to talk with them. It can also indicate a concern for that person's feeling when something is said that might upset them. Glancing may indicate a desire to gaze at something or someone where it is forbidden to look for a prolonged period.

Staring: Staring is generally done with eyes open wider than usual, prolonged attention to something, and with reduced blinking. It generally indicates particular interest in something or someone. Staring at a person can indicate shock and disbelief, particularly after hearing unexpected news. When the eyes are defocused, the person's attention may be inside their head and what they are staring at may be of no significance. (Without care, this can become quite embarrassing for them.) Prolonged eye contact can be aggressive, affectionate, or deceptive and is discussed further above. Staring at another's eyes is usually more associated with aggressive action. A short stare, with eyes wide open and then back to normal indicates surprise. The correction back to normal implies that the person would like to stare more, but knows it is impolite (this may be accompanied with some apologetic remark).

Following: The eyes will naturally follow movement of any kind. If the person is looking at something of interest, then they will naturally keep looking at it. They also follow neutral or feared things in case the movement turns into a threat.

Squinting: Narrowing of a person's eyes can indicate evaluation, perhaps considering that something told to them is not true (or at least not fully so). It can similarly indicate uncertainty. Squinting can also be used by liars who do not want the other person to detect their deception. When a person thinks about something and does not want to look at the internal image, they may involuntarily squint. Squinting can also happen when lights or the sun are bright. Lowering of eyelids is not really a squint but can have a similar meaning. It can also indicate tiredness. Lowering eyelids whilst still looking at the other person can be a part of a romantic and suggestive cluster and may be accompanied with tossing back the head and slightly puckering the lips in a kiss.

Closing: Closing the eyes shuts out the world. This can mean 'I do not want to see what is in front of me, it is so terrible'. Sometimes when people are talking, they close their eyes. This is equivalent to turning away so eye contact can be avoided and any implied request for the other person to speak is effectively ignored. Visual thinkers may also close their eyes, sometimes when talking, so they can better see the internal images without external distraction.

Rubbing: When a person is feeling uncomfortable, the eyes may water a little. To cover this and try to restore an appropriate dryness, the person may rub their eye and may even feign tiredness or having something in the eye. This also gives the opportunity to turn the head away. The rubbing may be with one finger, with a finger and thumb (for two eyes), or with both hands. The more the coverage, the more the person is trying to hide behind the hands.

Rubbing eyes or one eye can indicate disbelief, as if checking the vision, or upset, in which the action relates to crying, or tiredness, which can be due to boredom, not necessarily a need for sleep. If the signal is accompanied by a long pronounced blink, this tends to support the tiredness interpretation.

Blinking

Blinking is the rapid closing and opening of the eyes. It is a natural process whereby the eyelids wipe the eyes clean, much as a windscreen wiper on a car. On average, we blink 10 times per minute and every blink won't last longer than one-tenth of a second. The frequency of blinking indicates how nervous or worried a person is. Significantly, faster rates may reflect emotional stress, as aroused, for example, in the fight or flight response. Blink rate can increase up to a hundred times a minute. Blink rate is not a reliable sign of lying. Lack of blinking can indicate that he is in a trance, asleep with his eyes open, extremely hostile, or in a deep state of indifference.

The eye blink has been found to occur during vocalizations at the beginning of words and utterances, usually with the initial vowel of the word (Condon and Ogston, 1966). Some people have the mannerism of shutting their eyelids for up to two or three seconds every now and then while speaking. It signals that the person feels uninterested, bored, or superior and is trying to block the other out from his sight. This gives the listener a feeling of being left out and creates a distance between him and the speaker. People who are connected may blink at the same rate.

Infrequent blink rate can mean different things and so offers no single clue unless combined with other signals. An infrequent blink rate is probably due to boredom if the eyes are not focused, or can be the opposite—concentration—if accompanied with a strongly focused gaze. Infrequent blink rate can also be accompanied by signals of hostility or negativity, and is therefore not the most revealing of body language signals (Businessballs, 2011).

Tears

The tear ducts provide moisture to the eyes, both for washing them and for tears. Damp eyes can be suppressed weeping, indicating anxiety, fear, or sadness. It can also indicate that the person has been crying recently. Dampness can also occur when the person is tired (this may be accompanied by redness of the eyes).

Actual tears that roll down the cheeks are often a symptom of extreme fear or sadness, although paradoxically you can also weep tears of joy. Weeping can be silent, with little expression other than the tears (indicating a certain amount of control). It also typically involves screwing up of the face and, when emotions are extreme, can be accompanied by uncontrollable, convulsive sobs.

EYES IN INTERACTION

The facial expressions of listeners are an important feedback. The mouth and eyebrows can reveal that a listener is puzzled, or that he understands, agrees, or disagrees, or is pleased, annoyed, disbelieving, or angry. Those who look more during interactions are seen as attentive, interested, or willing to initiate interaction.

Argyle (1992) has found that listeners look a lot more than speakers, often 70–75 per cent of the time. Their purpose in looking is to pick up non-verbal accompaniments of speech. Argyle presumes that speakers do not resort to long, steady gazing so as not to compel listeners to strain themselves to pay attention to what they are saying.

People of high status tend to look more whilst they are talking but less when they are listening (Argyle, 1975). Meyrowitz (1985) notes that 'a person of high status often has the right to look at a lower status person for a long time, even stare at him or her up and down, while the lower status person is expected to avert his or her eyes'.

Nierenberg and Calero (1975) have also found that people tend to have greater eye contact while listening than while talking. As stated earlier, we have the capacity to listen to 650–700 words per minute (wpm), and a person speaks at the rate of 150–160 wpm. This implies that the average listener has three-quarters of his listening time to evaluate, accept, reject, or contest what is being said. But there is often the urge to interrupt the speaker, especially when dealing with an emotional topic.

If the listener looks away from the person speaking, it is a signal that he has reservations about what is being said; whereas looking at the speaker indicates interest and agreement. Looking at the listener while speaking would indicate that the speaker is confident about what he is saying, while looking away could mean that he is hiding his feelings, especially in front of someone who is critical or insulting. When people look away while speaking, it generally means they are not through explaining and do not want to be interrupted. When they lock gazes with listeners, it could be a signal to interrupt during an imminent pause. If they look away during the pause, it could mean that they are waiting for a response at that juncture, even though they have not yet finished speaking on the topic.

Fast (1970) records the outcome of interviews carried out at the University of Delaware under the supervision of Dr Ralph V. Exline. Two groups of 40 students each, with an equal number of men and women, were interviewed by a man and a woman. Half the members of each group were interviewed on intimate subjects—their plans, desires, needs, and fears, and the other half about their recreational interests—reading, movies, and sports. It was found that during the interview on personal matters, the students did not look at the interviewer as often as they did when interviewed about recreational subjects. Women looked at the interviewers more frequently than did the men.

Another study of eye contacts during interviews, by Nielsen (1968), reveals that people who speak a lot, look at their partners very little, while those who listen a lot, also look a lot. He found that when people start to speak, they look away from their partners. Nielsen explains that there is a subtle timing in speaking, listening, looking, and looking away. Most people look away either immediately before or after the beginning of one of every four interventions they make. They do this in order to concentrate on what they are thinking and not be distracted by the speaker's reactions or non-verbal behaviours.

On being asked questions that make them feel uncomfortable or guilty, however, people turn their gaze away. But when they are asked questions about or are reacting to a statement that makes them feel defensive, aggressive, or hostile, their eye contact increases dramatically, even to the extent that one is able to clearly see the pupils dilate.

Status or domination is reflected in the relative amount of looking while listening. People of higher status look relatively less while listening; they look more while talking. A high-powered person wants to be sure that others are listening and paying careful attention while he is talking; a low-powered person wants to ensure that he understands what the other is saying. If the listener adopts an attitude of superiority towards the speaker, he may look down his nose by tilting his head backwards and shutting the eyes. The eye block gesture is generally a cue to the speaker to change his approach so that is not viewed negatively.

In Asian cultures, looking at elderly or — in regard to a working hierarchy — more senior people directly into the eyes is often regarded as rude and aggressive as opposed to Western culture, where the same behaviour is often regarded as respectless.

NEURO-LINGUISTIC PROGRAMMING AND EYE MOVEMENTS

People's eyes move when they are thinking. We think primarily in one of three representational systems: pictures, sounds, or feelings. By paying close attention to a person's unconscious eye movements, we can determine which representational system they are using to access information. William James (*The Principles of Psychology*, 1890) first suggested that internal representations and eye movements may be related.

This observation was not explored further until the 1970s when Richard Bandler, John Grinder, Robert Dilts, and others conducted further experimentation in this area. According to neurological research, eye movement both laterally and vertically seems to be associated with activating different parts of the brain. In the neurological literature, these movements are called lateral eye movements (LEM); in Neuro-linguistic Programming (NLP) they are referred to as eye accessing cues because they give insights as to how people are accessing information.

Bandler and Grinder's (1979) findings suggest that the patterns of the eye movements while people think and speak are closely related with certain types of information retrieval behaviours.

While we think and talk, our eyes move in what is called 'eye-scanning patterns' as we try to access information stored or generated internally in the brain, in one or more of the representational systems. In the process of retrieving a memory or forming a new idea, we resort to particular behaviours which reveal the representational system we are accessing at a given moment.

The representational system groups are:

- Visual: the things we see
- Auditory: the things we hear
- Kinaesthetic: the things we feel (touch/emotion), taste, or smell

Lewis and Pucelik (1990) have delineated several eye movements. Their descriptions refer to patterns displayed by right-handed or left hemisphere-dominant people. These could be reversed for some left-handed people. The directions 'left' or 'right' refer to the seeing person's left or right. Generally, when accessing information, people 'look' internally, that is, they are 'not conscious of external visual stimuli'. Their focus is on stored memory or on concurrently generated images, sounds, words, and feelings.

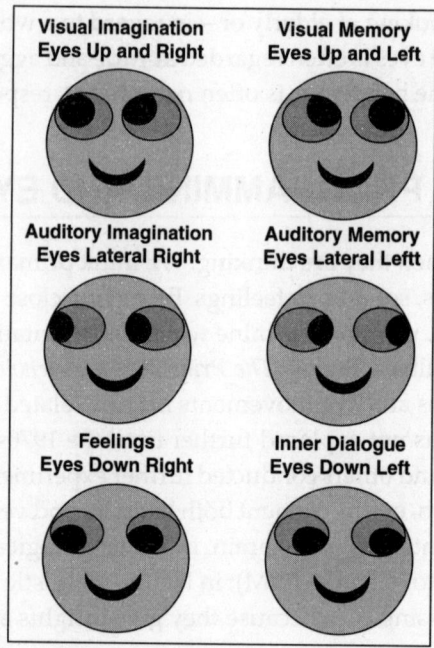

Visual Imagination
Eyes Up and Right

Visual Memory
Eyes Up and Left

Auditory Imagination
Eyes Lateral Right

Auditory Memory
Eyes Lateral Leftt

Feelings
Eyes Down Right

Inner Dialogue
Eyes Down Left

Looking up and to the right: Related to imagination and creative (right side) parts of the brain, this upwards right eye movement can be a warning sign of fabrication if a person is supposed to be recalling and stating facts. One must watch out for exaggeration of the truth or for complete lies.

When people keep looking up during a conversation, they are accessing visual information and have a greater sense of rapport. Visual thinkers speak a little faster, their breathing is shallow, and they make many hand gestures during conversation.

Up and to the right usually means that a person is imagining (constructing) something visually.

Looking up and to the left: This position is related to accessing memory in the brain rather than creating or imagining. It is a reassuring sign when the person is recalling and stating facts.

Looking level and to the right: The person responds to 'remembered sound', be it an advertisement jingle, a phone number, a swear word. The person may also be recalling 'auditory tape loops: messages stored in short, often tuneful or rhythmic patterns' which because of frequent repetition have sunk into the subconscious.

Creating here is basically making things up and saying them. Depending on context, this can indicate lying, but in other circumstances, for example, storytelling to a child, this would be perfectly normal.

Looking level and to the left: Here, a person is recalling from memory a particular sound.

Looking down and to the right: Here, a person accesses both derived feelings (emotions) and kinesthetic memories that are stored in the brain. This can be a perfectly genuine response or not, depending on the context, and to an extent the person. It may be clustered with a physical position often characteristic of a depressed person: hunched, head bent, and body drawn into himself.

Looking down and to the left: Here, the person is resorting to self-talk, perhaps even articulating his deepest thoughts internally. Occasionally, the words and exclamations may be uttered aloud, without the person realizing it.

Defocused eyes: This happens in all eye positions noted in the foregoing, often in a face-to-face interaction, and especially when one tends to look at the speaker while listening. Here, either eidetic or constructed imagery is accessed.

Closed eyes: People usually close their eyes to recall a particular taste or smell. The eyelids are closed, but a careful observer will detect movement below them. This movement can be any one of those mention above and can be interpreted in the same way.

Eye-scanning patterns provide instant and efficient information regarding the representational system a person is using by preference at a given time, as well as about how he is thinking. If interpreted together with breathing and posture, the patterns enable one to help a person become aware or change his pain-producing behaviours.

Learning to read eye-accessing cues will not make us mind readers but will give us a clue to the way the other person is thinking. With some skill we will notice the sequencing of eye patterns. For example, before answering a question, someone might always follow the pattern 'up left, across right, down right'. This suggests that they are remembering a picture, putting together some sound or words, and checking that the idea feels OK.

Once we know which representational system a person tends to operate in, we communicate our ideas in the same sequence and probably gain strong rapport and trust with the person.

EYE GLASSES

Peering Over Glasses

Peering over glasses signifies that the person is being critical or judgemental. Sometimes, instead of bifocals, a person may be wearing reading glasses; hence, rather than remove them, he finds it more convenient to drop them down the bridge of the nose and peer over the tops. This gesture nevertheless makes the one on the receiving end feel as though she is being judged or scrutinized. Hence, he may get on the defensive—generally crossing his hands and legs—and take a negative attitude. People who wear glasses would do well to remove them during a conversation, at least while speaking; they may put them back on when listening. This will relax the other person. It will also give the one wearing glasses control over the conversation, in that it can serve as a signal to the listener that the speaker must not be interrupted until he removes his glasses and gives the listener a cue to respond.

In the early 1960s, it was a fashion to wear dark glasses with lenses which were like a one-way mirror. The wearer could see out easily, like through any typical glasses that have tinted lenses, but the outside of these lenses reflected things like a mirror does, so no one could see the eyes behind them. Because of this characteristic, the glasses came to be known as 'cheaters' (Lewis and Pucelik, 1990).

According to Hall (1979), many Arabs wear dark glasses even indoors to hide their responses—which the eyes are quick to give away. Morris (1977) observes that the jade dealers of pre-revolutionary China used to wear dark glasses to hide their pupil dilations when they dealt with particularly valuable specimens of jade.

In a study using pictures of people's faces, it was found that when a person adds glasses to his face in a business context, respondents describe that person as studious, intelligent, conservative, educated, and sincere. The heavier the frame on the glasses, the more frequently these descriptions were likely to be used and it made little difference whether the face was male or female. This could be because the leaders of business who wear glasses use heavier frames. So in a business environment, glasses are a statement of power. Frameless, small, or spindly frames convey a powerless image and say that you are more interested in fashion

than business. The reverse holds true in social contexts but in these situations you are selling yourself as a friend or mate. We advise people in positions of power to wear stronger
frames to make serious points, such as reading a financial budget, and frameless styles when
conveying a 'nice guy' image or being 'one of the boys' (Westside Toastmasters, n.d.).

Dark Glasses

As noted earlier, some people hide their eyes by wearing dark glasses so as to conceal
their genuine feelings. They feel threatened or exposed when have to remove their glasses
and 'look one in the eye'. Not many people feel comfortable to look others in the eyes and
holding the gaze while communicating. In fact, this is often a giveaway. When people are
being dishonest or trying to hold back information, they make less eye contact. The person
wearing dark eye glasses feels protected and assumes that he can stare without it being
noticed. However, this is a deception because the other person usually feels that the one
wearing dark glasses is staring at him constantly.

Mannerisms

Seldom do we observe people playing with their glasses. One of the most common gestures
of a person wearing glasses is one arm of the frame placed in his mouth. This gesture can
be used to stall or delay a decision. This gesture may, therefore, appear towards the end of
a discussion. They may not need cleaning. If the person puts the glasses back on, it could
often mean that he wishes to 'see' or review the issue; if he folds the glasses and puts them
away, it is a clear signal that he wants to terminate the discussion. When a person moves his
glasses to the front of his nose, it is a sign of disapproval or of secretly telling the other person
off. When a person takes his glasses off with both hands, and holds on to them, it means he
is interested in the conversation but does not want to commit himself to any decision.

If a person takes off his glasses either too quickly or with undue emphasis, and throws
them on the table, he is signalling an emotional outbreak. He may be saying in non-verbal
terms that the other person has exceeded limits, or he could be non-verbally signalling the
person to be more patient. This gesture clearly indicates that the person is showing resistance to what is being said.

DISTINCTIVE TRAITS

There are a number of physical traits that give away the hidden attitudes and tendencies of
a person. We shall deal with a few of them, mainly summarizing from Whiteside (1975).

Large, brimming, saucer eyes, with only a little white showing in them, but a large iris or coloured part, tell us that the person is affectionate and emotional. 'All the feelings are on the surface. All the feelings are keen. This person will laugh more easily, cry more easily, show anger more vividly, show devastation of despair more completely, anguish more demonstratively, ecstasy more delightedly.'

Large-eyed people are keen observers of others. They are sensitive to how others behave towards them. They do not mind getting into personal matters and can warm up to a subject.

Conversely, someone with 'beady eyes' will be businesslike and dispassionate, and will tend to avoid personal talk and confidences. We can expect little demonstrativeness from a small-eyed person; rather, there will be some awkwardness in the show of emotion. 'Give the person some encouragement to help get the heart more out on top.'

There are people with a quality of eyes known as magnetic. Their eyes sparkle like jewels. Such persons will be alert and animated, and draw an audience wherever they go. They will be more fun to be with, stand out in a crowd, attract others with their charm, and be remembered. Such people make good receptionists and public relations officers.

Then there are eyes that are full of worry and show unhappiness and gloom. The whites show between the coloured part of the eyes and the lower eyelid. People with such eyes are preoccupied with problems; they are not light-hearted or cheerful. They need to be given a sympathetic ear so that they can unburden themselves.

There are people with shifty eyes. They avoid eye contact for several reasons: they may be uncomfortable with the transaction, or are too self-conscious, or are really not interested. Obviously, one may tend to be suspicious of such people and doubt whether they are dependable.

People with critical eyes, that is, 'eyes that slide down from the inner canthus to the outer corners', break up friendships by dwelling on the negative qualities of people or things. Such people could always be pointing out what is wrong, where you have failed, how clumsy or untidy you are.

There are eyes that can spell out direct action. Here, the upper eyelids are well exposed. People with such eyes are people of action, who do not sit on fences or postpone things. They are ruthlessly efficient. They do not require any provocation to begin to talk. If asked a direct question, they will give a direct answer.

Analytical eyes are characterized by a fold in the upper lids. People who have such eyes will probably answer your question with counter-questions. They will probe before they give a final yes or no.

Eye Feedback

There are a number of ways in which we receive feedback from eye movements.

In a negotiating situation, if we notice that the other person hardens the lower eyelid and sets its rigidly—we must realize that we have lost him or her; he or she will not yield to us. If during a conversation the other individual's eyes start wandering around the room, or he begins to look at his watch, he has lost interest.

When the other person's eyes go dull, it means we have said something he does not understand according to his make-up or which does not appeal to him.

When a hurt look comes in the other person's eyes, we are given a cue about something important to him or her. We must ask him what he feels bad about. If we know already that it is something we have said or done, we must apologize.

SUMMING UP

Our eyes convey a large variety of non-verbal messages that greatly support and strengthen our verbal communication. In several ways, using the eyes is the first step in establishing a relationship with the person we are communicating at a given time. We can develop a bond between ourselves and another, depending on our interest and respect for each other. In brief, eye contact:

- establishes our relationship with the other;
- helps us keep our mind on the message;
- involves us in the emotional and factual content of what we are saying; and
- encourages the other to continue interacting with us.

Eye contact also reflects our self-confidence and many of our other personality traits. Moreover, it expresses numerous emotional elements that are part of our personality at any given time, such as surprise, joy, satisfaction, sadness, shock, disappointment, anger, curiosity, warmth, respect, strength, and pride.

Since the eyes are our most powerful body language message transmitters, here are some general rules about using your eyes.

It is OK to look into the eyes of another person for longer periods of time than normal when you:

- like or love them;
- are apart and trying to improve your communication;
- are deeply interested in what they are saying;
- know they are extroverted and like being close;
- are expecting an answer or response from someone;
- are trying to dominate and intimidate someone.

Chapter 4

The Head and Torso

HEAD GESTURES

Introduction

The head can send a wide range of signals as described in earlier chapters. Here we focus just on movement of the head as affected by the neck muscles.

Head Movements

There are a number of head gestures which fall into clear categories with accepted meanings. The two most widely used head movements are the 'nod'—a positive gesture to signify affirmation or 'yes'; and the head shake—which usually means 'no'. Both are presumed to be inborn gestures.

Nodding

Head nodding can occur when invited for a response, or voluntarily while listening. Head nodding when talking face-to-face one-to-one is easy to see, but one must learn to detect tiny head-nods when addressing or observing a group.

Slow head-nodding can be a faked signal, so we must look for clusters of signals rather than rely on one alone. If the eyes are focused, for example, the slow head-nod will be genuine.

In most cultures, nodding up and down signals agreement. A vertical, up and down movement of the head is used to show agreement, approval, or comprehension while listening. This rhythmical cue for affirmation may as well be accompanied by smiling and other signs of approval. Rarely, if at all, do we hold our heads in a single position for longer than a sentence or two.

Nodding whilst the other person is talking sends approval signals and encourages them to keep talking. This may range from a subtle encouragement to agree to a rapid and aggressive tilt. We can non-verbally seek another person's agreement by synchronizing our speech with quick head-nods; nodding or shaking the head whilst talking encourages the other person to agree (and this works surprisingly often). While large or repeated nod indicate agreement, small ones show continuing attention.

A vigorous nodding probably indicates strong agreement. Emphatic head-nods while speaking or listening may indicate powerful feelings of conviction, excitement, superiority, or rage. Slow nodding may indicate conditional agreement (and so may be questioned if you want full agreement). A flexed forward, lowering motion of the skull is used to emphasize an idea, assertion, or speaking point. A short, sharp nod can symbolize a headbutt, indicating the desire to strike the other person (this may be in emphasis or for other reasons). A nod is also a common greeting, perhaps as a small bow. It may also be a signal of power, when a person presumes he is so powerful that people will notice even a small nod. Again it may be a deliberate concealment, sending covert agreement to a colleague.

Shaking

A head shake is the rotation of the head horizontally from side-to-side to disagree or to show misunderstanding of a speaker's words. Speakers may either stop and seek the listener's view or redouble their attempts to persuade them.

The head-shake is a universal sign of disapproval, disbelief, and negation (Darwin, 1965; Morris, 1994). A head tilted down whilst swinging may signal particular disapproval, indicating that the person does not even want to look at the other. In emotional conversations, a rhythmic, side-to-side rotation of the head expresses disbelief, sympathy, or grief. Shaking the head when saying something positive is a negative signal and may indicate that the person does not believe what he is saying.

Head gestures can prove to be a little tricky; they may conceal incongruency. For instance, if someone expresses agreement in words such as 'Yes, I see your viewpoint', or 'I find great joy in this job', yet shakes his head from side to side, the non-verbal gesture signals a negative attitude and contradicts the verbal conviction. Head movement is thus related not only to what we are saying but also to what is happening to us emotionally.

The strength of movement of the head usually relates to strength of feeling, and often to the force by which the head-shaker seeks to send this message to the receiver. This is an immensely powerful signal and is used intentionally by some people to dominate others.

Tilting

The head tilted to one side expresses non-threatening, submissive, thoughtful attitudes. It is also a signal of interest, and/or vulnerability, which in turn suggests a level of trust. Head tilting is thought by some to relate to 'sizing up' something, since tilting the head changes the perspective offered by the eyes and a different view is seen of the other person or subject. Exposing the neck is also a sign of trust.

People who tilt their head to the right by a few degrees are seen as trustworthy; those who tilt their head to the left are seen as attractive (Reiman, 2010). Sideward head-tilts have been decoded as signals of shyness in young children (McGrew, 1972) and in adults (Givens, 1999).

In a one-to-one encounter, if the speaker is convincing enough, the listener will tilt his head and lean forward in a hand-to-chin evaluation gesture, which indicates a positive response. If the listener tilts and nods his head, it means he has taken a negative, even judgemental, stance. A tilted head pulled back tends to indicate suspicion, as the uncertainty of the tilt is combined with a defensive pulling back. Head tilted downwards towards a person is commonly a signal of criticism or reprimand or disapproval, usually from a position of authority.

In a seminar, if the participants' heads are tilted, it signals interest. If the head is held straight up, it means that the listener has taken a neutral position on what he or she is hearing. Individuals sometimes stop tilting their heads to indicate 'information overload' and their indifference to additional data. This is evident in the way they change their gesture cluster: heads become erect rather than tilted, backs straighten up, then slouch; there are glances at the ceiling, at the watch, at others, and finally some repositioning so that their bodies point towards the exit. When a group has reached this stage, the organizer must respond to their signals for 'enough' and change tactics to get the group more involved or wind up the session.

Tilting can indicate curiosity, uncertainty, or query, particularly if the head is pushed forward, as if the person was trying to look at the subject in a different way in the hope of seeing something new. The greater the tilt is, the greater will the uncertainty be, or the greater the intent to send this signal.

The tilted head is a signal of interest, and/or vulnerability, which in turn suggests a level of trust. The tilted head exposes the carotid artery on the side of the neck and may be a sign of submission and feelings of vulnerability. Exposing the neck is also a sign of trust. If the head is propped up by the hand, it may be tiredness or an expectation of continued interest.

Lowering

Head lowering is generally a signal of rejection (of someone's ideas, and so on), unless the head is down for a purpose like reading supporting notes, and so on. Head lowering when responding to criticism is a signal of failure, vulnerability (hence seeking protection), or feeling ashamed. Head lowering is a sign of loss, defeat, shame, and so on.

Head down also tends to cause shoulders and upper back to slump, increasing the signs of weakness at that moment. Lowering the head to cover the neck with the chin is a defensive gesture in response to a physical or any other type of threat. It can also be a sign of defiance or caution, for example, when showing respect to an enemy, indicating that he is stronger and trustworthy. Lowering the head can be part of ducking as the person reflexively pulls the head down to avoid a real or imagined hazard. This makes the body smaller and protects the neck. Sometimes, lowering the head is just a sign of exhaustion. The head is rather heavy and a tired person's head will sag.

Lowering the head results in the eye being lowered, indicating submission: the person does not dare look at the other. However, in a given context, the typical lowering of the eyes can indicate that one is moved by affection towards the other, or fear that the other might hurt if looked at.

Head dip: When individuals walk between people who are having a conversation, they frequently 'duck' their head down in order to make sure that they do not get in the way and to apologize for any inconvenience they may have caused. Some people produce an involuntary dip of the head when they approach someone who is important, especially when that person is unfamiliar to them or is involved in a conversation with someone else.

Raising

High head position signifies attentive listening, usually with an open or undecided mind, or lack of bias. Darwin (1965) noticed early in his studies that animals as well as men tend to cock their head slightly whenever they hear something that interests them. From a level position, a quick flick upwards can be a sign of query, asking what the person means.

Raising the head and looking at the ceiling may signal boredom. It may also indicate a visual thinker who is looking at internal images. Another alternative is where a person wants to focus on the sound and is thus averting the eyes in order to concentrate on the sound.

The head is heavy and when tired, we may prop it up, either under the chin or at the side. Boredom makes us tired so propping the head may indicate this. Propping up the head also happens when a person is thinking or evaluating.

Chin up

The chin up is very similar to the raised head signal. Holding the chin up naturally alters the angle of the head backwards, exposing the neck, which is a signal of strength, resilience, pride, resistance, and so on. A pronounced raised chin puffs out the chest and it widens the shoulders. These combined effects make the person stand bigger. An exposed neck is also a sign of confidence. 'Chin up' is for these reasons a long-standing expression used to encourage someone to be brave.

Lifting the chin and looking down the nose is universally used as a non-verbal symbol of superiority, arrogance, and disdain (Eibl-Eibesfeldt, 1970). This is characterized by the snobbish head upwards, with the chin pointing forward, and slightly looking down at someone over his nose. This head position is taken by people who feel fearless, arrogant, or superior.

Rotating

Rotation of the head in a circle is a relatively rare gesture and may just be the person exercising a stiff neck; in a conference room, this could indicate they have lost attention and are feeling bored. In a conversation, turning the head away indicates lack of interest and attention; it may signal the person's need to wind up the conversation abruptly. Turning the head slightly so that only one eye of the listener is visible to the speaker can be very disconcerting to the latter. This 'one-eye' gaze may be used as an act of dominance.

Wiggling

Roberts (2004), an Australian, in his semi-autobiographical fiction *Shantaram*, writes about the 'Indian gesture' he calls the head-wiggle:

> No discovery pleased me more, on that first excursion from the city, than the full translation of the famous Indian head-wiggle. The weeks I'd spent in Bombay with Prabaker had taught me that the shaking or wiggling of the head from side to side—that most characteristic of Indian expressive gestures—was the equivalent of a forward nod of the head, meaning Yes. I'd also discerned the subtler senses of I agree with you, and Yes, I would like that. What I learned, on the train, was that a universal message is attached to the gesture, when it was used as a greeting, which made it uniquely useful.

> Most of those who entered the open carriage greeted the other seated or standing men with a little wiggle of the head. The gesture always drew a reciprocal wag of the head from at least one, and sometimes several of the passengers. I watched it happen at station after station, knowing that the newcomers could not be indicating 'Yes', or I agree with you with the head-wiggle because nothing had been said, and there was no exchange other than the gesture itself. Gradually, I realised that the wiggle of the head was a signal to others that carried an amiable and disarming message: 'I'm a peaceful man, I don't mean any harm'.

Wobbling

There is a gesture known outside India as the 'Indian head wobble' or 'Indian head bobble'. The head wobbling is a motion that is somewhere in between the up and down nod and the sideways head-shaking. So, it is somewhat rotational motion of the head—a light head-shake combined with a head roll. It means 'yes'. Though common in India, head wobble is a mystery to many foreigners, and even more confusing when made silently, without speaking a single word.

The wobble implies agreement on an opinion or topic of conversation. It is equivalent of up and down nodding, but most of the time with more empathy. In general, this motion means something like: 'Yes, I agree with you!', 'Yes, I understand what you mean!', 'Yes, I understand how you feel!', 'Yes, I get your viewpoint!', and so on.

A longer head wobble means better understanding or more in agreement. However, if the head wobble goes on for a few extra rotations, the listener *really* understands you. The head wobble may often accompany a smile—to show warmth and friendliness. It is an affirmative yes, but there is no element of surprise. It does not mean something like 'Oh, Yes!'. The wobble also means 'Ok, I am listening, tell me more ...'

Aspects of Head Gestures

Forehead

The forehead has its place in body language communications, often as a part of a wider set of signals. It is near the eyes and can be looked at without sending other signals (for example, looking the mouth can say 'I want to kiss you'), which can make even small movements with it reliably observed and hence significant. Its main limitation is that it can only make a few movements.

There are various gestures of head-touching. People tend to have preferred places they touch or stroke when they are experiencing certain emotions. They touch their faces when they are anxious. They cover their eyes, ears, or mouth when they do not want to see, hear, or say something. They touch the side of the nose or stroke the chin when they are thinking, making decisions, and judging others. Slowly rubbing the forehead can indicate deep thinking, as if the person was massaging their brain to get it going. Rubbing the temples on either side can indicate stress as the person tries to massage away the actual or implicit headache.

Tapping the head indicates self-chastisement and thus signals regret. For example, tapping the forehead with the heel of the hand, an open palm, or light fist says: ('I'm stupid!'). Again, depending on the context, this gesture can also be a signal that somebody else is considered stupid.

Touching the forehead happens in the greeting of a salute. A salute, in effect, is shading the eyes and says: 'You are so wonderful I am dazzled by your brilliance'.

Wiping the forehead can be to remove sweat. It typically indicates relief and can be a deliberate exaggeration. It can also indicate fear, even when the person is not sweating.

Note that we often sweat more from the forehead than other parts of the body, making it significant in sending moisture-related signals. Sweating can occur when we are hot, which can come from external temperature, exercise, and also inner energy and arousal. A cold sweat can indicate extreme fear and may be accompanied by damp eyes.

Wrinkles

Wrinkles here refer to creases—lines or marks of ridges or furrows made by folding, twisting, shrinking—that form on the face, mainly the forehead and the area around the eyes. Wrinkles could be either vertical or linked to worry or ageing, or horizontal lines which are more youthful, especially around the eyes.

Wrinkling the forehead is often connected with the movement of the eyebrows, particularly upwards, and hence acts as an amplifier of these signals. Raised eyebrows (and wrinkled forehead) indicate surprise or questioning.

Vertical wrinkles indicate a fussy and exacting person, a perfectionist. Wrinkles which fan out from the outer corner of each eye forming 'crow's feet' or smiling eyes indicate that the person appreciates the funny side of things. Successful people often have such lines.

Hair

The hair is a part of the body and hence is used in various ways for communication. Hair can be cut and shaped into a wide range of styles which contributes to the overall image and hence sends non-verbal signals. A conventional and tidy cut indicates a conventional person who follows basic social rules. Well-styled hair can indicate a desire to be attractive and so get the approval and admiration of others.

Hairstyles or hairdos are also indicative of an individual's personality; it is a non-verbal signature representing who and what we are. In some cases, a hairstyle identifies a person with a particular group or cult, not unlike a cap or hat. Hairstyles help us blend into the social scene.

Hands to Head Gestures

There are a few gestures in this area which are important to note.

Head in Hand

The head supported at the cheeks by one or both hands can signify despair, bereavement, prolonged thinking, boredom. It also indicates extreme interest. The accompanying eye gestures may strengthen the message. For instance, a person may use this gesture for boredom; the non-verbal behaviour here will be an open hand, on the side of the head in a gesture of regret, a lowered chin in the manner of nodding, (or the hand may be used to prevent the head from nodding), with the eyes half covered and drooping. If the head is fully supported, it indicates extreme boredom and lack of interest.

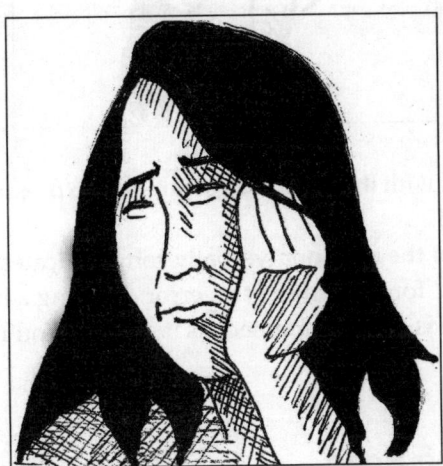

Head Buried in Hands

When a person supports his forehead with his palms, hands spread over his head, and elbows resting on a table, one may conclude he is in deep thought or in a desperate situation.

Slapping the Head

When a person slaps either his forehead or the back of the neck, it could have a variety of meanings. The most obvious one, perhaps, is that it signifies forgetfulness—with a person hitting himself as punishment.

These gestures could also indicate how one feels about the other person or the situation at a given time. Slapping the forehead could mean that he is not intimidated by the other person mentioning his forgetfulness. A person in grief will support his head in the palm of his hand. The other hand may be pressed against his heart or breast and the eyes shut.

Scratching the head with the hand is a gesture that expresses frustration or indicates that one is feeling flustered.

Slapping the back of the neck non-verbally communicates that the other person is literally a 'pain in the neck' for pointing out an error. Holding a hand flat against the forehead signals that the person is feeling harassed, as if saying, 'You're giving me a headache. This is too much'.

Hands behind the Head

This gesture is commonly used by professionals or people who are feeling confident, dominant, or superior about something.

Pease (1993) notes that if we could read the person's mind, he would be saying something like 'I have all the answers', or 'Maybe one day you'll be as smart as I am', or even 'Everything's under control'. It is also a gesture used by the 'know-it-all' individual, which most people find it irritating. Pease refers to research done in this gesture in a particular insurance company. It was found that 27 out of 30 sales managers were accustomed to making this gesture before sales people or subordinates but rarely used it before their superiors; rather, they used submissive and defensive gesture clusters in their presence.

Pease offers several ways of countering this gesture to make it work positively in a given situation. One approach: if you want to discover the reason for the person's superior attitude, lean forward with palms up and say, 'I see that you know about this. Would you care to comment?' Then sit back, palms fully visible, and wait for an answer. Another method is to compel the person to change his position, which will in turn change his attitude. This

can be accomplished by placing something just out of his reach and asking: 'Have you seen this?', forcing him to lean forward.

Copying this gesture is another good way of handling it. If you want to show that you agree with the other person, all you need do is copy his gesture, particularly if the person using the hands-behind-head gesture is in a reprimanding mood. Copying this gesture will non-verbally intimidate him. It is not clear how this gesture originated. Perhaps people, in the absence of high-decked chairs to which they may have been accustomed, would use their hands to support the back of their head. That might have become a habit so that they did it even when they sat in chairs with a headrest.

Knocking the Head about the Temple Areas with the Knuckles

This gesture is made with one hand or both hands; it indicates to the other person that he is being 'a hard nut', obstinate in his views or opinions, or response. It is generally a gesture of exasperation signifying a breakdown of negotiation or communication. Screwing the temples with the index finger is used to indicate that the other person is out of his mind, or insane, or acting stupid.

Tapping of Fingertips on the Side of the Forehead

This is a gesture which complements the aforementioned gesture. It is made with one hand or both hands when someone wants to tell the other that he is a 'hard-nut' to crack or does not have enough brains to comprehend an issue or idea.

THE NECK

The neck is used to support and rotate the head and hence controls some head gestures. It also may send a few signals of its own. When people feel threatened, they will protect the neck, pulling the chin down to protect the throat and possibly also raising the shoulders to protect the sides of the neck. Embarrassment or fear can lead to increased swallowing. A hand on the throat may cover up the signs of swallowing as the person seeks to hide this signal.

The neck can be rotated, both horizontally and vertically, thus giving the head several degrees of freedom and the ability to look in many directions. The eyes can also look without turning the head. Rotating the neck is useful for extending the range of vision. It can also be used deliberately to send a signal that the person is giving or removing attention. The neck can also become stiff from propping up the head and rotation of the neck may be done to exercise it. Exercising the neck can be a sign of tension. It may also indicate boredom.

When a person is uncomfortable with what they are saying or where they are saying it, then their neck muscles may tense, affecting their voice through constriction of the windpipe or tensing of the vocal chords. This can cause discomfort in the neck and the hand thus acts to sooth this irritation. There are also major muscles at the side and back of the neck and rubbing or squeezing these indicates tension, which may well be anxiety.

Hiding the neck by lowering the chin to protect it is a clear display of a judgemental, aggressive, or negative attitude in the person. It is a subconscious gesture used by a person who is aware that he has deceitful or bad intentions and therefore should protect his vulnerable throats and necks from being attacked by the other person if they were to find out what his thoughts were.

We shrug our shoulders to protect our neck and throat. We usually shrug our shoulders when we are in danger or feel helpless. For instance, when we hear a sudden threatening, loud sound, our immediate reaction is to hide our neck inside our shoulders. We shrug our necks and raise our shoulders trying to appear smaller and stop from being attacked when we pass by threatening persons or crowds.

Neck Touching

Neck touching and/or stroking is one of the most significant and frequent pacifying behaviours we use in responding to stress. Some people rub or massage the back of their neck with their fingers; others stroke the sides of their neck or just under the chin above the Adam's apple, tugging at the fleshy area of the neck. This area is rich with nerve endings that, when stroked, reduce blood pressure, lower the heart rate, and calm the individual down (Navarro, 2008).

Touching the front of the neck may indicate concern about what the person is saying in words. This may be because they are lying or otherwise are embarrassed or uncomfortable with what they are actually saying or are thinking of saying.

We not only touch our necks or massage our necks when there is an 'issue', we also do other interesting behaviours that communicate our discomfort or insecurity. Men will ventilate their shirts at the neck or sometimes by pulling at the ends of their collar. Women ventilate by stroking the back of the neck upward lifting their hair. In both cases it means the same thing. Obviously you may see these behaviours on a hot day, but when someone is dealing with something stressful or they are asked a question that is bothersome, you may see this behaviour as a reaction (Navarro and Poynter, 2010).

Neck Scratch

Scratching satisfies a physical need; it is also a non-verbal signal that the person is suffering from some psychological discomfort at the given moment. A slow, sustained scratch on the head, neck, chin, or cheek accompanied by the eyes looking down or up and away may mean the person is searching his memory for something. The same scratch when faster and with a peculiar headshake could indicate that he is embarrassed or has realized that he has made a fool of himself before others.

Neck Rub

A person rubs the back of his neck when he is desperately trying to convince the other to acknowledge a fact. A person also uses this gesture when telling a lie and wanting to avoid the other person's gaze by looking down.

This gesture can also signal frustration or anger. When this is the case, the hand first slaps the back of the neck and then starts rubbing it. People who are in the habit of rubbing the backs of their necks tend to be negative or critical, whereas those who habitually rub their foreheads to non-verbalize an error tend to be relatively more frank and carefree.

Neck Stroking

Neck stroking signals that one does not completely believe what the speaker is saying. We may call special attention here to how a woman disguises this gesture. When she says or hears something that makes her uncomfortable, she slowly and gracefully brings her hand to her throat. If she is wearing a necklace, the movement may give the (false) impression that she is only feeling whether the necklace is still there.

Palm to Back of Neck

When a person places his palm at the back of his neck, he may adopt two postures that look very similar but have quite different functions. One is the 'cradle'; the other is the 'catapult'. In both gestures, the hands are clasped round the back of the neck, but while the elbows are pulled back and the chest is expanded in the case of the 'catapult', the emphasis in the 'cradle' is on supporting the head. The 'catapult' is in fact a disguised gesture of aggression. By pulling his elbows back and expanding his chest, a man increases his apparent breadth and makes himself look threatening. While his hands appear to be taking refuge behind his head, they are actually waiting to ambush anyone who strays too close.

The purpose of the 'cradle' is completely different. Here the hands perform a purely supportive role—there is no sense in which they are being pulled back in preparation for attack. Both the 'catapult' and the 'cradle' can be seen in business settings when people feel threatened. The 'catapult' is likely to be used when one person wants to intimidate another; the 'cradle' when individuals feel the need to comfort themselves. The first is a disguised form of counter-attack, while the second is a surreptitious form of self-assurance (Collett, 2003).

THE TORSO

The torso is made up of the shoulders, chest, abdomen, and hips. In other words, the torso is the body excluding the head and neck and limbs.

It is remarked that the torso is the billboard of the human body. This is very true. We reveal and hide a lot of information in the torso area. This is where we have our badges, wear jewellery on show, may have shirts buttoned up or down. This is an example of really being what we wear, and this also sends a message in conjunction with the other tells we observe.

Shoulders

Our shoulders are a good spot to look for non-verbal cues. The soft skin and rounded shape of our upper arm area and the extreme flexibility of our shoulders have made this body region sexually appealing in men and women alike.

The flexibility and visibility of human shoulders—and the fact that they are moved by emotionally sensitive (that is, branchiomeric or 'gut reactive') muscles—renders them highly expressive as signs, like the shoulder-shrug. Their size and angular silhouette when squared, for example, bespeak dominance (Givens, 1999).

Both men and women unconsciously square their shoulders conveying dominance when they stand tall in an aggressive and dominant attitude. They are preparing for an 'attack' and they want to appear stronger and bigger.

Another important interpretation of the shoulder position is during conversation. In order to tell if someone is really interested or involved in the dialogue taking place, look at his shoulders. If they are facing the interlocutor, then he is focused in the conversation. If, instead, the shoulders are turning away in a different direction, that probably means he wants to leave and his attention is on something else.

Although the shoulders have limited movement when compared with other parts of the body, they can be used to convey various signals.

Positions

Raised

Holding the shoulders in a raised position requires that the whole weight of the arms be lifted. This takes continued effort, which is supplied if the person is aroused in some way. Shoulders hunched up can be a sign that the person is cold (they may be shivering too). Often, this is a sign of tension, often from anxiety or fear. Raising the shoulders and lowering the head protects the neck when the person fears attack (actual or virtual).

Curved forward

Curving the shoulders forward happens naturally when arms are folded. When curled forward with the hands down, this reduces the width of the body and can thus be a defensive posture or a subconscious desire not to be seen, for example, when the person is feeling threatened or when they want to stay 'under cover'.

Pushed back

Pushing the shoulders back forces the chest out and exposes the torso to potential attack. This posture is thus used when the person does not fear attack and may be used as a taunt to demonstrate power. If the body is pulled back when the shoulders are pulled back, particularly when the person is up against the wall, this can indicate a desire to hide the body and not be seen, or otherwise defensively move it out of harm's way.

Circling

Circling the shoulders may be done forwards or backwards, with one or both shoulders. This is often done to exercise a stiff shoulder, which may have been held tensely (and hence may indicate anxiety). This may also be accompanied by rotating or leaning of the neck and other muscle-exercising movements. This exercising can signal that the person is readying himself for action and perhaps combat, and hence may be used as a sign of aggression. When done whilst the other person is talking and when it would be polite to listen carefully, this deliberate breaking of protocol can be an insulting signal of power, indicating that the other is so unimportant as not to merit being listened to.

Shrug

Raising the shoulders is an integral feature of the shrug, which owes its origins to the innate 'startle response'. When we're exposed to a loud, unexpected noise, we instinctively raise our shoulders and pull our head down. This enables us to protect our head and neck from injury. Raising the shoulders as part of the shrug is also self-protective. When people shrug, they frequently place their head to one side. Often added to the shrug are raised eyebrows, down-turned mouth, and hands held to the side, with palms upward or forward (showing nothing is being concealed). Someone who shrugs is saying: 'I can't do anything about it', 'I don't know', or 'I'm not responsible' (Collett, 2003). The shrug commonly shows helplessness, resignation, and/or uncertainty.

A prolonged and animated shrug can be similar to the circling shoulders that indicate readying for aggression and can thus signal a threat. In a smaller form, it may indicate irritation or frustration.

Relaxed

We often carry tension in the shoulders and a person who is truly relaxed will have their shoulders held low, with arms that can move naturally, without jerkiness, and swinging free.

Leaning

When the person leans against a wall, they often contact the wall with their shoulder. This is usually a relaxed pose as galvanizing into physical movement would take more than a little effort, which puts the person in a position vulnerable to attack.

Turning

Turning shoulders is a key part of turning away. If a person turns his shoulders whilst still looking at you, it probably means he wants to leave (maybe because what you are saying is uncomfortable for him).

Shoulder Wear

Human shoulders are so expressive that, in every society, consumer products have evolved to accent their masculine, feminine, dominant, or submissive messages. Clothing may be designed to bare one or both shoulders, to accentuate their roundness, or to allow them greater freedom of movement. However, whether we dress them or leave them bare, or even the way we clothe them will convey different meanings.

Chest

The chest can send a few non-verbal body language signals.

Pushing the chest forward draws attention to it. Men thrust their chest out to display their strong chest muscles. Enlarged pectorals are, along with biceps, the most common muscles that are used to assess overall strength. Men show off their bulging chest muscles to indicate they are strong and as a warning to others not to confront them. When the thrust out their chest to women, they could indicate their strength in case there is need for offering protection.

When women push forward their chests, it could be a part of a provocative romantic display; they may thus be inviting intimate relations (or just teasing). Women wear high heels, which curves the spine to push out the chest and buttocks.

When the person stands sideways or at 45 degrees, the effect of a thrust-out chest is exaggerated as the person is seen in profile. Women may use this to display the curve of their breasts. Likewise, men may show their strong profiles.

When the chest is pulled back, this may well indicate that the person is trying to hide or appear inoffensive so as not to be hurt. Curling forward the shoulders may offer further protection.

The heaving of the chest is effected by the volume and depth of breathing. Deep breath may be used to help thrust out the chest. It also increases the oxygen intake and readies the person for action, thus indicating fear or anger. We also breathe deeply when we are experiencing intense emotions such as love.

A person who is particularly anxious may breathe too fast and deep and so hyperventilate, taking in so much oxygen that they get giddy (and can even faint).

When the body is held rigid, then breathing is more difficult and short breaths are more likely and may indicate tension. When a person in a state of hopeful suspense, he may hold his breath, as if breathing would either cause what is feared or destroy what is being enjoyed.

Touching the chest draws further attention to it. When a woman does this in front of a man, it makes the man think of doing this and is thus a highly suggestive and flirtatious act.

Rubbing the chest can also be a sign of pain of discomfort, perhaps from tension and stress.

Hands to Chest Gestures

The hands to chest gesture is by and large a male gesture. Females usually make this gesture to cover their breasts. In both cases it signifies honesty.

For centuries people have been known to put their hands on their chest to communicate loyalty, honesty, and devotion. The Romans saluted by putting one hand on the chest and thrusting the other hand outwardly toward the person they were greeting. Children, when they make a promise or an important statement, they want their friends to believe, raise their right hand with the palm exposed and touch their chest with the other hand for endorsement. Adults may do the same, though very rarely.

Stomach

The stomach is the area between the bottom of the ribs and the top of the hips. It is referred to variously as the belly, the tummy, the abdomen, or the paunch.

A flat stomach is considered desirable in both men and women as it indicates fitness and health. In men, at least, the ultimate is a 'six pack' where individual muscles can be seen.

People with protruding stomach may consciously pull in the flabby muscles in order to look trimmer. The stomach may stick out more as a counterbalance when we want to pull our vulnerable upper body and head away in a situation where we feel uncomfortably close to another person.

The abdomen walls contain significant muscles and we can carry tension here. Rubbing or holding them can thus indicate tension, for example, from excessive worry. Rubbing the stomach can mean that the person simply has a digestive problem.

Hips

The hips are at the base of the body trunk and are made up of the pelvis and covering tissue. Pushing the hips sideways makes the spine curve and rearranges the whole body to compensate. This can be a relaxed position as the person lets the body drop. The sagging can also come from disappointment or tiredness.

The hips may be used as a subtle pointer, indicating what the person really wants. Pointing at a person may indicate that they are found to be attractive. Pointing at the door can mean the person wants to leave.

Thrust Out

Pushing the hips forwards is difficult without losing balance, so this is sometimes done by leaning back against something like a wall to support the upper body whilst the hips are clearly foremost.

Men may use the hip thrust with other men as a signal of power (with reference to the sexual organs) or to warn another not to dare attack him.

Held Back

Holding the hips back is the opposite of thrusting them out. It defends and hides the genitals, seeking to protect them or avoid them being noticed. One way of holding them back is to sit down, folding the body over them. This may be compounded by crossing legs and covering the genitals with crossed hands.

Hands on Hips

Hands on hips is a very overt gesture that can be easily identified. People stand with their feet apart, for stability, and with the hands on the hips, in which the palms rest on the hips with the elbows flexed outward, bowed away from the body.

There are two main versions of this posture: the one-handed 'arm akimbo' and the two-handed 'arms akimbo'. The two-handed version is more spectacular, but the one-handed version can be pointed at other people in a way that the two-handed version cannot.

There are three components that make hand on hip postures dominant. Hands on hips pushes the elbows sideways, making the body look larger, and thus may be a signal of power or aggression; when both hands are used, the effect is doubled. Hand on hip postures also expand the territory that someone occupies. The elbows can be used to push through a large crowd for clearing a path.

The hands on hips posture displays the person's readiness to 'take steps' either to perform, to take part in, or to take charge of an event, activity, or work assignment. That is, as a non-verbal cue, the posture shows that the body is poised to 'step forward', for example, to carry out an order, to discipline or threaten someone weaker than oneself, or to defend oneself against those who 'overstep their limits'. The outward flexing of the elbows gives the impress of a widened, expanded, and enlarged upper body, making it look more powerful in size (Givens, 1999). This gesture is also associated with an 'achiever' who uses this pose when he is ready to tackle his objectives; for example, an athlete is waiting to take part in an event.

Bottom

The large padded area at the base of the back is referred to the bottom, or buttocks, or bum.

The bottom has a strange combination of meaning because it is related to the excretory functions of the body and also an orifice for pleasure. Pushing the bottom towards someone may thus be an insult or an invitation, depending on the situation.

Exposing the bottom can range from a slight push towards the person or significant extension, such as from leaning on a table (to retain balance) or bending over, such that the upper body is hidden and the bottom is highly visible. 'Mooning' is a semi-serious insult and involves exposing the naked bottom. This is a bit degrading and is often done with a certain amount of humorous intent.

Waving the bottom draws attention to it even more than pushing it out, although this tends to be more enticing than insulting.

SUMMING UP

The head usually has hair, ears, eyes, nose, and a face; thus, it has more complex and visible muscular effects than any other area of the body. The face, our eyes, and our hands are the most powerful parts of our body in sending body language signals.

The head is very significant in body language. Due to a very flexible neck structure, one can turn, jut forward, withdraw, tilt sideways, forwards, backwards. All of these movements have meanings when taken in a cluster. The head is used a lot in directional (likes and dislikes) body language and in defensive (self-protection) body language too.

Head movement is important to maintain a rapport during a conversation. Some positive signs in body language are nodding the head while talking and tilting it when listening.

The head—when our hands interact with it—is therefore dynamic and busy in communicating all sorts of messages, consciously and unconsciously.

Chapter 5

Arms, Hands, and Palms

PART ONE: THE ARMS

Our arms are an integral part of non-verbal communication. We use our arms to connect to people and objects, through our reach and our ability to grasp things. Our arms also help us defend ourselves against external threat. Moreover, the position of our arms as we sit, stand, or walk provides cues to our attitudes and emotions.

Relationships between people are frequently expressed through the physical connection of arms. Formal relations usually require handshakes, while more familiar relations might permit forearm clasps, shoulder clasps, or even hugs.

CROSSED OR FOLDED ARMS

Introduction

The 'crossed arms' gesture is made by neatly folding the arms over the lower chest or upper abdomen, with one or both hands touching the biceps muscles. It is a self-comforting, self-stimulating posture, unconsciously used to alleviate anxiety and social stress (Givens, 1999).

Originally, the purpose of placing the arms across the chest was to protect the heart and the upper body. When the arms are crossed, they form a 'barrier' to an impending threat or undesirable situation. It is reminiscent of childhood—a 'hiding' gesture—when we sought refuge behind solid objects whenever we felt threatened. Crossed arms, therefore, indicate a protective guard against an anticipated attack. It could also mean that the person has taken a fixed position and will stand his ground regardless of consequences. However, we must note that this is also a comfortable position and the gesture stands for relaxation. Professionals like doctors and teachers use this gesture when they are in the company of peers. Children use it when defying their parents' instructions.

When a person pulls his arms and elbows tightly into the body, the gesture may reveal acute nervousness or chronic anxiety. When the arms are held less tightly against the chest and the elbows are elevated and project outward from the body, the crossed arm presents a guard like stance, suggestive of arrogance, disliking, or disagreement.

There are different intensities of arm-folding. A child around six years old does it quite obviously by deliberately crossing the arms tightly across the chest. The teenager makes it appear less obvious by relaxing the arms a bit and combining it with a crossed leg gesture. Older people cross their arms rather casually, but this is taken for granted as the behaviour expected of elders.

Interpretations

Research

According to Darwin (1965), the crossed arm gesture is used worldwide to communicate defensiveness. The classical understanding of the crossed arm, according to Fast (1970), is that it reflects a closed mind. The person who makes this gesture is not willing either to listen to the arguments of the speaker or to agree with his views.

According to Nierenberg and Calero (1975), the crossed arm gesture 'tends to be the easiest to understand and sometimes the least recognized as a nonverbal indicator'. This gesture, and the attitude that goes with it, is easily imitated in a group situation. It could, very subtly, rally support for one side or the other. For instance, when a person uses this gesture while speaking to a group, those who are on the same wavelength will start crossing their arms, as if they have caught a contagion. Those with arms crossed form a subgroup, as it were, apart from the others who do not. Those with crossed arms may go on the defensive and cause dissension during the meeting. As long as the arms are crossed there could be resistance in the group; but once they are uncrossed, open communication can take place.

Pease (1993), thinking on the same lines, considers the crossed arm gestures as a signal from a person with a nervous, negative, or defensive attitude. Obviously, this person feels threatened, so he uses the arm as a shield behind which he withdraws from the task or person he fears.

In conversation, a person who has his arms crossed tightly over his chest has a negative attitude towards the speaker and pays less attention to what is being said. People with arms and legs uncrossed and relaxed, pay closer attention, and retain more. They also tend to respond to the speaker with greater openness. A common method salespeople use to break a crossed arms closed position is to give the person something to hold or otherwise ask them to use their hands.

General Observations

Arms can act as the doorway to the body and the self. When they are crossed, they form a closed defensive shield, blocking out the outside world. Shields act in two ways: one is to block incoming attacks and the other is a place behind which the person can hide and perhaps not be noticed.

Crossed arms may indicate anxiety driven by a lack of trust in the other person or an internal discomfort and sense of vulnerability. The extent of crossing indicates how firmly closed the person is. This may range from a light cross to arms folded to arms wrapped around the person. An extreme version which may indicate additional hostility is a tight close with hands formed as fists. If legs are crossed, too, it reinforces also then this adds to the signal.

The hands in an arm-cross may also be used to hold the person in a reassuring self-hug, for example, holding upper arms in a folded arms position or wrapped around the torso, holding the sides. If the thumbs are up, this may indicate some approval or agreement with what is being said.

Not all crossed arms gestures indicate defensive. Sometimes folded arms, for example, are just a relaxed position. Crossed arms are also used when the person is cold (this is typically done with hands tucked under armpits to keep them warm).

Range of Crossed and Folded Arms Gestures

There are a variety of crossed or folded arm gestures. We will consider the main ones here:

The Standard Arm-cross

When both arms are folded across the chest, it is a universal gesture that signifies defensiveness or negativity, an attempt to 'hide' from an unfavourable situation. The gesture is common in places where people feel insecure or uncertain, like at public meetings, queues and lifts, or in the company of strangers. The gesture can also signal disagreement, discomfort, or discontentment. A forced smile at times serves as a cover-up for these emotions.

In a group discussion situation or at a public meeting, people take a crossed arm position when they disagree with the speaker. They remain in that position for as long as they hold contrary views. Speakers who notice the gesture must make an attempt to get the audience to become more receptive and not continue with their train of thought.

In a one-to-one dialogue situation, if a person folds his arms across the chest, he is nonverbally expressing that he disagrees with what the speaker has stated. In some cases, this gesture may be accompanied by the incongruent head-nod which signifies agreement—though in reality the person does not accept the speaker's line of thinking.

In order to change the attitude and gesture, we may resort to certain tactics. One approach is to give the person something to hold—like a file or a pen—so that he will be forced to break up the crossed arm gesture. Another is to ask him directly if he has something else in mind, so that he opens up both mentally and physically.

Reinforced Arm-cross

Crossed arms with fists

This is the standard arm-cross gesture but with the fists tightly clenched. It signifies a hostile or offensive attitude. It may be accompanied by a gesture cluster like blushed cheeks and gritting teeth. The person is about to attack—verbally, at least.

If apart from crossing their arms, the fists are clenched, it is a sign of strong hostility as well as defensiveness. It is an aggressive and attacking attitude used by policemen standing guard.

Partial arm-cross

In order not to betray their fear through the full crossed arm gesture, some people substi-tute it with the partial arm-cross, which is more subtle. While one arm lies at the side, the other hand is placed across the body to hold it. This gesture is made by a person who lacks

self-confidence while meeting with strangers. It is also seen among public speaker, recipients of awards when on stage, subordinates in the presence of superiors.

Disguised arm-cross

This is a very subtle and sophisticated crossed arm gesture. It is resorted to by those who are in public dealing, for example, marketing executives, politicians, teachers, and actors. It resembles an ordinary crossed arm gesture—with one arm swinging in front of the body to grasp the other. However, the arm does not fold; instead, it reaches out to touch some part of the other hand, playing with the strap of the wristwatch, fingering a bracelet or cufflink, or grabbing a handbag. The arm only partially crosses the body. Another form of partial arm-cross is when a person who is drinking holds the glass with both hands. Although he may be totally unaware that he is making this gesture, a trained observer will immediately detect the disguise and identify the nervousness that lies behind it.

Arm-cross and thumbs

In this gesture, the arms are folded, with the fingers tucked into the armpits, and thumbs sticking out. The gesture occurs when a subordinate faces his superior whom he considers his equal. The thumbs sticking out indicate that the person is 'cool' and self-confident in the presence of a superior. The gesture shows that though he is in control, he still maintains a level of protection with the crossed arms, just in case. This gesture can also be seen in an exam, where the student feels confident about his abilities to answer correctly yet still feels a bit threatened by something going wrong.

ARM POSITIONS

One Crossed Arm

This type of body shield is a single arm crossing the chest and grabbing or touching the bicep or elbow of the opposite arm; as young children, our parents would embrace or hug us when we were going through a distressful moment, as adults we try to recreate that same comforting feeling by doing it ourselves. It resembles a self-hug and is more popular amongst woman than men. This arm gesture can be seen in social group situations where a stranger feels low in self-confidence.

Subtle Arm Crosses

People who are constantly in the limelight choose subtler ways of crossing arms for self-assurance. Men like adjusting their watches or shirt cufflinks, fiddle with their ring, scratch their wrists, check inside their wallets or mobile phones. These actions make the arms get in front of the body when they feel nervous and in full view of others.

Women, who generally carry accessories, 'adjust' and fiddle around with their jewellery or use their purse as a barrier when they feel self-conscious or insecure.

A communally used subtle arm-cross is, when seated at a table, to so place their glass that they will have to move their arm across their body to reach it.

Arm Gripping

In this gesture, the hands grip the upper arms tightly, so as to reinforce the position and prevent the arms from sliding back to a relaxed position. At times the grip can be so firm, like a stranglehold, that the knuckles and fingers get drained of blood and appear white. This gesture shows a negative, suppressed attitude. It is a response to the fear of impending 'danger'. It may be observed in places like waiting rooms of doctors or in the security lounge of an airport among people afraid of flying.

Arms behind the Back

Persons experiencing inner conflict resort to this gesture. They clench their fist and hold the wrist of the clenched hand or restrain the entire arm by locking it behind their back. This happens when the person is standing, but the gripping of the wrist happens while either standing or sitting.

While in a standing position, when a person tries to hold himself back from taking aggressive action, he will either clench his hand and hold the wrist, or restrain the entire arm by locking it behind the back.

Holding one arm behind the back and clenching the hand lightly, while the other hand grips the wrist or arm, is a gesture people use to disguise their emotions of anger, frustration, or fear with this gesture of self-control. A worker or salesperson kept waiting outside the boss' office may make this gesture out of nervousness. The longer the delay, he may begin to get upset, and in turn he will move the hand up the back, raising it higher the angrier he gets. The person who holds the other hand high up on the arm, however, can be seen to be exercising greater self-control than the one who grabs the wrist or the back of the hand.

Unclenched hands behind back is a gesture of superiority or confidence. They expose the person's vulnerable areas like the stomach, heart, and throat in an unconscious show of fearlessness. It signals that he feels quite relaxed and confident, and in a position of authority. Members of the royal family and the aristocracy, and persons in authority (policeman, headmaster, managers) are observed to make this gesture.

GESTURES WITH THE ELBOWS

The elbows are the lesser noticed parts of the human anatomy, but they provide a few non-verbal messages both individually and as a part of a wider cluster.

Displaying Size

Elbows are like the wings of a bird. When we push them outwards, we puff ourselves up and appear bigger larger than we are. When we place our hands on our waist and stick out our elbows, we could be displaying aggression in the face of unreasonable demands, aggravations, or insurmountable tasks.

A more subtle form of the gesture is when the chest is expanded and the elbows are pushed slightly out. The body remains stationery. When this gesture is accompanied by a relaxed S-shaped body curve, with one foot pointing forward at the target person, it results in a more relaxed attention-getting pose.

Elbows as Weapons

Elbows are bony and sharp. They can be used to nudge, lever, or prod people out of the way without causing the kind of offence that might arise if one were to use one's hands. In this respect the elbows are a 'second-grade weapon', but a weapon nevertheless. This makes it possible for the elbows to be used in an understated, almost subliminal way. If we push with our arms on our hips, the message is subtler—the elbows threaten people without them being fully aware of what is happening.

Elbows as Props

When seated, we may take a more relaxed pose by putting out and cupping our hands to support our head.

ARM POSITIONS WHILE SLEEPING

| FOETUS | LOG | YEARNER | SOLDIER | FREE FALLER | STARFISH |
| 41% | 15% | 13% | 8% | 7% | 5% |

Non-verbal plus body language speak volumes about how one actually feels. When one seeks to appear interested and engaged, posture straightens, arms are unfolded, and eye contact is maintained during conversation.

But scientific evidence suggests that posture during sleep reveals insight into the psyche. According to the BBC in London (BBC, 2003), Professor Chris Idzikowski, director of the Sleep Assessment and Advisory Service and a visiting professor at the University of Surrey in Southern England, studied a thousand Britons and their various sleeping positions to see if they provided a clue to their personalities. He identified six of the most common sleep postures and how they relate to personality type. This is the first time a link has been shown between the various sleeping positions and elements of personality.

Positions

Foetus or *Foetal* **Sleeping Position** is the most common sleep posture, with 41 per cent of the 1,000 people tested falling asleep on one side, with their knees pulled up towards the chest and arms in a prayer position with hands by the face. Those who curl up in the foetal position are described as tough on the outside but sensitive at heart. They may be shy when they first meet someone, but soon relax. More than twice as many women (51 per cent) as men tend to sleep in this position.

Log **Sleeping Position (15 per cent):** These people fall asleep on their side, with both arms down by their side. They are easy-going, social people who like being part of the 'in' crowd and are trusting of strangers. However, they may be gullible.

This is not a relaxed and stretched out posture. These people are calm, peaceful, and steady. They are easy-going and do what is expected of them. They want to be liked and be part of the group. They are not driven or aggressive. Some research says people who sleep on their side with their right arm stretched over their head are said to be blessed with power and fortune.

Yearner **Sleeping Position (13 per cent):** People who sleep on their side with both arms out in front tend to have an open nature but can be suspicious and cynical. This person is slow to make up his mind, but once a decision is made, he is unlikely to ever change his mind.

This position is similar to the log. The sleeper lies on their side but has their arms reaching out towards the other side of the bed. The yearner is so named because the sleeper looks like they are trying to bring something towards them (Deasey, 2006).

Soldier **Sleeping Position (8 per cent):** These folks lie on their back with both arms pinned to their sides. People who sleep in this position are generally quiet and reserved. They do not make trouble but set high standards for themselves and for others.

Freefall **Sleeping Position (7 per cent):** These types lie on their belly with hands around the pillow, head turned to one side. Described as gregarious and brash people, these personalities can be nervy and thin-skinned underneath and find criticism or extreme situations difficult to accept.

Starfish **Sleeping Position (5 per cent):** Those who fall asleep on their back with both arms up around the pillow make good friends because they readily listen to others and offer help when needed. They generally don't like to be the centre of attention.

According to Idzikowski, the research reveals most people stay in the same position all night and only 5 per cent lay differently night by night. Also interesting is that the study showed only one in 10 people cover their bodies entirely with a blanket, with most people exposing an arm, leg, or both feet.

Added Inputs

Wood (2011), a body language expert, commenting on Professor Idzikowski's research, makes the following comments and adds some positions from her own observation.

The Foetal Position

The Full-foetal Position: The full-foetal is the characteristic womb position. Sleepers lie curled on their sides, with knees pulled all the way up, heads bent forward. Usually a pillow or blanket mass is centred at the stomach. These people are highly emotional, sensitive, artistic, and have intense one-on-one relationships.

The symbolism is that of a baby in the womb. People who sleep in this position would have the innocence and unaffected personality of a child. If they are hugging a pillow, they need a lot of love and support. They are sensitive and trusting. They tend to see the world as full of goodness as if they are wearing rose-coloured glasses. They are friendly and social. They give support. They are the ones who bring the birthday card for everyone at the office to sign; a sense of community is important to them. They long for what they had in the womb: security, warmth, and intimacy. They give joy to others. If the position is tightly curled up, it may show a slight degree of insecurity. A sudden change to this position could show stress and a need to return to the womb.

Semi-foetal Position: The most common position, the semi-foetal, has sleepers lying on their sides with knees slightly bent, one arm outstretched above the head, the other resting comfortably on the opposing upper arm to cradle the head. Conciliatory, compromising, non-threatening, non-shakers, sleep experts claim this to be the optimal sleep posture position.

The Yearner (side sleeper and reacher): The same research shows that this position is used by 13 per cent of sleepers.

The Crab (lying face down): The sleeper is face down on the stomach with arms extended and bent, usually framed above the head, this position has quite different meanings. I feel when a sleeper suddenly takes on this position, it shows they are afraid of something. They may not want to face something or they are dealing with intense stress. Research says that sleepers who regularly sleep in the prone position tend to have strong compulsive tendencies and stubbornness in their personalities and are persistent and goal-oriented. The symbolism is of someone who refuses to see others' viewpoints. They are serious and stubborn. They hold strong beliefs and try to have everything done their way and will use force to gain compliance. They are tense and focused in order to get things done. They do not give ground easily. If their hands are in fists, they could be showing hidden aggression. They are 'my way or the highway' people.

The Soldier (on back and face up, arms at the side): According to American researchers, 43 per cent of the population sleeps in this position. The non-verbal symbolism indicates that of someone facing life; you are secure and self-assured. Professor Idzikowski's British research says that only 8 per cent of the population use this position. I guess there are a lot more soldiers in the USA. The soldier position is held by lying on your back with both arms pinned to your sides. Professor Idzikowski says that people who sleep in this position are generally quiet and reserved. They don't like a fuss but set high standards for themselves and others.

The Royal Position is the geometric opposite of the prone. The royal sleeper lies supine, fully on the back, with arms slightly akimbo at the sides. It's an open, vulnerable, and expansive position, and these people display self-confidence and self-involvement. Workaholic businessmen and entrepreneurs often prefer this position.

The Star (on back, face up with the legs open, and arms spread wide): You are a star and freedom-loving. You are comfortable taking over the space. This is the sleep position of an extremely confident person. You are not only assured, you are open to the world. You're ready to hug the world. Sleeping in this position shows you have a sense of well-being. You're confident and optimistic and not particular keen on planning or scheming, but you can be surprised by scheming of others.

Starfish (on back with both arms up around the pillow): British research says that these sleepers make up 5 per cent of the population, make good friends because they are always ready to listen to them, and offer help when needed. They generally do not like to be the centre of attention. I disagree and give a specific assessment based on the position of the hands on top and I call it 'The Crown'.

The Crown (hands are on top of the head or arms are crossed to support the head): They are putting a crown on their heads because they think they are kings. They listen so they can be the wise sage and then tell people what to do. They think they are supportive and merely giving helpful advice. The crowned sleeper is highly intelligent and enthusiastic but some of their ideas are only good to them.

The Twister (tied up in knots): People who sleep all tied up in knots (twisted) or with limbs flung out all over the bed are experiencing stresses. They are under constant pressure. It is difficult to always feel that life is a struggle and these people often feel that they are falling short. The tension will eventually wear them down, hopefully leading to a new approach to life that is less stressful.

PART TWO: HANDS

INTRODUCTION

The most revealing aspect of body language, perhaps, is what people do with their hands. If a person says one thing and means something else, his hands will be a dead giveaway, because there are very few movements of the hands that are accidental. Practically all hand movements have hidden meanings. What a person does with his hands, fingers, and arms is directly related to what is going on in his mind.

The hands have 27 bones and are very expressive parts of our anatomy. Neurologists speak of a vast network of 'telephone lines' that link the hands directly to the brain. Scientists have observed that there are more nerves between the brain and the hands than any other part of the body. The hands thus act as a kind of mental earphone or 'listening device' that reveals what a person is thinking.

A hand signal may be small, perhaps betraying subconscious thinking. It may also be exaggerated or done with both hands to emphasize the point. It is worth noting that gestures with the hands vary significantly cross-culturally.

Hand gestures show conviction and enthusiasm. Hand gestures, to be most effective, must be made above your elbow and away from your body. They should be vigorous and definite to show conviction. A sweeping wave of your arm to show distance will add more to your message than a half-hearted hand wave. Hand gestures also should be full and varied rather than partial and repetitious; making the same movement over and over is distracting. Make your hand gestures larger for large audiences to ensure that even people in the back of the room can see them.

COMMON HAND SIGNALS

There are a variety of non-verbal gestures of the hands.

Individual Hand Gestures

Holding

Hands may be used to hold items such as pens or cups, which may be used as comfort objects, for example, where a person hugs a cup (the cup represents the person, so they are effectively hugging themselves). Holding an item with two hands effectively creates a closed position. Items may also be for distracting activity that releases nervous energy, such as fiddling with a pen, clicking it on and off, or doodling with it.

Holding imaginary objects as they are talked about can show importance. Things which are important (and perhaps with fear of loss) are held close and tight. Things which are not wanted are held further away (or even tossed away).

Hands may also hold the self, such as when people hold their own hands, typically for comfort. Holding the self can also be an act of restraint. This can be to let the other person talk. It can also be used when the person is angry, effectively stopping them from attacking.

The two hands can show different desires, for example, with one forming a fist and the other holding it back, restraining the desire to punch the other person.

People who are lying often try to control their hands, and when they are kept still (often holding one another), one may suspect deceit.

Hands are even ideas to express the volume of an idea. The bigger and more important the idea, the wider the arms are held. Generally, people make gestures as if they are holding a basketball; this is suggestive of passing it to others. A wide-armed hold may indicate the whole world or something massive.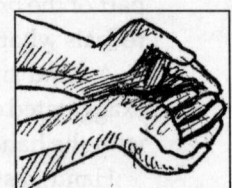

Cupping

Cupping is holding one or both hands, individually or together (giving an exaggerated effect), in the shape of a cup or a container. Cupped hands can symbolize delicacy or hold a fragile idea. They may also be used for giving. Gripping can show possessiveness, ownership, and desire (the tighter the fist, the stronger the feeling).

Cupped hands may be used to indicate weight, which often is used as a metaphor for importance. Single-handed weighting bounces the cupped hand up and down, for example, when an argument is being proposed. Two hands are used to indicate discussion of one individual against the other. The hand which seems to hold the heavier weight will be the one which the person thinks is most significant.

People cup their ears with their hands in order to cut off distracting sounds so as to focus on something they are special attention to and want to hear more distinctly. This is also used to ask the speaker to raise his voice for what he is saying cannot be clearly heard. When people do not want to hear something, they cup their ears.

Shaping

People gesture shapes by carving the air with their hands. This non-verbally communicates by creating visual metaphors out of literally nothing.

Cutting

The side of a flat hand can appear as a knife, cutting the air like a karate chop. The cutting hand may strike the other palm, creating visual and aural impact. A side-swiped cut with palm down tells others to stop what they are doing, for example, when a person on stage asks the audience to stop clapping so they can speak. A short side swipe may also signal 'no' in any conversation. Cuts can signal aggression, particularly when coupled with an aggressive face. They may also indicate decisiveness, chopping with each point. A side-swiped cut can chop away someone else's argument.

Covering

People use their hands to cover their ears or eyes to indicate that they do not wish to hear or see something. They may put their hands to their mouth (or that of another) when they want to say something but feel restrained. A hand may also cover a rudely open mouth, which may be opened in such as surprise or a yawn. Hands covering the mouth when speaking may be an indicator of lying, although it may also just indicate uncertainty.

Hands can cover other things. A hand to heart may seek to protect it from shocking harm. A hand to the groin may protect from dangerous attack. Hands can also cover one another. Sometimes a tense fist may be covered by the other hand.

Hiding

Hands are often used in communication and hiding the hands may indicate a desire not to communicate or not to collaborate, saying 'I don't want to talk with you' or 'I do not agree with you'. This may be done in a deliberate gesture of defiance, such as stuffing hands in pockets.

Putting hands in pockets or behind the back can also be to just feel relaxed.

Liars may hide their hands behind the back to prevent any giveaways while lying.

Waving

The wave is a gesture in which the hand is raised and moved back and forth, as a greeting or sign of departure. The gesture can be used to attract attention at a distance. Most commonly, though, the gesture means quite simply 'hello' or 'goodbye' (Armstrong and Wagner, 2003; Cooke, 1959).

Two-hand Gestures

Applause is an expression of approval made by clapping the hands together to create noise.

Whatever is an expression made with the thumb and forefinger of both hands to form the letter 'W'. It is used to signal that something is not worth the time and energy. It as popularized by the movie *Clueless* (Paumgarten, 2005).

Victory clasp is used to exclaim victory by clasping the hands together and shaking them to one's side.

Hand Positions

Limp Hands: A limp, or hanging hand, signifies boredom, restlessness, or tiredness. Depending on the context, it can also indicate frustration or disgust. It can be used in certain situations to indicate contempt, snobbishness, or a desire not to get one's hands dirty.

Flat Hands: A hand held flat, palm upward or outward, has come to symbolize the silent question 'Why?' and 'I don't know' or 'Search me'.

Relaxed Hands: We can tell a person's mood simply by observing his hands. The hands of a person who is calm, confident, and self-assured will be at rest, moving little. They may hang limply by his sides, or if he is seated, rest gracefully one over the other, or folded neatly, finger to finger. Even if occupied, the hand movements will be steady and relaxed.

Restless Hands: If a person is uneasy, nervous, or jittery, his hands will be rather active and restless; picking, biting, or sucking the fingers are common movements in such circumstances.

Raised Hand/s: People raise a hand to call attention to themselves or to show their readiness to respond to a question or a request.

Hands raised with palms facing outward could be a signal for parting—waving goodbye. Politicians and celebrities use this gesture to acknowledge the greetings of the public.

In India, the holy gurus may hold out their hand straight up in front of the body with palm facing outwards to signify peace, reassurance, or even blessing.

Clenched Hands: To clench means to close together tightly or to grasp firmly. This gesture has a number of meanings depending on the context and the mood. Bacon (1875) states that the clenched hand signifies extreme emphasis, vehement declaration, fierce determination, or desperate resolve.

Clenched hands also often indicate tension and frustration (the sense of having one's hand 'tied') restraint, anxiety, or negative thoughts, and even anger. People often try to cover up their feelings by flashing a happy, smiling face, but are betrayed by their clenched hands.

The degree or intensity of a person's feeling of negativism or level of frustration seems to be connected with the height at which the hands are held. When held high, it could indicate a strong negative attitude. When a person is in this position, it will be rather difficult to get him to agree to one's point of view or clinch a deal.

Hands may be clenched and placed in front of the face while sitting, with the elbows resting on the table, or in front of the stomach or crotch while standing.

In a win–lose situation, the person who feels threatened by the aggressive partner tenses up and clenches his hands tightly. Even though verbally he may pretend to be open, the opponent can observe the person's closed attitude from the clenched hands.

People who have their hands tightly clenched are tense and very difficult to relate to, and it will not be possible to convince them to do anything in a favourable manner unless they are made to 'open up', shed their tension, and relax. One technique by which such people can be made to unclench their fingers and expose their palms is by offering them something to hold. Another effective technique is to lean towards them while talking.

Sportspersons resort to the clenched hand gesture after a successful game. The player throws himself on his knees and presses tightly clenched hands to his forehead. This gesture resembles someone deep in prayer.

Covered Hands: When a person displays the back of one or both hands in a gesture, it can signal the person's insecurity or even his attempt to hide his feelings.

Clinging Hands: When a person is confused or feels insecure, he seeks support physically by clinging to something, be it a table, the armrests of his chair, or his files. It is a clear indication that he is uncertain about facing a situation.

Wringing Hands: To wring means to twist and compress, to turn and strain with violence, to squeeze or press out causing pain. Wringing hands denote discomfort or tension when facing a trying situation or an overbearing person.

A clenched hand could turn into a hand wringing gesture should the person be in a tight spot and has to face some reprimand or charges. This gesture is evident when a subordinate approaches an overbearing boss who looks down his nose at him; the subordinate will keep wringing his hands. The situation can change where an understanding boss notices the hand wringing gesture; the wringing stops when the boss, comes around to the subordinate and leans towards him in a gesture of assurance.

Clapping of Hands: Besides applause, this gesture is used to call someone's attention, whether the person is near or far.

Making a Fist: Making the hands into fists is a gesture related to the clenched hand gesture. It is generally done by males; it is rather unusual for a woman to make a fist while talking. Darwin (1965) observed that the clenched fist signifies determination, anger, and possible hostile action. Furthermore, he noted that a person gesturing with his fist causes an interaction that can make his opponent also clench his fist, which can result in a heated argument or other display of hostility.

Fists are also indicative of emotional arousal, in anger or excitement. Protestors raise their fists, as do enthusiasts at a game. The fists also signals nervousness, anxiety, or disagreement. According to Morris (1994), the closed fist is a universal gesture of power and triumph, as well as a display of force, emphasis, threat. It is an infant's transition to sleep, 'Fists closed for more than several seconds indicate increasing fatigue or distress ...' (Papousek and Papousek, 1977).

People who clench their fists may allow them to be clearly seen, but more often, they conceal the gesture by thrusting their fist into their pocket, or tucking both fists under the armpits in a crossed arm gesture, or putting both hands behind the back.

People tend to clench their fists under stress; if the stress becomes unbearable, they will resort to table-pounding or some other physical action.

The two hands can show different desires, for example, with one forming a fist and the other holding it back, restraining the desire to punch the other person.

Fist shapes and movements are often symbols of inner aggression. When moved towards a person, even a small amount, they signal aggression towards that person. A shaking fist signifies a strong desire to strike someone. Punching the air indicates triumphal excitement.

In protest rallies, people make a fist and raise their hands to express their grievances. This gesture is often accompanied by slogan-shouting.

Supporting Hands: When someone uses his hand to support his head, it is a clear sign of boredom and an attempt to restrain himself from falling asleep by finding a support point to rest his head. There are different degrees of support which reflect the degree of boredom. It can imply with a thumb being used to support the head, followed by the fist or clenched hand, and in the deeper scenarios the whole hand being used to wrap the face in a hand pedestal while resting the arm on a desk or arm rest.

The hands may also lightly support the head, either as a single hand gently under the chin or with fingers intertwined with elbows on table and chin touching the fingers. Particularly when looking at the other person, it draws attention to one's face and may thus be an enticing position.

Evaluating: Someone who is paying close attention to and is genuinely interested in what you are saying will close his hand and rest it on his chin or cheek occasionally using their index finger to point upwards, if what you are saying is something he feels negative towards or does not agree with; he will start resting his heads on his or hand's lower palm while still maintaining the index finger upwards and fist clenched to appear interested, sometimes using the index finger to rub his eye or scratch under it to reinforce his critical thoughts about what you are saying.

Thinking: When someone is making a decision or thinking about something, you will notice how they slowly raise their hands and start stroking their chin; they might also play with their beard if they have one or sometimes fiddle with their lips stretching them out or squashing them together; it can often be seen at the supermarkets when someone can't decide if they should buy the low fat yogurt or risk it and venture into the unknown to purchase the new flavoured full-fat yogurt that just came out.

GESTURES WITH FINGERS

Gestures

Fingers are very flexible and allow for gestures that can be very subtle.

Pointing

Pointing Index Finger: This gesture is used in a harmless way to indicate where something is placed or to indicate a particular direction. More often it could also accompany words of warning or a threat. In heated arguments, fingers may be pointed to the other person almost like a sharp instrument used for piercing. However, a smiling face mellows the threat.

The pointing finger is often used by parents, authority figures, preachers, politicians, when scolding, demanding discipline, or driving home a point. A pointing finger indicates

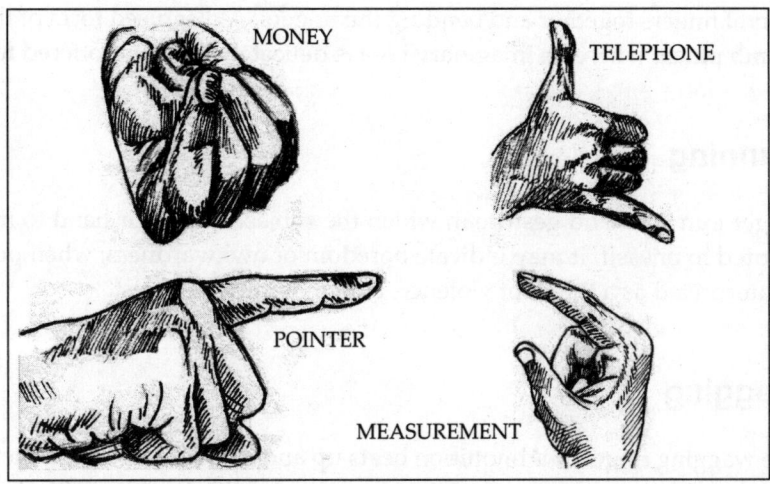

direction. To indicate a long distance, the finger may be pointed diagonally upwards, as if firing an arrow. The index finger is usually used, though the middle finger or even all fingers may be used. When a finger is pointed towards a large audience, the gesture is rarely effective as a threat because it is easy to believe that one's neighbour is the one being referred to.

People dislike being the target of a pointing finger. Some people take offence at this and may either 'turn off' or become hostile towards the person who does it. People who are angry tend to point more, including at themselves (when they feel hurt or insulted) and at those who they feel are to blame. Research in early infant pointing gestures and hand babbling validates the hypothesis that pointing is a universal and fundamental means of communication (Givens, 1999).

Glasses are sometimes used as an extension of the index finger, to point at a person being admonished or reprimanded. They are also so used when a point is being emphasized.

Prodding

To prod is to jab or poke with a pointed object. The finger prod can act like a stiletto knife, stabbing forward at the other person. This is usually the index finger, although the middle finger is sometimes used. This is often very threatening and felt as a personal attack. The prod may also be used to prod downwards at an imaginary item in front. This is less threatening than pointing directly at the person. The prod can also be made less threatening by bringing several fingers together and bending the fingers. A disguised form of this is the finger and thumb pinch, where an imaginary idea is delicately held and offered forward.

Gunning

Finger gun is a hand gesture in which the subject uses their hand to mimic a handgun. If pointed to oneself, it may indicate boredom or awkwardness; when pointed to another, it is interpreted as a threat of violence, either genuine or in jest.

Wagging

The wagging finger of admonition beats up and down as if striking the culprit. This can be with a stable hand and just a finger way. It may also be done with the whole arm, giving an exaggerated striking movement.

A more polite version points downwards as it beats out an important point, perhaps tapping on something like a table.

The forefinger held up and stationary means 'wait'; it could be used to serve as a warning or as a threat.

Beckoning

A beckoning sign is made with the index finger sticking out of the clenched fist, palm facing the gesturer. The finger moves repeatedly towards the gesturer (in a hook) as to draw something nearer. It has the general meaning of 'come here' (McNeill, 1992).

Pinching

Fingers pinched together hold something small and delicate. This may be finger and thumb or may involve more fingers (finger and thumb is less frequent as this forms an 'O' which can have many different meanings). It may be used when saying 'you must grasp this idea'. Held out towards others, it offers them the idea. Pushed down, it holds the idea whilst beating out the key points.

Placing the tips of the thumb and forefinger together is often used to emphasize a line of argument. Usually, the hand moves agitatedly to and fro, and the speaker often concludes the gesture by abruptly baring his open palm at the other party (Haas, 1970).

Pinching the fleshy part of the hand is done for reassurance. Though men also do this, the gesture is found to be more common with women.

Clawing

Curved and separated fingers form a claw. With palm facing down, the claw may threaten to reach forward and grab, scratch, or tear. If the fingers are held loosely, the shape is more of an open cup and may thus hold something. Held downwards, it may gently restrain.

Clicking or Snapping

Finger clicking or snapping can have different meanings. It is used to call someone's attention. It is done spontaneously to convey that one has found some solution that one was working on, or in response to a brainwave one has just received. People snap their fingers to signify that they have remembered something. In Latin America and Asia, a finger snap often means 'hurry up!'. When fingers are snapped close to another's face, it is considered an offensive gesture.

Shush

Shush gesture is used to demand or request silence from those to whom it is directed. The index finger of one hand is extended, with the remaining fingers curled towards the palm with the thumb forming a fist. The index finger is placed vertically in front of the lips (Roberts, 2007).

Emotions

The nerves of the fingers of the human body are linked to the areas of the brain that control speech. Hence, finger movements are a reflection of 'unvoiced thoughts and concealed opinions' (Givens, 1999). When you feel strong and confident, the space between your fingers grows making your hands more territorial; your thumbs will rise more often as you speak, especially if your fingers are intertwined in front of you. When you feel insecure, that space disappears; in fact, you tuck your thumbs under your fingers when under a lot of stress.

There are varieties of finger gestures, usually conveying a person's anxieties, inner conflicts, and apprehensions. We shall consider here a few of the most common ones.

Slightly Raised Fingers

In this gesture, the hand may be resting on the table while sitting, or bent at the elbows while standing, but appears lifeless, with the first two fingers slightly raised in a 'weak-willed' effort to make a point. This gesture may be seen in a person in a group discussion; such a person makes out as if he wants to say something, or is about to say something, and raises a finger ever so slightly. It is the same as a person who starts to say something but then stops, for whatever reason. This gesture is used by timid people; it indicates fear or uncertainty. An aggressive person who notices this gesture may take advantage of the timidity or weak will of the other person and push him around. Another, more subtle use of the gesture of the slightly raised finger or hand is when it is made between friends, as a sign of caution; that is, two friends are in a discussion with a third person present, and one of them suspects that what the other is saying—or likely to say—may prove injurious or harmful in some way.

In another context, the slightly raised finger—or raised finger—when used forcefully is almost universally a sign of warning, as if to say 'Don't do that!'. It is generally used by those in authority, such as a parent, a policeman, an employer, or a supervisor.

Crossed Fingers

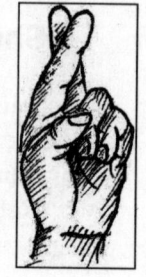

The most common message of the gesture of crossing the middle finger over the index finger is that the person making it wants to assure the other that he is telling the truth. Often, it is used as a figure of speech ('Keep your fingers crossed'), without the gesture accompanying the spoken word. Some use it superstitiously as a plea for good luck, or to avert evil. Feldman (1969) considers this gesture 'a magic gesture, a defence against evil, whether the evil comes from within ourselves or from outside'. It has been observed that in tense situations, after a person makes a request or demand of someone, he crosses his fingers slightly to signify that he hopes the same will be granted or fulfilled.

Nierenberg and Calero (1975) trace this gesture to the childhood action of crossing the middle finger over the index finger and saying alongside: 'I cross my fingers and hope to die, if you ever catch me in another lie'. Youngsters cross their fingers while telling 'a little white lie'. In adults, this gesture may be used often, but in a rather subtle way—the fingers are crossed quickly and then uncrossed. Crossed fingers are also used to nullify a promise.

Steepling

Some people join their fingertips and form what might be described as a 'church steeple'—that is, the tower that has a pointed spire. In steepling, the tactile pads of the fingertips of one hand gently touch their counterparts on the other. Steepling is a gesture generally used by people who are feeling confident or superior, or those who make minimal or restricted body movements. It is frequently used in a superior–subordinate interaction. 'This technique is a powerful adjunct you can use, not only to project your own power, but also to turn off another person's play for power' (Van Fleet, 1984).

This is one of the rare gestures that can be evaluated independently on its own symbolism rather than taken in a gesture cluster. The steeple cue reflects precise thought patterns. The body movements preceding the steepling gesture can indicate the attitude of the steepler. If the steeple follows a series of other positive gestures, one may expect a positive result. If it follows a series of negative gestures, such as arm folding, leg crossing, looking away, and hand-to-face gestures, it could mean that the outcome may be negative. In both cases the gesture signifies confidence; the difference is in the outcome which could be either positive or negative.

The raised steeple expresses opinions or ideas. When the fingers are pressed while steepling upwards, the person may well be thinking, evaluating, or deciding. When the raised steeple position is accompanied with the head tilted back, the person assumes an air of smugness or arrogance. The more important the steepler considers himself, the higher will he hold his hands while steepling. At times they may be at the level of the eyes and the steepler looks through them. This happens often in a superior–subordinate relationship.

The steeple forms a barrier against the other person and may be held lower when the person wants to connect more, such as when they are listening. The lowered steeple is used while listening rather than speaking.

There are open and covert forms of steepling. In its covert form, the hands are positioned on the lap or in front of the body about the waistline while the person is standing, and the fingers joined slightly about the belt level.

A more subtle form of steepling occurs when the hands are joined more closely, while the arms assume any one of the basic steepling positions.

Dovetailing

The fingers of the two hands are intertwined. The palms of the hands are either pressed together or kept loosely apart, creating a sensation that is very similar to holding hands or having one's hand reassuringly held by someone else.

I Love You

The 'I love you' sign is a combination of the American Sign Language letters I, L, and Y.

I = Little finger raised, other fingers bent
L = Thumb and index fingers raised, other fingers bent
Y = Thumb and little finger raised, other fingers bent

The ILY sign combines the letters 'I', 'L', and 'Y' by extending the thumb, index finger, and little finger while the middle and ring finger touch the palm. The one-handed sign (ILY) is an acronym that means I love you.

Movement

Touched or Screw Loose

Making a circling motion of the index finger at the ear or side of the head signifies that the person 'has a screw loose', that is, is speaking nonsense or is crazy.

Blah-blah

In this gesture, the fingers are kept straight and together, held horizontal, or upwards, while the thumb points downwards. The fingers and thumb then snap together repeatedly to suggest a mouth talking. The gesture can be used to indicate that someone talks too much, gossips, is saying nothing of any consequence, or is boring (Armstrong, 2003).

Fiddling

Sometimes people fiddle with things on their person. That is, they do subtle irrelevant gestures that do not appear to be much or in context with the moment but can have an important meaning. The popular ones used are fiddling with a button, jewellery, piece of paper or metal, playing with hair, even picking lint from their clothes, doing any of these things while looking downwards or away. Fiddling can indicate the person is secretly hiding his opinion because he feels it will be perceived as negative if he shares it.

Ring Twisting

This is a gesture of touching and moving the ring around the ring finger and it signifies nervous tension. In case a person does not wear a ring, he will rub the finger where the ring would have been. This gesture may also indicate a sense of guilt.

Drumming

Drumming a flat surface with the fingers can indicate frustration; for example, when another person is speaking and the person wants to interrupt. It may also mean that the person drumming wants to leave. The louder the noise and faster the drumming, the greater the tension the person is feeling. Drumming with the nails makes an even louder noise and hence sends a more urgent signal.

Drumming can also indicate that the person is thinking and that the frustration is with internal thoughts and perhaps that an easy solution cannot be found.

Tapping

Waiting gesture is made by rapidly tapping with the fingers on a rough surface. The thumb is usually not used, and the other four fingers hit the surface in turn; the tapping sequence may be repeated a few times. The gesture denotes either impatience or feeling mildly insulted.

Drumming or finger tapping, whether on tables, while holding a cup, or on the remote control, is always a sign of impatience or anxiety; it can commonly be found at dentist waiting rooms, students waiting to take final exams, and so on.

Knocking on Wood

Knocking on wood is a superstitious gesture used to ensure that a good thing will continue to occur after it has been acknowledged. However, it is sometimes used after speaking of a plausible unfortunate event, so that it does not actually occur.

Poking

Poking, tapping, or jabbing a person with an extended finger may be used to call for attention to tease the person poked.

Cracking of Knuckles

This is a non-verbal signal of anxiety, nervousness, boredom, restlessness, and an unresolved state of mind.

Signs

Okay Sign

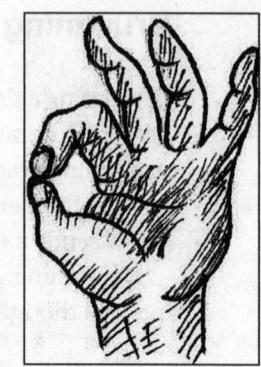

In this gesture, the tips of the thumb and index finger meet in a circle to form an 'O' and holding the other fingers straight. There are several interpretations to this gesture in relation to the abbreviation 'OK'. It may signal the word okay before venturing on a task.

Pease (1993) provides different views on this gesture. Some believe the 'OK' stands for 'all correct', which was misspelled as 'oll korrect'. Others consider it as the opposite of 'KO' or 'knock out'. In all English-speaking countries and in parts of Europe and Asia, the gesture means 'all correct'. In France it means 'zero' or 'nothing'. In Japan it indicates 'money'. In some countries in the Mediterranean, it is used as an orifice signal. It also indicated 'perfect' as when a photographer is pleased with a pose, or someone is satisfied with a job well done.

V Sign

V sign is made by raising the index and middle fingers and separating them to form a V, with the palm facing outward, to signify victory. It is very commonly used today, chiefly by sportspersons or competitors after each round of success. It is also used to mean 'peace'. If the sign is done with the palm facing inwards of the person making the gesture, it would mean 'two'. If the back of the hand faces outwards, this could be an offensive gesture.

Drinking Sign

The gesture for drinking is made by putting the back of the thumb just below the lower lip, while the other fingers are close together as if holding an imaginary mug or glass, tipping it repeatedly. This gesture can also be used to imply that somebody is thirsty, needs a drink, or is going off to have a drink. The gesture is also used to indicate that someone is drunk, either literally or insultingly.

Money Sign

The thumb rubs repeatedly over the tip of the index finger and middle finger. This gesture resembles the act of rubbing coins or bills together and is generally used when speaking about money (Armstrong and Wagner, 2003).

Rubbing the thumb and index finger together indicates expectation of money. It could be used when someone is making a request for money or a loan or by a salesperson while he is negotiating a reduction in the price.

The 'Cut-throat' or Throat-slash Sign

Throat slash is made by moving one's finger across one's throat; the gesture imitates cutting a person's throat with a blade. The gesture indicates strong disapproval, extreme anger, or displeasure with others or with oneself (Armstrong, 2003). It can also be a direction to another party to bring an action to an end and is done in order for the sign initiator to avoid speaking, whether for social decorum, for audio recording purposes, or inability to communicate vocally.

Positions

Cup

Fingers held together and curled upwards form a cup that can contain things more securely than the plate. Relaxed fingers form a loose cup, whilst tense fingers form a more closed cup. Two hands together form a big cup (to hold bigger things). Cups may be used to plead for something to be given or offer something forward to others.

Plate

Fingers extended and closed join with the palm to form a plate. The plate holds symbolic things, such as ideas, often gently. The plate may be proffered forwards, offering the held item to others. For large things, both hands may be held together. Held under the chin, it presents the face as an object to be admired and is often used in flirting.

Telephone

Thumb and little finger outstretched, other fingers tight against palm. Thumb to ear and little finger to mouth as though they were a telephone receiver. Used to say, 'I'll call you', or may be used to request a future telephone conversation or to tell someone of a call (Haviland, 2005).

Thumb Gestures

Thumbs Up

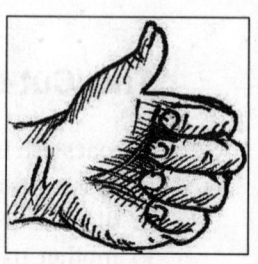

The thumbs up gesture has three meanings according to Pease (1993): it is commonly used by hitch-hikers who are thumbing a lift, it is an OK signal, and when the thumb is jerked sharply upwards, it becomes an insult signal, meaning 'up yours' or 'sit on this'. The thumb is also used with other gestures, as a power and superiority signal and in situations where a person is trying to get someone 'under his thumb'.

Thumbs up signals approval and agreement. Thumbs down signals disapproval. Held sideways (and perhaps waggled) indicates uncertainty.

Thumbs up when arms are crossed or a single hand is held across the chest is a subtle sign of approval. It can also be an invitation to others to show approval of what you are saying.

Thumbs Sticking Out

Thumbs sticking out when hands are in pockets is often a sign of confidence, feeling relaxed, and in control. It can thus be both a sign of authority and also of friendliness.

Those who wish to display dominance and aggression tend to make this typically male gesture.

Men are accustomed to concealing their feeling of dominance by sinking their hands into their pockets—the front or sometimes the back one—and letting their thumbs stick out.

Thumbs Pointing

When the thumb is used as a pointer, it indicates ridicule or lack of respect. For example, if a person points his thumb at the captain of a team and says, 'All his players are like him', he is showing disrespect. He may turn the gesture into ridicule by jerking his pointed thumb at the same time that he makes the statement. Sometimes a person may reinforce his sarcastic remarks by closing his fingers and pointing with the thumb.

The thumb may be used to point to something or someone as it is jerked over the shoulder.

Another common gesture is the thumbs pointing upwards from arms folded across the chest. This conveys a double message: the folded arms show defensiveness or negativity, while the thumbs display superiority. A person may gesture only with the thumbs while speaking.

When you feel confident, your thumbs will rise more often as you speak, especially if your fingers are intertwined in front of you.

Patience

Palm up, index and middle fingers touching the thumb, remaining fingers folded against the palm, and wrist bending slightly, up and down about three times, so that the touching fingers move towards and away from the gesturer. This gesture is used as a reproachful and exasperated request for patience in response to a request to be served immediately out of turn or for something to happen faster than is possible.

HANDS IN MOTION

Hands to Face Gestures

Gestures, we have discussed earlier, have to be interpreted in clusters. The hands are the most versatile part of the body and make for several combinations of gestures. For the sake of convenience, we took each gesture in isolation to better understand its singular interpretations. Now we will deal specifically with gestures of hands touching the facial area and certain parts of the body and treat these individually. However, if the movements are to be fully understood, they must not be interpreted in isolation but in clusters.

Most of the hand(s) to face gestures have negative connotations, for instance, doubt, deceit, exaggeration, apprehension, and uncertainty. Since the gestures can be subtle and the dividing line between these emotions not very clear, an accurate interpretation of the sets of gestures involving the hand and face combination is difficult. It requires keen observation skills and patience. Further, we must be careful to take each gesture in its context, as well as analyze the sequence of gestures that precede it. Otherwise we may reach wrong conclusions and make a false assessment of the gesture involved.

Mouth

Mouth-covering

The hand-to-mouth covering gesture indicates astonishment at or apology for a wrong remark that one lets slip. It is almost as if they wish to shut off the flow of words which they have uttered (Darwin, 1965). This gesture is very noticeable in children who, when confronted for some wrongdoing, invariably bring their hands to the mouth if they are lying. When they wish to lie but tell the truth by mistake, they immediately cover their mouths with their hands. People who give in to spontaneous outbursts of excessive laughter, too, may cover their mouths in embarrassment.

In conversation at table, the steeple gesture may be used to cover the mouth. When one agrees with the other's viewpoints, one lowers the hand and may even show open palms; when disagreeing, the hands are brought up front.

Mouth guard

People use the mouth-guard gesture to suppress a lie that they are telling. In this gesture, they cover their mouths with their hands, with the thumb pressed against the cheek; or they put several fingers into the mouth; or they shove a closed fist in the mouth. Some people use a clever trick to disguise their 'mouth guard' or at least to make it appear less obvious: they bring their hands to their mouth and give fake coughs.

When this gesture is used by the one speaking, it becomes quite obvious that the person is lying. However, when a listener resorts to this gesture, it is a signal that he is of the opinion that the speaker is lying. In a public meeting, if several people suddenly use the mouth-guard gesture, it could put the speaker in a rather embarrassing situation. It would be wise for the speaker to stop speaking and call for a response from the audience to what he has said, thus providing a forum for objections and clarifications.

Putting objects in the mouth

It is not uncommon to see individuals putting things in their mouth, or sucking or chewing objects when they are busy with something. This gesture clearly indicates that the person is under great pressure and is biding time. When a person makes this gesture while speaking, it would mean either that he is procrastinating or that he is 'hungry' for more information.

The fingers-in-the-mouth gesture is considered an overt manifestation of an inner need for reassurance. People use a variety of things as 'mouth feeders'. Grown-ups sometimes substitute objects for fingers; they use pens or pencils for biting gestures, or cigarettes, pipes, and so on. Some even use paper or fabric, or the arm of their glasses.

Nail biting

Nail biting is an inwardly redirected aggression borne of fear, or some other suppression of behaviour. Later nail biting becomes reinforced as a comforting habit, again typically prompted by frustration or fear. Stress in this context is an outcome. Stress doesn't cause nail biting; nail biting is the outward demonstration of stress (Chapman, 2010).

Lips

Lip suppressors

People sometimes place their index finger to their lips as though to seal them and stop the words from coming out. It is a common gesture when we want others to 'shut up'—that is, stop speaking. It is the popular 'silence please' gesture of teachers in schools or of parents who do not wish to be disturbed.

Sometimes a person clips his lips together with thumb and forefinger to demand silence or to indicate that he wants the other person to stop speaking.

Lip-touch

The lip-touch is a hypersensitive, self-stimulating gesture to relieve anxiety or indicate 'boredom, excitement, fear, horror, and uncertainty'. When a person stimulates his lips, he diverts attention either from his own disturbing thoughts or from people who may be upsetting him. 'As a self-consoling gesture, the lip-touch is equivalent to infantile thumb-sucking' (Givens, 1999).

Pinching the Nose

When a person pinches the bridge of his nose, it may indicate that he is in deep thought or engaged in a decision-making process. This gesture is usually accompanied by closed eyes and lowered head, particularly if the person is experiencing self-conflict. A simple explanation for the cause of this gesture is that a person, because of the predicament he is in, pinches his nose to make sure that things are for real and that he is not imagining or dreaming up the situation.

Pinching of nostrils with thumb and forefinger signifies the presence of bad odour. Sometimes it is a symbolic gesture to 'tell' a person that he 'stinks' or what he or she is saying is in poor taste.

Rubbing

Eye rub

People rub their eyes to ease some physical irritation or when they are in doubt or trying to deceive. The action, especially while lying, is an effective way of avoiding eye contact with the other person. Liars tend to rub their eyes vigorously when lying. Women may make small, gentle rubbing motions just below the eye, either through force of habit or in order not to smudge their make-up; they may also look at the ceiling to avoid the listener's gaze.

Ear rub

The ear-rub gesture has several variations. It is reminiscent of the hands-over-both-ears gesture of young children when they want to block out their parent's reprimands. Grown-ups, however, resort to a more sophisticated version of the gesture; they put their hands around or over their ear to indicate that they are blocking out some malicious remark.

There are other forms of this gesture, like the rubbing of the back of the ear, the finger drill (where the fingertip is screwed back and forth inside the ear), and tugging the earlobe or bending the entire ear forward to cover the earhole. This last gesture is a signal that the person is losing patience with the speaker or has heard enough and is eager to speak. Rubbing behind or beside the ear with the index finger is a variation of the nose rub. It is very often accompanied by the facial expression of doubt.

The ear rub could take a rather curious turn. An individual in an audience who wants to intervene may raise his hand to call the speaker's attention, but if he is not noticed, or he changes his mind, he reaches for his ears. Also, if the interrupter raises his hand four to six inches from the desk and then changes his mind, he does not usually return the hand to its original position immediately, but subtly tugs at the earlobe before taking his hand back. When it is not an interrupt gesture, the ear rub could be a mannerism that signals nervousness and anxiety, especially when done in a rhythmic motion.

There are two other gestures related to the ear that are noteworthy:

Fingers in the ears: People generally push their index fingers into their ears to 'tell' the other person that he or she is 'too loud' or that what is being said is either offensive or indecent and hence not worth listening to. It is an indication to the other person to stop speaking because he has extended his limits, enough has been said. Holding a palm or both palms behind the ears is an indication for someone to 'speak up'.

Holding of earlobes with forefinger and thumb: This a typically Indian gesture to say, 'I'm sorry; I won't repeat it'. Sometimes the arms are crossed in this gesture with the left hand holding the right earlobe and the right hand the left. Often, the lobes are tugged simultaneously.

Nose rub

In this gesture, a person touches the nose or rubs it slightly. Birdwhistell (1971) has found that the nose rub is a sign of rejection—like 'no'. It can also be a gesture of doubt. The nose rub is not an uncommon gesture. It is used by many articulate speakers when they are not sure how to approach a subject or what the reaction of the audience might be.

Basically, the nose-rub gesture is a subtle, disguised form of the mouth-guard gesture. It can have some variations, for instance, several light rubs below the nose or one quick, almost unnoticeable touch. Women tend to use this gesture more gently in order not to smudge their make-up.

According to Pease (1993), one explanation for the origin of the nose-touch gesture is that, as a negative thought enters the mind, the subconscious instructs the hand to cover the mouth, but at the last moment, in an attempt to appear less obvious, the hand pulls away from the face and a quick nose-touch gesture is the result. Another explanation is that when a person resorts to telling a lie, the delicate nerve endings in the nose tingle, so the rubbing action takes place to ease this feeling.

There is a distinct difference between the mannerism of rubbing one's nose due to an itch and rubbing it as a gesture of negation or doubt. People who rub (or scratch) the nose usually do it vigorously, whereas those who make the other gesture do it very lightly. The latter is subtle and often accompanied by a gesture cluster, such as squirming in the chair, twisting the body into a silhouette position, or physically withdrawing. A person who touches his nose (during a game of cards, for example) indicates that he is unsure of his own next move, his partner's next move, or both (Pease, 1993).

Similar to the mouth-guard gesture, the nose rub, too, can be used both by the speaker to disguise his own deceit and by the listener who doubts the speaker's words.

Collar pull

People make the collar-pull gesture when they are telling a lie or when they feel that the lie has been detected by the opposite party. According to sociologist Morris (1967), research has shown that when a person tells a lie, there is a tingling sensation in the delicate facial and neck tissues which necessitates a rub or scratch to ease it. Pease (1993) concludes that when a person is lying or realizes that the other person suspects his deceit, it may cause a slight trickle of sweat on the deceiver's neck, which urges him to loosen his collar. This gesture is also used by an angry or a frustrated person who needs to pull the collar away from his neck so as to allow the cool air to circulate around it.

Hands to Cheek and Chin

In body language, there are a variety of feedback gestures involving the hands and the face. In general, we have the boredom, evaluation, and decision-making gesture clusters which occasionally show up in certain combinations, each of which reveals a person's attitudes. These could include, for instance, stroking of the chin while the person simultaneously evaluates a proposition and makes a decision.

Hand on Cheek

When a person places his hand on his cheek, and his eyes blink, it signifies that he is in a process of evaluation, or in deep reflection. It could also indicate attention and interest. A closed hand resting on the cheek, often with the index finger pointing upwards, is an evaluation gesture. When a person's interest is on the decline, and he pretends otherwise, he will support his head with the heel of his palm. Genuine interest is indicated by the hand on the cheek, but not used as a head support.

When the index finger points vertically up the cheek, and the thumb supports the chin, it could indicate that the listener is having negative and critical thoughts, and is cynical about the speaker or his subject. Often the index finger may rub or pull at the eye as the negative thoughts continue. This gesture is often mistaken as a signal of interest, but the supporting thumb reveals the critical attitude.

Hand Supporting Chin or Side of Face

Usually the forearm is vertical from the supporting elbow on a table. People who display this signal are commonly assessing or evaluating next actions, options, or reactions to something or someone. If the resting is heavier and more prolonged, and the gaze is unfocused or averted, then tiredness or boredom is a more likely cause. A lighter resting contact is more likely to be evaluation, as is lightly resting the chin on the knuckles.

Palms Covering Cheeks

When a person presses his palm flat against his cheek, it suggests that he is being patient, or resigned, or feeling helpless. When a person presses the palms of both hands against his cheeks, and at the same time raises his eyebrows and opens his mouth, he could be expressing shock, wonder, or surprise.

Chin Stroking

Stroking the chin is a universal gesture which people make when going through a decision-making process or are in deep reflection. Siddons (1822) stated: 'This gesture signifies the wise man making a judgment.' It follows the flow of choices the person is deliberating upon regarding the proposition under consideration. A gesture that may accompany the stroking is a light squinting of the eyes, which gives the impression that the person is 'seeing' the solution to the problem somewhere in the distant background. One can observe this gesture in a game of chess when a player has to make the next move; or, in a group when the members are challenged or asked to give their opinion.

Facepalm is an expression referring to the physical gesture of striking one's own face in a display of exasperation. In internet discussions, the term is used as an expression of embarrassment, frustration, disbelief, disgust, or general woe. It is also used when the person making the gesture does not believe that words can express the level of idiocy.

An example of its online use is by linking to a photograph of Jim Horne, a model, whose use of the gesture typified the 'disgust' aspect.

Another commonly used example is linking to an image of Captain Jean-Luc Picard from the television series *Star Trek: The Next Generation*, who was seen making this gesture on a number of occasions (Wikipedia, 2011).

Hands to Ears

To express remorse or honesty in India, people will grasp their earlobes. This is a gesture used by servants when they are scolded.

PART THREE: GESTURES WITH PALMS

There are a few self-revealing palm gestures. Oaths are still taken with the palm of the hand over the heart. Even footballers do this when singing the national anthems before international games. The palm is held in the air when somebody is giving evidence in court of law. One of the most valuable clues to discovering whether someone is being honest and open or not is to watch for palm displays. The body language of palms were originally like the vocal cords of body language because they did more 'talking' than any other body part and putting them away was like keeping one's mouth shut!

PALM POSITIONS

Open Palms–Uplifted Palms

The gesture made with palms clearly visible, facing upwards is associated with truth, honesty, allegiance, and submission. From an evolutionary perspective, the gesture shows the person holds no weapons; it became modified over the centuries and gestures like the single palm raised in the air, the palm over the heart, and

many other variations developed. It is used in courts of law while taking the oath: the left hand on a holy book and the right hand with the palm open held up in clear view of all present. Positive ideas or appeals are made with the palm facing up.

People who want to declare their honesty or total openness hold one or both palms out with a remark like, 'To be very honest ...' When a speaker is being truthful or opening up, he will unconsciously and spontaneously expose all or a part of his palms. Anyone who habitually keeps the palms open will most likely be a sincere and frank person.

Uplifted palms is a gesture that suggests a vulnerable or non-aggressive pose which appeals to listeners as allies, rather than as rivals or foes. It is a non-threatening gesture, reminiscent of the pleading gesture of a street beggar. Throughout the world, palm up cues reflect moods of congeniality, humility, and uncertainty. Accompanied by 'palm shows', our ideas, opinions, and remarks may seem patronizing or conciliatory rather than aggressive or 'pointed'. Held out to an opponent across a conference table, the palm up cue may, like an olive branch, enlist support as an emblem of peace (Givens, 1999).

Palm up gesture are used to ask questions: 'who', 'what', 'when', 'why'.

The open palm up hand-shrug is a sign of 'helpless uncertainty and confusion' (Ekman and Friesen, 1969).

Hand outstretched and palms facing upwards are a common plea gesture, 'begging'. Hands with palms pressed together indicate a more anxious pleading. This gesture may be done with fingers upwards in a clear prayer position ('Please do not harm me!') and possibly thrust towards the other person. With fingers pointing down, this may be more concealed or a less anxious desire for agreement. A variant of this is to have fingers interleaved but otherwise making the same shape and movement.

Downward Palms

While gesturing with the palms, negative ideas or appeals are made with the palms facing down.

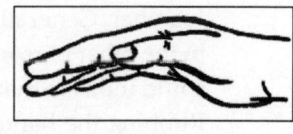

The gesture indicates authority. A mother disciplines her child using overturned palms to accent her words. A boss' palm down request will be complied with by a subordinate, while an equal's palm down request may be resented.

While speaking or listening, palm down gestures show confidence, assertiveness, and dominance. Accompanied by aggressive, palm downward 'beating' signs, our ideas, opinions, and remarks appear stronger and more convincing. The palm down above a conference table may appear as a judge's gavel. Palms down is a worldwide speaking gesture used to 'hold down' an idea or 'calm down' the mood of an audience (Morris, 1994: 194–95). It is a gesture of restraining.

Common palm down signs include the corporate table slap, the athlete's high five slap of victory, and the football fan's two-fisted triumph display (Givens, 1999).

The Palm Closed, Finger Pointed Position

When the palm is closed into a fist with the index finger pointing, it is a sign of authority; it suggests that the finger is like a 'weapon' which, as it were, threatens the object into submission. It is a highly unpleasant gesture and causes much irritation, especially if it beats time to the speaker's words.

The gesture is also used for directions; it is also commonly used when telling someone something to do like that is unpleasant.

Rubbing the Palms Together

People rub their palms together to non-verbally communicate some positive expectation; for instance, when a high-jumper is about to attempt his qualifying jump or a carom-player is about to take his final shot which he knows is easy and will bring him victory. The palm-rub gesture is sometimes a spontaneous response to a happy announcement: a child may rub his palms together while announcing to his parents that he has been selected to play with the hockey team; or it could be used by a master of ceremonies while introducing an exciting party game; or a waiter at a restaurant returns the bill with the change and, while waiting for the guests to rise, may rub his palms in the expectation of a tip.

In this gesture, the outcome of the expectations could be for the one who rubs his palms or for the other people involved. This is reflected by the speed at which the palms are rubbed together. Generally when the palms are rubbed quickly, it is meant to create expectations in the other person who will be at the receiving end of something good; if the rub is slow, it could indicate that the one rubbing the palms stands to benefit from the expected outcome. Rubbing the hands together can also mean that the person is feeling particularly gleeful about something.

There are people who tend to rub their palms together in a washing motion before venturing on some activity; this gesture reveals their intense interest in the activity. People who rub their sweaty (wet) palms against their clothes communicate nervousness and a lack of self-assurance. Men usually use their trousers, whereas women usually use a handkerchief.

Other Palm Gestures

There are other palm gestures that are noteworthy. The palm facing up at an angle, and doing a chopping motion, indicates that the other person deserves, or is going to receive, a good beating. A palm held up, usually in front of the face, means 'stay away from me'.

In Kerala, a state in South India, when people wish to show contempt, they hold their finger tips together and then release them in a jerky, sprinkling motion repeatedly.

Slapping the Palms

This gesture is quite a common sight on the playfields, to signify exuberant victory: for example, when a goal is scored, the jubilant players of a team slap each others palms at arms length or with hands raised. It is also used during other team activities like a quiz or a competition. This gesture is referred to as 'high five' by North Americans.

Tapping the Palms

Tapping of palm, generally of the right hand, during a conversation, is a typical Indian gesture. It is used when a clever or witty remark is made by one person, who then holds out his open palm to the other for him to tap it. It is also used when a general consensus is reached or one person seeks the approval of the other to a proposal or agreement. The gesture may occur spontaneously, with both persons bringing up their hands together and tapping each others palms. The tapping may be gentle or hard depending on the intensity of emotions.

Striking

The hand can strike openly, with the palm or closed as a fist. The fist can strike forwards, sideways, or downwards. One hand is often used for symbols as two hands as fists can be an invitation to fight (two hands held inwards can also indicate extreme tension).

Fist shapes and movements are often symbols of inner aggression. When moved towards a person, even a small amount, they signal aggression towards that person. A shaking fist signifies a strong desire to strike someone. Punching the air indicates triumphal excitement.

Palms behind the Back

Some people, like army officers, policemen on patrol, principals at school, may hold their hands behind their back, while walking around on duty.

The total opposite of crossing your arms, this hand/arm gesture exposes the vulnerable chest with its vital organs, stomach, crotch, and neck in an attempt to demonstrate fearlessness, superiority, and self-confidence.

Holding of palm over hand is a sign of authority. Gripping the wrist with the other hand behind their back is a display of frustration and self-control, as if refraining the person from using that hand to punch or slap someone. The higher up the arm the grip of the hand is, the more frustrated he is; some even gripping themselves at the elbow. This gesture can commonly be observed at court rooms when lawyers are interviewing the accused.

HANDSHAKES

Experts in the field of body language trace the origin of the handshake to the era of cavemen. When cave dwellers encountered one another, they used to raise their arms with the palms exposed to indicate that they were not carrying weapons. Later, the greeting evolved into the Roman Salute, a hand-to-chest gesture. During the era of the Roman Empire, men grasped each other's forearms instead of the hand, and gesturing a 'sawing' motion, back and forth, to assert the friendship between them. The gesture got modified over the centuries till it evolved to the modern-day handshake. It consisted of grabbing the wrist of the other person. When the handshake is the first physical contact a person has with another, it can reveal telling signs about that person's personality and feelings.

The handshake is a gesture of welcome: the interlocking of palms signifies openness and the touching signifies solidarity. Handshaking customs vary across cultures. For instance, the French shake hands on arrival and departure; the Germans do it only once, either on arrival or on departure. When women express feelings of sympathy to other women, especially in times of crisis, they do not shake hands but gently hold the other woman's hands in theirs and communicate their feelings through congruent facial expressions; rarely do women use this gesture with men. In traditional Indian society, women may not shake hands with men, but they greet each other with folded palms, in the *'namaste'* form of gesture (see box at the end of the chapter). In a Westernized set-up, however, a man does not extend his hand to a woman, unless the woman first offers her hand to a man in the stance of a handshake.

The handshake can be a spontaneous gesture between friends, with each offering his hand at the same time. At formal meetings, it is usually the 'superior' or older person who must be allowed the initiative in the handshake. Salespersons are trained not to be the first to extend their hand for a handshake to a customer when they are meeting for the first time or who is not expecting them. Taking the initiative in this case may produce a negative impact on the customer and may have adverse effects. If the customer does not offer his hand, the salesperson can merely nod his head as a sign of greeting.

A proper handshake should last from 3 to 6 seconds, be equally balanced, meaning each persons hand is vertically side by side, thumbs must be locked around each others upper hand, and fingers have a firm grip, always put the same amount of pressure you are receiving, mentally give a calculation from 1 to 10 of what strength they are using and adjust accordingly.

Styles of Handshake

Our styles of handshake are generally governed by our attitudes, especially when we encounter someone for the first time, and form our 'first impressions'. There are essentially three main attitudes depending on our approach: (*a*) *dominance*—when we sense that the other person is likely to dominate us, and we feel threatened, our handshake may be either dominating or cautious; (*b*) *submission*—when we feel that the other person will yield easily to our wishes, so we need not display any aggression; and (*c*) *equality*—when we feel that the person we are about to greet is affable and sociable. The level handshake denotes equality. We may not be conscious of our attitudes every time we shake hands, but they have their effect, which in turn may be unconsciously felt.

The common view that a firm handshake is the sign of a strong solid person may not be correct. Firm handshakes are a sign of outward confidence, which could mask deceit or a weak bullying nature, or indicate a strong solid person. Strength of a handshake is not by itself an indicator of positive 'good' mood or personality, and caution is required in reading this signal.

Experts in non-verbal communications have labelled the different styles or types of handshake (see Pease, 1993). We will discuss each of these briefly.

The vigorous handshake: Here the other person's hand is gripped, squeezed firmly, then released. A vigorous pumping handshake may indicate a sense of attempting to transfer energy and enthusiasm, literally, towards the other person, the meeting, situation, or project.

The palm down thrust: In this handshake, when taking the receiver's hand, the giver turns his hand so that his palm faces downward, though not necessarily parallel to the floor, while the receiver's palm faces up. This gesture signifies dominance or aggressiveness. It gives the receiver little chance to establish an equal relationship. It communicates the message that the giver wishes to take control of the interaction that is to follow, because the stiff arm with palm facing downward forces the receiver into a submissive position—as he is forced to respond with his palm facing up.

In case both parties are dominant, each party may make an effort to get the upper hand—to turn the palm of the other into a submissive position. The outcome will be a very firm handshake, with both palms in the vertical position, and the attitudes changed to one of sociability and acceptance.

There is another way to counter the palm-down thrust. When the giver turns the receiver's palm down, the latter must take hold of the top of the giver's hand with his left hand so as to 'disarm' him and then shake it. By this, the role of dominance is reversed, with the receiver getting the upper hand—the superior position—because even his or her hand will be facing down. This must, of course, be done with discretion because it is bound to embarrass the giver.

Pease (1993) provides one other technique to disarm the giver while receiving a dominant handshake: invade the dominant person's 'personal space'. This must be done in stages. First, step forward with the left foot as you reach out to shake hands. Next, bring the right leg forward, moving in front of the person towards his right leg and into his personal space. Then, as you shake hands, bring the left leg in line with the right. In this position, you may be able to bring the palms to a vertical position or even turn the other person's palm down. Shaking hands with the left foot forward tends to 'neutralize' a dominant handshake.

The palm-up position: Some people impose themselves on the other person by rotating their forearm so that their own hand ends up on top and the other person's below. Even though they may not be consciously aware of what is happening, the person who manages to get his hand on top—in the prone position—automatically gains an advantage over the person whose hand is below, in the supine position. That is because prone positions are associated with dominance and control, while supine positions are connected with submission and passivity. The person whose hand is on top will feel more dominant, and the person whose hand is below will feel more submissive.

The glove handshake: This is recognized as the 'politician's handshake'. It is done by grasping the hand with the right hand and cupping it with the left, to communicate that one is trustworthy and honest. The glove handshake must be used only with people one is familiar with. New acquaintances tend to be suspicious and cautious about the giver's real intentions.

Hand hug: The hand hug is popular with politicians; it is used when they choose to wrap the other's hand handshake with their left hand creating this warm cocoon protecting one's hand. When done to the right person, they are perceived as being warm, friendly, trustworthy, and honest; sometimes it is reciprocated creating this pile of four hands, but this type of handshake is only done with people who share close bonds, as similar to hugs. It is seen as an invasion of intimacy when done by people who have just met.

Some people use their left hand to grasp the other persons forearm, elbow, bicep, and even shoulder while shaking hands. People stretch out their arms to shake hands to keep people out of their personal space and protect their body. The higher up the arm the other person is seen putting their left hand, the closer the bond those two people share (or at least the person doing the double hander handshake believes they do or want to portray it.

The dead-fish handshake: This weak handshake (known as the wet fish) is done by offering a flaccid, lifeless, and sometimes cold and sweaty hand. It is believed that people of weak character use this handshake, because their palms are easily pliable. However, strong but passive people can have gentle handshakes. Old people can have weak handshakes. A weak handshake might be due to arthritis. Young people unaccustomed to handshaking can have weak handshakes.

People who are in professions where the hand is used a lot—for instance, artists, musicians, and surgeons—are careful about their hands and may have the dead-fish handshake. Athletes, too, are very cautious not to expend too much of energy; so they use little pressure when shaking hands.

Cold and clammy handshake: A person may offer a hand that is cold with sweat. This is sometimes associated with weak character or lack of energy used by passive or pathetic people. More commonly, however, it can be found in nervous people whose hands are drained of blood.

The knuckle-grinder handshake: This handshake characterizes the 'rough and tough'. In this handshake, the giver crushes the palm of the receiver. And there is hardly any way to counter this. The over-strong handshake indicates someone who is either dominant or maybe someone with emotional issues who is trying to get noticed. Depending on the pressure, it is also used with less strength by individuals with a desire to dominate occasionally out of weakness or fear they will be dominated by others if they do not do it first.

The handshake that makes your knuckles grind each other when shaking and leaves your hand in numbing pain afterwards.

The stiff-arm handshake: This is the 'invasion handshake', where someone fully extends his arm so that the handclasp is forced to take place in the other person's space rather than his own. The arms are kept stiff, thus placing the receiver at 'arms length', literally out of ones 'intimacy zone'. The giver may lean forward or even balance on one foot while extending his arm for a shake.

The fingertip-grab handshake: This takes place if the giver offers a stiff arm and then stays short of the receiver's outstretched palm, ending up in grabbing only the fingers. This handshake reveals the giver's lack of confidence in himself. Here, too, the handshake keeps the receiver at a comfortable distance, away from the giver's intimacy zone, so as not to get physically too close to the receiver.

Queens fingertips: This is quite common in male–female encounters, as women need more personal space than men, they will stretch out their hand (sometimes in an awkward position) from a distance allowing the other person to barely grasp the two or three fingers without a good grip of the hand. It is also used by individuals who feel superior to the other person.

Keep-back handshake: This handshake is used by the aggressive type with the main purpose of keeping the other at a distant and away from his personal space as he might feel threatened; he leans forward or balances on one foot to achieve the needed distance.

The arm-pull handshake: This 'yank and pull' or 'huddled handshake' is considered a power play. One person pulls the other person into his personal space, thereby creating a handshake that is on his own terms. There are three possible reasons for this: the person is insecure and needs you to be in his own territory in order to feel comfortable and safe, or he come from a culture/city that requires smaller space needs, and, finally, he want to take control and get you off balance, literally. In any of these cases, he should be considered manipulative because he wants things done a certain way.

The double-arm handshake: In this, the initiator uses both his hands during the handshake. It is characterized by two significant elements: first, the initiator uses his left hand to communicate more than his usual feelings—be they of confidence, sincerity, affection, or whatever—to the receiver; second, he expresses the degree of intensity of his feeling by holding the lower or the upper parts of the receiver's hands. That is, while his right palms grasps the receiver's right palm in the handshake, the initiator's left hand holds the receiver's right wrist to transmit that extra bit of feeling. If he wants to convey even greater feeling, he will grasp the arms above the wrist, like the elbow, upper arm, or shoulder. The higher the grasp, the more intense the feeling expressed.

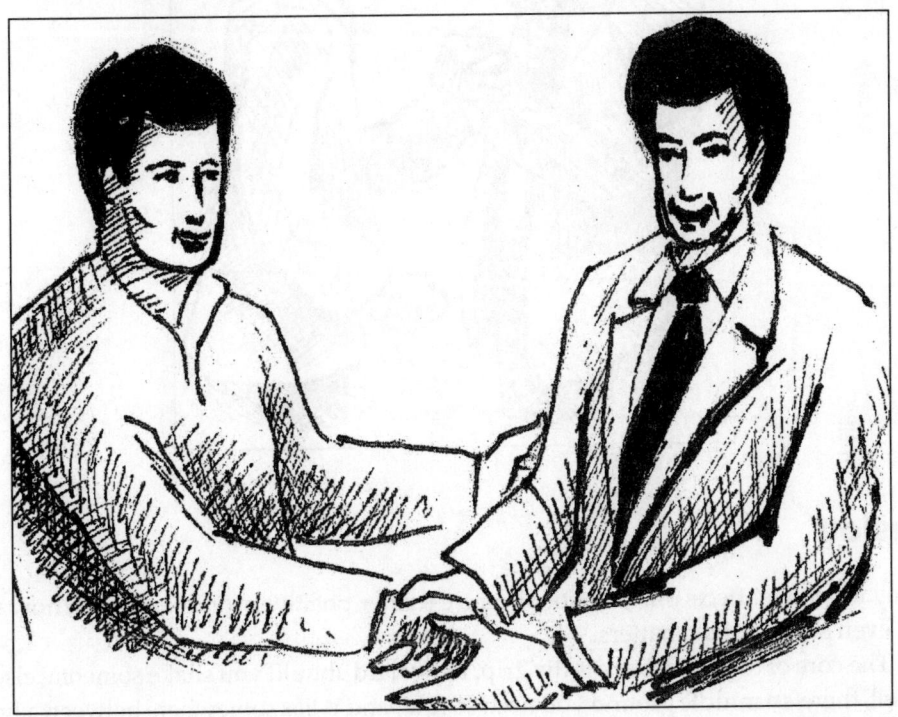

The double-arm handshake indicates a certain degree of intimacy between the initiator and the receiver. Those who are not either relatives or close friends of the initiator may find the holding of the wrist and elbow acceptable. However, the upper arm and the shoulder grips, particularly, will be acceptable only to those who have close emotional ties with the initiator.

In case the initiator and receiver do not have extra feelings for each other, the double-handed handshake will have an adverse effect; that is, the receiver will suspect and mistrust the motives of the initiator.

The grasp: Here the initiator holds the hand of the receiver firmly at chest level.

Conclusion

Any touching affects our emotional centre (either positively or negatively); how we touch or even shake hands matters.

The core of the handshake is the grip. How hard should you shake someone else's hand? Well, there's a middle ground you need to find, and it lies somewhere between a limp grasp and a bone-crushing one. If you have shaken enough hands, you've no doubt experienced both ends of the spectrum and you know that neither is especially pleasant.

The limp shake is decidedly feminine, which, of course, is not in and of itself a bad thing. If you're a woman heading out on a blind date and you want to make sure your suitor knows that you are a soft-hearted female, by all means, use the limp shake. However, most handshakes are offered and accepted in the business world—which is often defined by an air of masculinity, even in this day and age. Therefore, once you put on a suit, the limp handshake should be left out of your repertoire, no matter what your gender.

How can you tell if your grip is adequate? First, make sure you are inserting your hand far enough into the shake. A limp shake often generates from one person attempting to limit her exposure to the other person's palm; the weak shaker does his best to only touch the other person's fingers or to lightly touch the inside of the other person's palm. Handshakes should mirror the other person's handshake with good eye contact.

Quite often, people are careful to shake hands in a positive way when they first meet you. They have trained themselves to do so. It is a good idea to see if they shake hands in a different way when you say goodbye. People rarely train themselves to do this positively and the 'real' person might appear.

While a great handshake can make you seem wise and powerful, a weak shake can give you an aura of fearfulness or insecurity.

NAMASTE

The namaste is an age-old tradition of greeting one another in India. It is practised in some other countries as well; it is also a gesture of prayer in certain religions.

Etymologically, the mantra namaste is compounded from two Sanskrit words: *namah* ('bow' or 'bend') and *te* ('to you'). In the gesture, 'the bowing of the head is accompanied by the action of joining the palms and drawing them towards the breast'.

In its proper form, all five fingers of each hand must close in one over the other correspondingly, and the thumbs must turn back to touch the 'heart'. The greeting is reciprocated in similar manner.

There are variations of the namaste gesture. '*Mahatmas* in India do it in their general intercourse without uttering the word *Namaste*. They do it in silence.' In some cities in India, the greeting is done with only one hand being drawn to the breast.

When the hands are occupied or are holding something, only the word namaste is used in welcome. At times people greet each other only with a namaste without folding their hands.

The namaste can be distinguished from the handshake as a form of greeting. A handshake involves two persons and has physical limitations. The namaste can be used by an individual to greet large crowds collectively and be reciprocated. In this case, a bond gets established in spite of the physical distance involved.

Source: Nambiar (1979).

SUMMING UP

There are many movements we make with the various parts of our body, especially our hands and arms, to add emphasis to our messages. To be effective, all gestures must be appropriate for our purpose and natural to our *personal* style.

We must carefully avoid the following inappropriate and awkward gestures, lest they detract from our message and alienate us from others:

- pointing at others;
- touching others to emphasize a point;
- being too familiar (putting our arm around someone we do not know very well);
- invading people's personal space;
- conveying obscenities with fingers, hands, and other body parts;
- holding someone's hand longer than a few seconds during a handshake.

Chapter 6

Postures

OVERVIEW

Posture refers to a bearing, pose, or stance of the body or it parts: for example, a crouched posture or a fixed, stationary body position as opposed to a fluid body movement. When sustained (that is, held longer than two seconds), a body movement such as a bowed head may be considered a posture. Though duration varies, postures frequently are more expressive of attitudes, feelings, and moods than are briefer gestures and fleeting motions of the body (Givens, 1999).

How we hold our bodies can also serve as an important part of body language. The term posture refers to how we hold our bodies as well as overall physical form. Posture can convey a wealth of information on our personality, about how we are feeling, our characteristics, such as whether we are confident, open, or submissive. Sitting up straight, for example, may indicate that a person is focused and paying attention to what is going on. Sitting with the body hunched forward, on the other hand, can imply that the person is bored or indifferent.

A lot of people feeling down will give that information by the way they hold their shoulders. Not only do we see it in their body posture shoulders sagging and head down, but also in the way they have very little eye contact. They say to the world in fact that they are not interested in their environment or the people in it. In contrast, someone who walks straight and looks up immediately gives another impression of how this person is feeling. Our body posture often reflects quite well how we feel. By changing our posture we can alter our feelings. If we walk upright and look around when we are feeling a bit low, we will notice that such a simple posture already influences our mood positively.

Our body posture can also communicate interest and respect for someone else. Turning our body to someone when they are talking to us indicates that we are interested in hearing what they have to say. It is an act of friendliness and respect and often rewards itself when we get it back from the other person. A small effort in this way can make the difference between being accepted by others or not.

A body posture can be closed or open. People who do not feel too comfortable when they are with someone else will often assume a closed position. They will possibly have crossed arms or legs or will hold an object such as a bag in front. The bag as well as the crossed arms and legs provide a bit of a barrier and protection for feeling vulnerable.

There are mainly *two categories* of posture in which every posture can be placed:

1. Standing
2. Bent-knee positions (sitting, kneeling)

These fall under the following *three types* of postures:

(a) *Inclusive or Non-inclusive*: Inclusivity or non-inclusivity refers to the way in which the members of a group include people or fail to include them. They do it by positioning their bodies, arms, or legs in a certain way. The arms and legs of the members of the group are unconsciously used to protect the group from intrusion.

(b) *Face-to-face or Parallel*: The second category assumes that two persons can relate with each other in terms of posture, face-to-face, sitting beside each other, or maybe facing towards a third person. The face-to-face position is usual in a teacher–student relationship or a doctor–patient relationship where emotions or information are being transmitted. Parallel positions occur, for example, among two or more students listening to a teacher. Parallel arrangements, when freely adopted, indicate that those persons are probably in a neutral situation, at least at that moment. The way a couple position themselves in a social gathering also says a great deal about their relationship.

(c) *Congruent or Incongruent*: This category refers to the ability of the members of a group to imitate each other. When a group is in congruence, the positions of their bodies mimic each other, in some cases like mirror images. Interestingly, when one member of a congruent group changes his position, everyone does so with him. The congruence of position of a group usually indicates that all the members are in agreement. If the group has two points of view, the defenders of each opinion will adopt different positions; each subgroup will be congruent within itself but not congruent with the other subgroup. The leader in any social or family gathering often selects the position for the group and they all invariably follow him or her.

Points to Note

Changes in Posture Can Be

- an extension of gestures;
- altering the distance between yourself and a person or object.

Postures and the use of them are influenced by culture and specific social groups.

Characteristics of Posture Are

Immediacy/Relaxation:

- Immediacy consists of body posture, forward leans, and other non-verbal means of communication, like touching or gazing. Immediacy expresses liking and trust.
- Relaxation consists of asymmetrical leg position and backward lean.

Status

Congruent body position: Persons with a similar status will have a similar posture.

Incongruent body position: Persons with a different status will use different postures. A more relaxed posture is used by members of a higher status, while a more tense posture is used by members of a lower status (for example, interview situation).

Gender

Male and female posture 'stereotypes' are created by culture and education. Eakins and Eakins (1978) described unladylike behaviour (see Malandro, Barker, and Barker, 1989): it is considered unfeminine or unladylike for a woman to 'use her body too forcefully, to sprawl, to stand with her legs widely spread, to sit with her feet up ... to cross the ankle of one leg over the knee of the other. And depending on the type of clothing she wears, 'she may be expected to sit with her knees together, not to sit cross-legged, or not even to bend over'.

Males show a dominant behaviour and body posture (staring, taking more space, legs apart, head erect, hands on hips), while females show a submissive behaviour and body posture (lowering eyes, cocking head, knees together) (Malandro, Barker, and Barker, 1989).

THE LEGS

Introduction

Our legs and feet transmit valuable information about what we are sensing, thinking, and feeling. We generally pay so much attention to the face and other parts of the body that we forget the importance of these vital appendages. In many ways, the feet and legs are the most accurate part of our body. They reflect our true emotions and intentions, unlike our face and other parts of the body (Navarro, 2008).

The legs can reveal whether those around you are open and comfortable, negative and uncertain, dominant or submissive, or ready to move away. The positioning of the legs (crossed, close together, held apart) can convey relaxation, tension, modesty, seduction, and so on. Shaking ones foot (or thigh) can signal impatience, anger, or nervousness, while stamping can reflect authority, arrogance, or contempt. Both feet placed firmly on the floor can indicate that one feels one is on firm ground, secure, and confident.

Those who make conscious effort to control their body language generally focus on their upper body. Their lower body including the legs and feet may not be in sync with the rest of the body, thereby betraying their hidden feelings and attitudes.

Legs and feet body language is more difficult to control consciously or fake than some body language of arms and hands and face. Legs and feet can therefore provide good clues to feelings and moods, if you know the signs (Chapman, 2010).

The most potent messages of submission are those associated with vulnerability, especially in the way that people arrange their arms and legs. Standing and sitting postures are full of clues because dominant people tend to adopt 'open' postures, while submissive people tend to adopt 'closed' postures.

STANDING POSITIONS

Open

Legs which are set apart when standing provide a stable base for the person. Standing with feet about the width of the shoulders is a normal, relaxed pose. A wide stance takes up more territory and makes the body appear wider and bigger, a signal of power and dominance. It indicates that the person feels grounded and confident.

Taking a stable position is readying the body in case of attack and can indicate caution. Standing with one foot forward and the other behind can be taking an extra stable position in case of frontal attack (as with martial artists). Straight legs indicate an open mind. This person is likely to be open to influence or is at ease with the conversation. Persons who stand with legs straight subconsciously make those around them feel more at ease.

Dominant individuals frequently adopt a 'straddle stance', with their legs straight and their feet wide apart. Subordinate individuals, on the other hand, are more likely to adopt the 'parallel stance'. The straddle stance offers more stability than the parallel stance.

Because the feet are set apart, the straddle stance is also a posture of immovability; it shows that the person does not intend to go. If you watch a group of young men standing in a circle, say, in a sports club after a match, you will often find them adopting the straddle stance. This posture is an expression of their solidarity. By standing with their legs apart, they display their manliness.

People who spread their legs far apart and stand with both feet firmly on the ground send out a non-verbal message that they are firmly grounded. This is usually interpreted as a sign of dominance. It is a stance taken by confident men approaching women but most notoriously found in superior officers giving instructions to the charges. Hands on hips support the interpretation.

Closed

There are several closed standing postures. One is the 'parallel stance', where the legs are straight and parallel, body quite upright, shoulders back, arms by sides, the feet are planted close together, and the weight of the body is evenly distributed between them. It is like the military 'at attention' posture and is often a signal of respect or subservience adopted when addressed by someone in authority. Schoolchildren adopt this posture when they are talking to their teacher, soldiers use it when addressing a superior officer, and employees assume it when talking to their boss. A person who stands with feet together (or less than a relaxed shoulder width) may be expressing anxiety. People who adopt the parallel stance are usually non-committal in ordinary relationships.

A fully closed standing position has knees touching. Increased desire for protection may be indicated by the person turning slightly to the side, leaning forward a little or pulling the hips back. A person also takes the closed position when feeling cold.

Crossed Leg

People sometimes stand with their legs crossed, adopting a 'scissors stance', where the legs are straight and one is crossed, just as if they were the blades of a pair of scissors; or the body weight is on one leg and the other is bent, with the foot positioned either in front or behind, with just the toes touching the ground. The scissors stance is the classic posture of immobility. People who are shy or lacking in confidence also adopt these postures. Because it is completely devoid of any suggestion of impatience, the scissor stance also comes across as a gesture of submissiveness (Collett, 2003).

In a group of 'strangers', there is a 'warming up' period; people take time to get acquainted and to accept each other. Initially, their legs and arms are crossed; as they gradually get familiar with each other, they uncross them, with some leaning on one foot with the other one pointing towards the members of the group. On the contrary, if a person standing crossed leg is tense, the legs are held rigidly and with jerking movements.

Often, people (though most commonly women) who are shy or timid will entangle their legs, creating a sort of over- and under-leg cross in an attempt to lock that negative emotion in place and make themselves as narrow and small as possible in order to appear non-threatening. Another common shy leg twirl is, while standing, to cross one leg in front of the other and hide the foot of that leg behind the knee of the other leg as if scratching it.

Ankle Lock

Sometimes, while standing or sitting, people lock the ankles of their feet. This is usually coupled with the clenched hand gesture. These gestures together signify a 'holding back' of strong feelings, attitudes, and emotions. They spell out a defensive, negative attitude. The ankle-lock position could also display tension, for instance, in people waiting outside a doctor's office or those waiting for a job interview. This gesture can also be made by people whose bladders are full and who have to wait to relieve themselves.

There are slight differences in the postures of men and women. The man who locks his ankles may also either clench his fists and rest them on his knees or firmly grip the arms of the chair. Women hold their knees together, with their feet on one side, and the hands side by side, or one on top of the other on the upper leg.

Unlocking of the ankles can bring relaxation as well. For instance, while resting in bed if we notice that our ankles are locked, we can deliberately uncross them; we will feel the whole body relax instantly.

Knees

In non-verbal communication, the knee can act as a subtle pointer, just like the elbow. When pointing towards something or somebody, the knee can indicate desire. Pointing away, it indicates the opposite. Twitching of the knee towards a person may be a desirable pointing and it may also be a desire to hit them.

Generally, seated persons direct their knee or knees towards the point of interest. Converse, legs tend to point away from something or someone which is uninteresting or threatening. When legs are crossed, the upper knee indicates interest or disinterest according to where it points. The more direct and obvious the position, the keener the attraction or repellent the feeling (Chapman, 2010).

SITTING POSITIONS

Sitting postures are essentially about comfort, convention, and communication. When somebody sits down, they usually arrange their legs so that they feel comfortable, so that they do not violate any social norms, and so that their posture conveys a certain message. The message that a sitting posture conveys need not be intentional. In fact, it is more likely to be motivated by unconscious desires. However, the fact that people are not always aware of the messages that they are sending via their sitting postures does not mean that other people are impervious to those messages. Although they may not react consciously, it is often evident from their responses that they are affected by how you sit (Collett, 2003).

Open

A person sitting with slightly open legs indicates that he is relaxed and comfortable. One or both legs may be flopped down sideways as far as they can go. Sitting allows a wider opening of the legs and can thus be even more of a sexual 'crotch display'. If the person is concerned about this, he may place his hands between his thighs.

In sitting positions, open uncrossed leg positions generally indicate an open attitude, contrasting with crossed legs, which normally indicate a closed attitude or a degree of caution or uncertainty (Chapman, 2010).

Closed

The ankle lock simply involves crossing one's legs directly at the ankles. The ankle lock can mean that the person is holding something back. For example, you ask them: 'What do you think of this' and they respond: 'Nothing at all' and cross their ankles. The person can be hiding feelings such as anger, sadness, or even happiness.

When we lock something, we think it is safe; we do the ankle lock, it is to put us into safety. For example, when in a group that is discussing something, then suddenly start making fun of a person, he will want to lock himself away into safety so he will simply cross their ankles without saying a word. Many patients will cross their ankles due to discomfort of being in the dental chair.

The male version of ankle lock is that it is often combined with clenched fists resting on the knees or with the hands tightly gripping the arms of the chair. The female version varies slightly—the knees are held together, the feet may be to one side, and the hands rest side by side or one on top of the other resting on the upper legs.

An ankle cross with legs tucked under the chair can indicate concealed anxiety. The concern may be more obvious if the person is leaning forward.

Crossed

The normal crossed leg position while sitting is one leg crossed neatly over the other, usually the right over the left. It may indicate a nervous, reserved, or defensive attitude. People often sit like this during lectures or if they are on uncomfortable chairs for long periods. When the crossed legs gesture is combined with crossed arms, the person has withdrawn from the conversation.

People often sit with the legs crossed to indicate discomfort, tightness, withdrawal, and resistance to any attack on them. Crossed legs tend to indicate a degree of caution or disinterest, which can be due to various reasons, ranging from feeling threatened to mildly insecure.

Generally, the upper crossed leg and knee will point according to the person's interest. If the knee points towards a person, then it signifies interest in or enthusiasm for that person; if it points away from a person, it signifies disinterest in, or a perceived threat from, that person. Signs are more indicative when people first sit down and adopt initial positions in relation to others present. Signs become less reliable when people have been sitting for half an hour or so, when leg crossing can change more for comfort than body language reasons (Chapman, 2010).

Thighs

While sitting, opening the thighs makes one vulnerable to attack; however, this move may also be a power display, saying: 'You dare not attack me because I am so powerful.' Closing the thighs by pulling them tightly together sends the opposite signals.

Crossing the thighs, standing, or sitting takes the defensiveness of closing further. It is often a strong 'closed' signal, very much like crossing the arms right across the body. When the upper body is open and the thighs are closed, this may be a symptom of the person applying deliberate control to their upper body but forgetting their legs. This can also be a relaxed position, particularly when the muscles seem loose.

When people are about to stand up, they may put both hands on the thighs to push themselves up. This may also be a signal of readiness ('I'm ready to go!'). Putting both hands on the thighs with the elbows out sideways can be a sitting version of hands on hips, widening the body and showing displeasure or threatening action.

CONVENTIONAL SITTING POSITIONS

Three basic sitting postures can be identified on the basis of where people place their feet: 'straight-leg' postures, where the legs are extended, 'step' postures, where the feet are placed directly under the knees, and 'tucked' postures, where the feet are pulled back under the chair.

Dominant people prefer to adopt 'straight-leg' sitting postures. By stretching out their legs, they symbolically place more of the public space under their personal jurisdiction, thereby reducing what's available to others and creating the impression that their own needs matter more than those of other people.

When people adopt the 'step' sitting postures, the position of their knees convey reliable information about whether they are feeling dominant or submissive. People who sit with their knees apart send clear, although usually unintended, signals that they are feeling dominant.

Depending on the angle at which a person spreads his or her legs and thighs while sitting reveals a positive or negative attitude. Sitting styles vary between males and females. A woman generally keeps her knees close together while seated, even if she is wearing pants.

Men and women sit differently, which needs to be considered when reading leg body language. Partly due to clothing and partly due to sexual differences, men naturally exhibit more open leg positions than women, which should be allowed for when interpreting signals. Certain open-leg male positions are not especially significant in men, but would be notable in women, especially combined with a short skirt (Chapman, 2010).

The 'Maharaja' Posture

Sitting in a chair with both feet planted firmly on the floor and apart, and arms resting flat on the arms of the chair, signifies an open attitude. Maharajas are portrayed in this posture. For Westerners, it is known as the 'Lincolnesque' position.

This is a confident, dominant posture. Two people seated facing each other in this manner will be agreeable to each other's ideas. There will be hardly any resistance; hence, neither will feel threatened by the other. This is not a gesture popularly used by women, especially in formal situations and not in a skirt. Regardless of gender, this posture is also combative because it requires space and makes the person look bigger. The impression of confidence is increased when arms are also in a wide or open position.

The Standard Cross-leg Position

In this 'standard' or European leg-cross position, the legs are crossed casually with one knee resting on the thigh of the other leg. The person occupies the full chair, with his back supported by the back of the chair. It is a position used by both men and women, for example, during lectures or when they have to sit in uncomfortable chairs for an extended period. A person taking this position may be nervous, withdrawn, or on the defensive, or merely feeling cold.

We can distinguish between a defensive position and legs crossed on account of cold weather conditions. The person who feels cold will usually have his legs straight, stiff, and pressed against each other; in contrast, a defensive person will have a more relaxed crossed leg posture. If together with the crossed leg position a person also crosses his arms, it means that he has reinforced his defensive position; in conversation, it is a sign of withdrawal.

Nierenberg and Calero (1975) have observed leg behaviour in the course of negotiations between two individuals. When issues are presented and discussed, or there is an argument, one or both parties will have their legs crossed. Significantly, when there is a change of approach, the negotiators tend to uncross their legs and move closer to each other; the issues then get settled amicably. It can thus be concluded that when an individual crosses his legs, we may be sure that we have to face competition and that the individual requires a great deal of attention. It would be unrealistic to expect a favourable response until the legs are uncrossed. When together with crossed legs the individual crosses his arms, we are up against an adversary. When a person with crossed legs moves his foot in a slight kicking motion, he is probably displaying boredom with the given situation.

Indians sit cross-legged on the floor, as is customary, irrespective of status. Depending on the situation or the availability, they may also use a low stool or cushion. Certain functions—like praying, meditating, eating, performing rituals, at a gathering of mourners—Indians sit cross-legged.

The Figure-4 Crossed Position

Birdwhistell (1971) describes the figure-4 position as one leg horizontally crossed with the ankle resting on the other knee. It has the same implications as the standard crossed leg position.

In an interaction between two people, if one or both have their legs in the figure-4 position, it means that they have taken a highly argumentative or competitive attitude in the discussion. One cannot hope to reach an agreement or be granted a favour when the opponent has adopted this position. To break the deadlock, one of them can use a gesture of open appeal—like leaning forward and exposing his palms—and then appeal to the other to reconsider his opinion.

Often, to strengthen his attitude, the person using the figure-4 position may place one hand or both hands on the crossed leg to 'clamp' it. This makes the going tough; it means that the individual is stubborn, and it will take some effort and skill to break through his resistance.

The figure-4 leg cross is a far more confident posture than the conventional 'both knees' leg cross. It typically causes the upper body to lean back. The crossed leg is nevertheless a protective barrier, and so this posture is regarded as more stubborn than the 'both knees' leg cross.

A fair amount of suppleness and stamina is required to perform the figure-4, which is why the posture is associated with youthfulness. When someone adopts the figure-4, they are more likely to be seen as youthful, relaxed, and dominant (Collett, 2003).

Typical Asian Positions

Squatting: To squat is to sit in a crouching position with knees bent and the buttocks on or near the heels. In weightlifting, the lifter squats and stands while holding a weighted barbell supported by the back of the shoulders. Squatting is a posture where the weight of the body is on the feet (as with standing) but the knees are bent either fully (full or deep squat) or partially (partial, half, semi, parallel, or monkey squat). In contrast, sitting involves taking the weight of the body, at least in part, on the buttocks against the ground or a horizontal object such as a chair seat. Crouching may involve squatting or kneeling. It is possible to squat with one leg and assume another position (such as kneeling) with the other leg. In adults, squatting (including the use of the squat toilet) is more common in Asian cultures.

Sitting on the floor: The most common way of sitting on the floor involves bending the knees. One can also sit with the legs unbent, using something solid as support for the back or leaning on one's arms.

Sitting with bent legs can be done along two major lines: one with the legs mostly parallel and one where they cross each other. A common cross-legged position is with the lower legs folded towards the body, crossing each other at the ankle or calf, with both ankles on the floor, sometimes with the feet tucked under the knees or thighs. The position is known in several European languages as *tailor style*, from the traditional working posture of tailors.

The *lotus position*, common in yoga and meditation, involves resting each foot on the opposite thigh so that the soles face upwards. If only one foot is brought into this position, it is called a *half-lotus position*. There are a variety of yogic sitting postures.

The traditional Indian way of eating is by squatting on the floor. Mats or wooden planks are at times used for seating. Eating is done with the hands.

VARIED SITTING POSTURES

Sitting on Edge of the Chair

Persons who move to the edge of the chair indicate that they are ready to compromise, cooperate, accept, or agree, or conclude, reject, or abandon. It is a gesture that is very obvious and leads to action.

When a person sits forward in a chair, feet on tiptoes, and displays a cluster of positive gestures, he non-verbally communicates his readiness for some positive action. When one notices someone in this position, one can consider it an opportune moment to strike a deal or ask a favour.

When a person sits forward in the chair, feet on tip toe, and displays a cluster of positive gestures, he non-verbally communicates his readiness for positive action. When one notices someone in this position, one can consider it an opportune moment to strike a deal or ask a favour.

When a person leans forward with both arms gripping the chair or placed on the knees, he is displaying a negative attitude. He non-verbally signals that he is ready to terminate an encounter or a conversation. In this situation, it will be next to impossible to obtain a favourable response. To preserve one's self-respect, one must discreetly withdraw from the scene.

Leg Over the Arm of the Chair

When a person has a leg over the arm of a chair, he appears to be relaxed, open, cooperative, and informal. However, this is only an eyewash because opposite attitudes exist. This position indicates that he is generally indifferent, or even hostile, to others' feeling and needs. Besides, since he non-verbally communicates a dominant or superior stance, it may become difficult to relate to him.

Straddling a Chair

Straddling a chair, that is, sitting with the chair around so that its back faces the other person, is a show of dominance or aggression, although to all outward appearances it gives the impression that one is only being informal and cooperative.

The back of the chair serves as a 'shield' to protect the straddler from attack, especially from other members in a group situation. The straddler will try to take control of the others, particularly when he feels bored with their discussion or conversation.

In a group situation, it is possible to 'disarm' the straddler by positioning oneself behind him—either sitting or standing. He will begin to feel vulnerable and change his position; he will then become less aggressive.

If the straddler is on a swivel chair and can turn around with the back of the chair still forming a shield, he must be 'disarmed' by another nonverbal tactic. One must walk up close to the straddler, keep standing, and looking down at him. This will disconcert him; he will change his position and become more yielding.

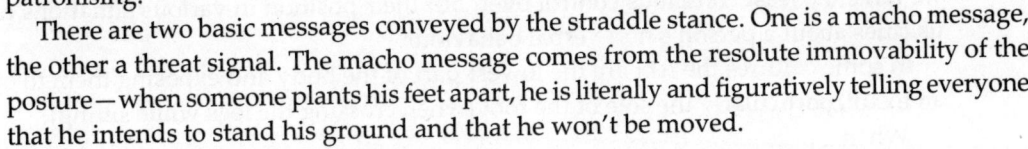

Sitting on your hands reveals a lack of maturity in adults. It is a very common in children, but in children it suggests a desire to grow up fast.

Sitting with your feet hooked around chair legs is an attitude acquired in childhood. Someone who sits like this feels like the person speaking to them is being patronising.

There are two basic messages conveyed by the straddle stance. One is a macho message, the other a threat signal. The macho message comes from the resolute immovability of the posture—when someone plants his feet apart, he is literally and figuratively telling everyone that he intends to stand his ground and that he won't be moved.

Rocking or Swinging in the Chair: Some people are used to rocking in a chair either forward or backward, or from side to side. This movement indicates that the person feels that he is in control of the situation and is confident that things will work out in his favour.

Fidgeting: In a tense situation, people tend to fidget, for instance, move restlessly in their chairs and continue to do so till they feel comfortable—not necessarily in the chair, but with the situation. Nierenberg and Calero (1975) list several reasons for people fidgeting in their chairs: they are tired; they are not stimulated by the speaker so they find it difficult to listen intently; their bodies are programmed to follow a certain rhythm (for instance, they have set lunch time) so they are telling them it is time for a break; the chairs are uncomfortable so their backs may be hurting; or they are distracted or preoccupied with something else. The fidgeting may continue till they stop paying attention completely and get immersed in their own thoughts.

Another peculiar behaviour in the sitting posture is of a person pulling his pants when engrossed in a decision-making process. He may do this a lot if he is having a difficult time reaching a decision, and may also fidget in his chair.

Desk Drawer Movements: While communicating across a desk, a person may pull out the bottom drawer and place a leg on it. This gesture indicates 'getting a leg up' on someone or a situation. It has been observed that many aggressive and goal-oriented executives use this gesture not only in face-to-face communication but even while talking over the telephone.

Sometimes when confronted with a rather complex problem while on the telephone, a person may repeatedly open and close the top drawer of the desk. As soon as he reaches a solution, he will shut the drawer with a deliberate movement, stand up, and communicate his answer in a firm tone over the line.

THE FEET

Like hands, our feet are neurologically gifted. As smart parts and sensory feelers, for example, they are well connected to diverse areas of the brain. Our feet are highly expressive and play major roles in non-verbal communication worldwide (Givens, 1999). The feet receive a lot of attention from the brain if the body is in 'fight or flight' mode when feeling threatened or uncomfortable. Nevertheless, of all of our body parts, the feet are probably the part that we have the least conscious control over, but their position in various situations can give us clues about a person's non-verbal behaviour.

In some cultures the feet are the lowest part of the body and exposing them to others is an insult, particularly the sole of the foot (when crossing the legs while sitting).

The Foot Lock

The foot lock or ankle lock, in which the foot locks around the other foot at the ankle or the lower calf, is like have a closed sign hanging over the door. Individuals who are not revealing information generally lock their ankles; when they finally allow emotions to flow, they unlock the ankles. Passengers who are uncomfortable or nervous during airplane take-offs display the same foot-lock gesture.

The ankle-lock gesture signifies a negative or defensive attitude. While males do combine this gesture with clenched fists resting on the knees or with the hands tightly gripping the arms of the chair they are sitting on, females do hold their knees together and the feet may be on one side with hands resting side by side or one hand on top of the other resting on the upper legs. One can see people showing ankle-lock gestures while in courts, interview halls, or during police interrogation.

This gesture is especially common among shy and timid women. In a state of intense defensiveness, a woman may lock the top of one foot around the other leg. This gesture almost always indicates that she has withdrawn into herself. To reassure her, one must show caring and concern and speak in a mild tone.

Pointing

As with other parts of the body, the feet can be used for pointing, since they are elongated. However, being down on the ground, foot gestures often go unnoticed, particularly when they are very subtle. The direction our feet point at reveals what our mind is focusing on.

We all have a dominant foot (right or left) that leads us when we are walking; when speaking to someone we are interested in, our lead foot will point towards them. When we are in a situation where we feel uncomfortable in and from which we wish to escape, our foot will point towards the nearest exit.

We can observe similar behaviours in others. Whether a person is standing or sitting, if his feet are pointing to a door, this would likely indicate that he wants to depart from the current situation. When a person points his feet towards an area of the room or even an individual, it show where his interests lie.

If a person's foot is resting on the heel with the sole pointing outward, this could be a dominance symbol, because the person is exposing a tender body part, he or she feels comfortable in their surroundings. If the person is resting his foot on the side with the sole pointed inward, however, this could indicate discomfort or nervousness because he is unconsciously protecting the bottom of his foot.

If a person is sitting with both feet resting on his knees and the soles of his feet pointing behind them, this could indicate either apprehensiveness or comfort. To distinguish between the two emotions, one must check other body signals. If the body is hunched forward, the person might feel uncomfortable in his surroundings, but if the person is leaning back, then he is taking up more space and thus displaying confidence in the current situation. If one foot is resting on a knee, the direction of the foot may indicate an object or person of interest to the individual.

The physical distance between people is directly related to the degree of intimacy between them. Also, the angle at which people orient their bodies gives many non-verbal clues about their attitudes and relationships.

Curling: We cannot move the foot a great deal and pretty much all we can do is curl the toes up or down. Curling the feet can be a sign of extreme pleasure (or extreme pain).

Stamping: Stamping is bringing down the foot heavily on the ground. We can stamp with the whole flat of the foot or the heel. Stamping makes a noise and can be an attention-getting signal—'Hey! Listen to me!' It can often be a signal of frustration, anger, or aggression, particularly when used with other noise-making devices such as shouting, perhaps to frighten the other person into submission or flight.

Shifting: Shifting from foot to foot indicates that a person is worried about getting found out for a wrongdoing. It also indicates that a person is feeling out of place and would rather be somewhere else quickly. Shifting may be accompanied by other gestures like looking out the door, backing up towards the door, half-facing the other person and half-facing the door, and so on.

Moving: The motion of the feet will tell you whether the person you are talking to wants to be in the room or not. Tapping of the foot, a restless leg, or restless swaying from side to side belie the person's intention to leave the room and get away from your boring conversation. If you notice movement of the legs, it is an activation of that person's flight response—on a very subtle level, they feel endangered by how disinterested in the conversation they are! Moving the feet is also a common indicator of a person lying, particularly if he is sitting and his feet are hidden under a table.

There are, what are termed 'happy feet' movement. It refers to people who walk restlessly up and down in a small space, out of anxiety; this happen with a speaker moments before he has to deliver a speech.

Foot-tapping can be a sign of impatience as the person gets into a kind of tense repetitive state. The foot becomes literally like a clock's pendulum, with rhythmic movements.

WALKING GESTURES

Each person has a distinct walk; seldom do we identify people by their walk. Our walk is shaped on the basis of our individual body structure and emotions. These control our pace and length of stride, and our posture. A person who is happy will be light-footed and the movements quick and lively. A depressed person will walk with heavy steps, as if he had leaden feet, and stooped shoulders.

While we walk on our hind limbs to commute from point A to point B, the manner and style of our gait (for example, marching, mincing, or swaggering) telegraphs information about our status, feelings, and moods. The two-point rhythm of our bipedal walk lays neurological foundations for the syncopated beat of music and the oscillating movements of dance (Givens, 1999).

When you are called up to speak before an audience, walking confidently to the dais or stage is important. If you walk very slowly while you are looking at the floor can convey the impression that you would rather be elsewhere. Walking rapidly while not looking at the people you talk to could convey the impression that this conversation or speech is not important to you.

The following are some walking styles:

Arms swinging: When people walk, their arms swing through an arc in the plane that is in line with the movement of their body through space. The full extent of the arc, forward and back, provides an index of vigour. Young people tend to swing their arms higher at the front and further up at the back, than older people. Swinging the arms across the body also helps to create an impression of masculine strength. The person is identified as being goal-oriented and on a definite mission.

Hands in pockets: People who tend to walk with their hands in their pockets may possess a character that is prone to being critical and secretive. They can often be found speaking disparagingly of others. It is quite possible that they are facing dejection themselves, especially if they move about with the head bent, as if measuring the floor. Another characteristic that might accompany this gesture is sloppiness.

Hands on hips: Walking with hands on hips is the typical mark of a 'rusher'—one who wants to be up and on the move without wasting time. Such people will generally use efficient means to fulfil their goals in the shortest possible time and via the shortest possible route. They are known to work in fits and starts; they act on impulse, then settle down briefly to plan their next move.

Meditative walk: People who are preoccupied with some problem may tend to walk at a slow pace with head down and hands clasped behind their backs. They may stop every now and then to intently examine an object on the ground, be it a stone or a scrap of paper.

Confidence walk: This is the walking style of a 'strutter'—chin raised, arms swinging exaggeratedly, legs somewhat stiff, and the pace impressively deliberate, calculated. This style exudes confidence.

Leadership walk: This refers to people who 'set the pace' of walking. They walk with deliberate steps, clearly indicating that they are headed towards a specific, desired goal; hence, others may take the cue and follow, if they so wish.

Pacing: This is walking with measured steps and with a particular gait. People pace up and down a limited area: a room, a veranda, a courtyard. They resort to this movement while attempting to solve a complex problem or when they are faced with a difficult decision. They naturally prefer to be left alone and not interrupted lest they lose their chain of thought.

Swagger: A swagger is a slight or moderate exaggeration of the side-to-side movements of walking. It is usually a masculine style of upper-body strutting, with somewhat exaggerated arms-swinging. This is almost exclusively a male gesture. It is a visual means of filling-up space or of occupying a greater expanse of personal territory. A man who approaches another with a swagger in order to greet him is displaying 'power, strength, and dominance' (Givens, 1999).

SUMMING UP

For body language to be interpreted as positive and genuine, it is important to be 'natural'. Always stand erect and walk with your shoulders back and stomach in, so people will recognize your self-confidence, awareness, and enthusiasm.

There are non-verbal behaviours that you must avoid if you do not wish to transmit lack of self-confidence. These are:

- hunching your shoulders;
- slouching in a chair;
- leaning forward with head or chin resting on one of the hands;
- constantly shifting position while sitting or standing.

Chapter 7

Zones and Spaces

INTRODUCTION

A fascinating area in the non-verbal world of body language is that of spatial relationships or proxemics: the study of people's appreciation and use of space.

We have an invisible space around us that we treasure as our own possession, which we carry along with us wherever we go; that is, we walk around inside a sort of private bubble, or body buffer zone, which represents the amount of airspace we feel we must have between ourselves and others. Our interactions have to do with people entering or 'invading' this space or keeping away or being kept away from it. In our dealings with people, we move close to them or keep a distance, as required, either deliberately or unconsciously. How we guard our personal space boundaries and how we enter into the others' personal space is integrally connected with the way we are related with other people. This bubble is created in childhood and it varies depending on the location one grew up in—crowded cities or spacious countryside.

Power is frequently linked to territory. High-status individuals occupy more space: they have bigger houses, cars, and offices. They also use up more of the space around them, and other people usually acknowledge their claims by allowing them extra space. High-status people seem to create an invisible boundary around them—not unlike a military exclusion zone—which other people approach with caution. Indeed, it is often the hesitant way that people approach the invisible boundary around a dominant individual that provides the most telling clues about how important they are, and that serves to reinforce that person's feelings of superiority.

SPECIFIC ZONES

Dr Edward Hall was one of the pioneers in the study of human personal space. He coined the word 'proxemics' (proximity or nearness) for his study of territory behaviour among humans.

Hall (1969) explains that body spacing and posture are unintentional reactions to sensory fluctuations or shifts, such as subtle changes in the sound and pitch of a person's voice. Social distance between people is reliably correlated with physical distance, as are intimate and personal distance.

Every person has his own territorial needs. Hall classified these needs, so as to standardize the science of proxemics, into four distinct zones: the intimate, personal, social, and public. We shall discuss each zoning distance briefly.

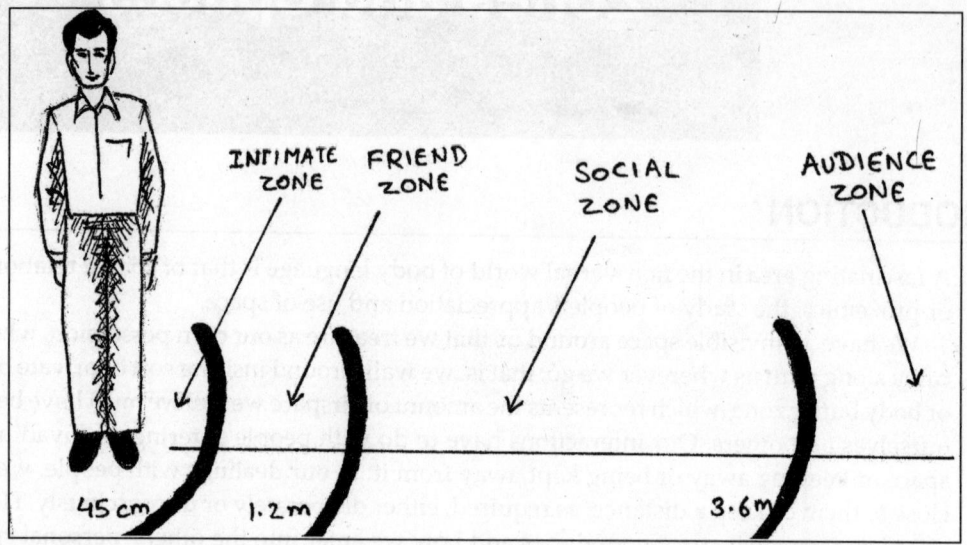

Intimate zone: The distance for embracing, touching, or whispering

> *Close phase:* Less than 6 inches (15 cm)
> *Far phase:* 6–18 inches (15–46 cm)

Friend zone: Personal distance for interactions among good friends or family members

> *Close phase:* 1.5–2.5 feet (46–76 cm)
> *Far phase:* 2.5–4 feet (76–120 cm)

Social zone: The distance for interactions among acquaintances

> *Close phase:* 4–7 feet (1.2–2.1 m)
> *Far phase:* 7–12 feet (2.1–3.7 m)

Audience zone: Distance used for public speaking

> *Close phase:* 12–25 feet (3.7–7.6 m)
> *Far phase:* 25 feet (7.6 m) or more

Intimate Distance Zone

This zone can be categorized into '*close*' or '*far*'. The individual guards it like his or her own property. The close intimate zone may entail actual physical contact and extend to about

6 inches, and so understandably it is reserved only for those who are emotionally close. These include family, relations, friends, and lovers. The zone is used for the most intimate interaction, for instance, caressing someone or making love. Within this zone, people can be overwhelmed by the sensory inputs of the other—heat from the body, stimulation from the other touching the skin, the sound of breathing, the fragrance of perfume. They might even talk in whispers. However, visibility of each to the other is low.

The far intimate zone ranges from 6 to 18 inches, within touching distance. It is crossed in crowded places, but here people observe rigid rules of behaviour. They hold themselves as stiff as possible trying not to touch their neighbours. If they do inadvertently touch them, they either draw away or tense the muscles of the area that is touching another's. They may also apologize. It is important to note that in crowded areas, leaning against a stranger can cause problems.

While we will tolerate strangers moving within our personal and social zones, the intrusion of a stranger into our intimate zone causes physiological changes to take place within our bodies. The heart pumps faster, adrenalin pours into the bloodstream and blood is pumped to the brain and the muscles as physical preparations for a possible fight or flight situation are made. This means that putting your arm in a friendly way on or around someone you have just met may result in that person's feeling negative towards you, even though he may smile and appear to enjoy it so as not to offend you. If you want people to feel comfortable in your company, the golden rule is 'keep your distance'.

Personal Distance Zone

The personal zone is the rather large area which an individual owns, has exclusive use of, or controls. Personal space is the area an individual maintains around himself in which

others cannot enter without causing discomfort. Thus, this space affords the person privacy or social intimacy as the case may be.

Some examples of personal territory are the house, garden, vehicles, and office. Temporary territories include a room in a hotel, a table and a seat at a restaurant, a desk in a library. A territory may be established simply by repeated occupation of a particular seat or table. In most homes, each member of the family has a bed, a chair, or an area—like the kitchen or the backyard—which is regarded as his or her own domain.

Two or more people in a large gathering or in a public place may indicate that they are for the time being a closed group, by their spatial positions, and also by their arm positions, low tone of voice, and so on. If they are open to new members, they will stand side by side with a greater distance between them and look around at others present. When a person passes through a group, especially a closed group, he does so quickly, with lowered head, avoiding eye contact, and with some embarrassment.

The personal zone, too, can be either close or far. The close area ranges between 1½ and 2½ feet. Here, outreach is still possible. The far area ranges between 2½ and 4 feet; this affords some amount of personal privacy. We literally keep people 'at arm's length', which is the distance we keep from others at parties, social functions, and get-togethers. This is the distance from which it is possible to touch the other by reaching out.

Social Distance Zone

The social zone also has its close and far phases. The close phase is between 4 and 7 feet; this is the distance generally maintained in routine business transactions and at casual social gatherings. We maintain this distance while interacting with people we do not know well, or with a new employee, or the postman, or a shopkeeper. A boss may utilize this distance in order to dominate a seated employee, for instance, a secretary or receptionist. In this position, the boss appears to loom large, thus non-verbally conveying the message 'You work for me'.

The far social phase is between 7 and 12 feet, and is used in formal relationships—social or business. The boss in an office may observe this distance by sitting behind a large desk, for it has a dominating effect. From this vantage point, he can still maintain his superiority despite being seated. In other cases, this distance allows a certain protection; for instance, workers separated by this distance on the floor of a workshop can either stop work and chat, or communicate with each other while working, without appearing to be rude due to lack of eye contact. At this distance, interactors use a high level of gaze and need to speak louder; their body movements, however, are visible.

Public Distance Zones

The public zone too has its close and far phases. The close phase is between 12 and 25 feet; this is suitable for a lecture or a conference. The far phase is 25 feet and beyond; this is the distance maintained by, say, politicians for security reasons and by actors on stage. In this phase, facial expression is difficult to see, a louder voice is needed, and bodily movements need to be exaggerated.

SPACE

Spatial Requirements

All the senses—and not the vision alone—perceive and establish spatial distances. According to Hall (1959), auditory space is perceived by the ears, thermal space with the skins, kinesthetic space with the muscles of the body, and olfactory space with the nose. The emotions also have a direct effect on the *size* of a person's territory. The space bubble of someone who is angry or under stress expands, and the person needs more space.

There is a great deal of variation in the distance of these boundaries from person to person and from culture to culture. According to Hall (1959), overcrowding in urban areas induces feelings of stress in people. He observes that people are more tolerant of crowds early in the day; but owing to the stress they accumulate in the course of the day, their tolerance level decreases, and by the end of the day they easily begin to lose their temper if pressured by crowds. Stress leads to a need for greater space. People need places that provide relief from constant overstimulation of their nervous system.

Brown (2006) identified four types of psychological boundary:

Soft: A person with soft boundaries merges with other people's boundaries. Someone with a soft boundary is easily manipulated.

Rigid: Persons with rigid boundaries are closed or walled off so nobody can get close to them either physically or emotionally. This is often the case if someone has been physically, emotionally, or psychologically abused. Rigid boundaries can be selective which depend on time, place, or circumstances and are usually based on a bad previous experience in a similar situation.

Spongy: Persons with spongy boundaries have a combination of soft and rigid boundaries. They permit less emotional contagion than soft boundaries but more than rigid ones. People with spongy boundaries are unsure of what to let in and what to keep out.

Flexible: This is the ideal. Similar to selective rigid boundaries but the person has more control. The person decides what to let in and what to keep out is resistant to emotional contagion, manipulation, and is difficult to exploit.

Personal Space

Here are some examples of personal space. At home the different members, especially the elders, might 'reserve' their particular spaces—a chair, for instance, by leaving some personal object on it, like a cigarette lighter, a magazine, or reading glasses. A woman's private territory may be the kitchen and she may not take kindly to those who invade that space when she is using it. In college, students might want to occupy a certain chair in the library and get upset if it is occupied by someone else. So they may 'reserve' their particular places by leaving a book, file, or some other personal object there while they are away at lectures or have to step out for a while.

Appropriation of Space

Physical Setting

The physical setting conditions and controls our spatial positions and movements. Argyle (1975) lists several settings:

1. Certain areas like the counter in a hotel or a desk in an office acquire significance because they are the exclusive territory of some person or group. To move into this

territory to transact business, or to move out of it to welcome someone into it, would entail a deliberate move towards being sociable.

2. Certain areas are considered to have high or low status; for example, the dais, high table, and front seats in a lecture or concert hall are of high status. To move into or away from such areas is a distinct social act.

3. Certain areas or seats are associated with particular social roles—for example, in a law court, the judge's seat and the dock; and at an interview, the candidate's seat, the chairman's seat, and the other interviewers' seats.

4. The different parts of a house acquire a distinct symbolic significance: for instance, upstairs as against downstairs, sitting room as against the bed room, and the front against the back areas. There are rules and taboos about which member of the family or which outsider may use the different areas.

5. The shape and size of a room as well as the arrangement of the furniture can determine the distance at which people interact with one another and the position they

take while seated; for instance, they may have to sit closer or at an angle different from the one they prefer.

6. Physical barriers, a narrow table, for instance, may constrain people to sit much closer than they would otherwise.

7. Cultural differences play a major role in determining the physical proximity in distance to be maintained with people. For example, in a gesture of welcome or greeting, people in some cultures embrace each other; in other cultures they either kiss or shake hands, or join the palms to do namaste.

Scheflen (1972) has demonstrated that within any given culture, postural configurations in relationships are orderly and standard. From the observed postural configurations, he abstracts three 'dimensions'.

Public Behaviour

It is easy to identify how people use their space in keeping with their personalities at social gatherings. Some sit or stand aloof, or facing a door or looking out a window. Those in pairs or groups give many non-verbal cues. The 'type' of group indicates its status. The position that particular people take in a group non-verbally communicates their relationship with the others—at the head or centre, or at the fringes. How much space a persons appropriates by keeping a distance from or having proximity with others, or the space others give him, are all tell-tale signs of ones personality and relationship.

In crowded places, there is inevitable trespassing over intimate territories. In such a situation, people tense their muscles and hold themselves stiff; this is a signal to others not to intrude upon their space, and, particularly, not to touch them. They also avoid eye contact. Walking along a crowded street seems to expand personal space slightly as people move in a stream of strangers, taking care not to bump into anyone.

Pease (1993) lists a number of 'unwritten rules' that people observe in a crowd:

- Silence must be maintained; there should be no exchange of words with anyone, including acquaintances.
- Eye contact with others must be constantly avoided.
- Emotions must not be displayed; one must wear an expressionless 'poker face'.
- One must appear totally engrossed in a book or newspaper, should one have one.
- One must remain still, rigidly stiff as a pole, and avoid any physical movement, especially if the crowd is large.
- In a lift, one must keep one's eyes on the floor numbers above one's head.

Regulating the distances between us and other people provides us with several benefits, including:

- Safety: When people are distant, they cannot surprise attack us.
- Communication: When people are closer, it is easier to communicate with them.
- Affection: When they are closer still, we can be intimate.
- Threat: The reverse can be used — you may deliberately threaten a person by invading their body space.

GROUP INTERACTIONS

Posture

In groups, one can distinguish between inclusive or non-inclusiveness postures. This has to do with how a group defines the space for the activities and delimits access to and within the group. It includes the proxemic and postural behaviour of members of a group, who may, for example, form a circle to keep others out, or, if standing in a line, may at the end of the line extend an arm or leg (what Scheflen [1972] terms 'bookending') with the same intention. In a rather similar way, people who would otherwise form dyads (for example, pairs that might engage in courtship or arguments) which might detract from the group's purpose are prevented from doing so by a member of the group who places a part of her body between the two. The closer people are forced to be, the more likely they are to adopt blocking postures like crossing their arms and leaning backwards.

Orientation

Orientation means where we sit or stand in relation to the people we are talking to. The angle at which people orient their bodies gives a number of non-verbal cues regarding their attitudes and relationships. When we align our upper body with the person we are talking to, we non-verbally express agreement, liking, and loyalty. Then, when two people are conversing with their bodies forming a right angle, it could be a non-verbal invitation to a third person to join the pair and complete the triangle.

The right-angle position, with two persons not facing each other directly, also suggests that what they are talking about is not personal or private; they have thus left the option of someone joining them open. When a third person does join them, they may both move slightly to face that person. However, if the third person is not acceptable, they will turn only their heads towards him or her, as a sign of recognition, but their bodies will non-verbally communicate that he or she should not remain longer in their company. This could also happen when there are three people involved in a conversation, forming a triangle; they will not pay attention to an 'intruder'. It also happens often that when three people form a triangular group for a conversation, eventually two may break the triangle by facing each other, thus giving the third person the cue that they want him or her out.

When two people having a conversation want to be left alone, because of the intimate nature of their discussion, they will physically so place themselves that they face each other squarely.

There seems to be an inverse relationship between proximity and orientation, except in intimate relationships. Orientation also changes naturally to suit the kind of interaction, roughly like this:

- competition: face-to-face
- cooperation: side by side
- conversation: 90° angle

How people orient their bodies towards others can convey messages about dominance. When a man is talking to his boss, he usually shows his respect by orienting his body towards his boss. The boss, on the other hand, is much more likely to orient his body away from the subordinate. In their separate ways, the subordinate shows that he is totally focused on his boss, while his boss shows that he is dominant and keeping his options open.

There is, however, an entirely different set of messages conveyed by body orientation. We present vulnerable parts of our body, including our flanks, when we want to show that we do not have aggressive intentions towards someone else. So when an aggressive-looking stranger approaches, we are much more likely to present him with the side of your body than to face him directly. Standing face-on might suggest that we are ready for a fight, whereas exposing our flank shows that we are vulnerable and undefended, and do not present a threat.

Therefore, body orientation can convey very different meanings in different situations. That is, because the meaning of orientation depends on whether or not people know each other. When two people are not acquainted and there is a lot of uncertainty, direct orientation is more likely to be interpreted as a prelude to attack. But when they do know each other, it is more likely to be seen as a sign of respect.

Vis-à-vis or parallel body orientation: This gives evidence about the types of social activities. In the vis-à-vis orientation, people sit or stand facing each other. They tend to engage in conversation, courtship, instructing, or arguing, typically an interaction which involves an exchange of information. These interactions are *reciprocal* — the participants *must* interact.

In the parallel orientation, people sit or stand side by side, oriented towards some third party, task, or object the two participants are likely to be engaging mutually towards some third thing or person, for example, lending each other support in arguing with a third party. Such relationships do not require two people; they can equally be performed by a single individual.

Congruence or non-congruence: This indicates association, non-association, or dissociation of group members. Postural congruence (also referred to as mirroring, imitating, or interactional synchrony) can be found even in relatively large groups of, say, six or so people. Once congruence is established, it tends to be maintained; when one member of the group changes posture, the others tend to follow suit quite rapidly.

In some groups there may be two congruent sets ('split postural congruence'), with two separate sets of members. In such a case it is likely that two points of view are being presented. Old friends will often shift into postural congruence when they are disagreeing, almost as if to signal that their relationship continues amicably despite the temporary disagreement.

Defending Personal Space

The guarding of zones and space is one of the first basic principles of non-verbal communication according to Fast (1970). An integral part of our relationships has to do with how we approach and enter others' zones and how we guard our own. The way in which we defend our zones and react when someone intrudes upon our space, as well as the way we trespass into the territories of others, can be observed and mapped out so as to serve a constructive purpose in our life.

People are highly sensitive to any invasion (that is, the dramatic or sudden entry into their personal space) of their personal space. If a person stands too close to another, the other's first instinct is to back up. In case that is not possible, the other will lean away or pull himself in, tensing the muscles. If the intruder does not sense the discomfort he has caused, or ignores it, the other may try to protect himself using a briefcase or anything else he has in his hand. If all efforts at 'cueing' fail, the other may move to another spot, or get behind some furniture. Territoriality is established very rapidly. For instance, in a seminar, after the break, most of the participants return to their original seats; and should the seat have been occupied by someone else, the former occupant might express a fleeting irritation.

People send 'keep off' signals in other situations, too, to maintain the privacy of their physical space as well. For instance, when we sit at a vacant table and wish to discourage others from joining us, we may adopt two procedures. One would be avoidance, that is, we will take a position at the corner of the table, with our back to the entrance. Here, the message we send out is clear: 'Share my table if you must, but leave me alone; I'm sitting in a corner with the hope that you will occupy the other corner as far away from me as possible.' The second approach is to seek privacy by keeping the entire table to ourselves by sitting somewhere at the centre of either side, facing the entrance. Here, the message would be: 'Leave me alone; if you join me I will feel annoyed.'

Mehrabian (1968) suggests that people feel most at ease when addressing a low-status person, less so when relating to peers, and least of all when dealing with a higher status person. They may take extreme attitudes and relax either very little or very much when relating to someone they like. They experience extreme tension when dealing with a threatening individual and extreme relaxation when dealing with someone who is non-threatening, or whom they dislike.

Territorial Gestures

When a person leans against an object or another person, he is signalling territorial possession of that object or person. Touching (an object or a person) signifies an extension of one's body and, consequently, possession or intimacy with that object or person; for instance, friends put their arms around each other, lovers hold hands, a manager stretches his legs out on his office table, and a person rests his foot on a vehicle he owns.

To lean against 'property' that belongs to someone else is a sign of domination and intimidation, be it an office chair or a vehicle. Leaning against someone else's doorpost is another kind of space usurpation. When a man sits with one leg over one of the arms of his chair, he signal's his ownership stand. This gesture, however, also sends a clear message that one need not be formal in his presence, but can take a relaxed, carefree attitude.

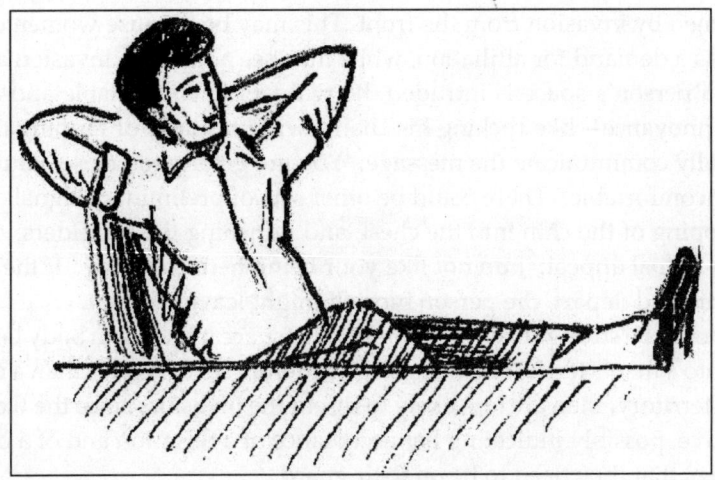

A boss may stretch out both his legs on his office table to declare dominance. However, should his *boss* appear on the scene, he will use subtle forms of dominance; for instance, he may lower his legs from the table but still keep his position by placing his foot on the lower-most drawer of the table. If there are no drawers, he may press his leg against a leg of the desk to retain his position of dominance.

In a negotiation situation, the person who has his legs over the arm of his chair or on the desk may take on an indifferent, even hostile attitude. It is possible to disarm him by placing something a little out of his reach so that he has to lean forward to scrutinize it. This will change his posture and attitude.

Space Invasion

One can invade another's zone or space in several ways, for instance, by moving physically close, looking or listening, making a noise, using the facilities, or by contaminating or disturbing parts of the territory. Invasion into another's territory creates feelings of discomfort and annoyance.

The individual, whose personal space is invaded, will avert his gaze, using his arms or a pile of books as a barrier, turn his face, lean away, or resort to hostile gestures and glances. If none of these work, he will try to increase his distance from the intruder or leave the place.

Discomfort is proportional to the degree of invasion. Typically, people start to feel a little uncomfortable at 28 inches, moderately so at 20 inches, and extremely uncomfortable at just over 12 inches. The degree of discomfort depends largely on who the intruder is. For instance, if it is a close friend or an attractive person, the disturbance will be less than if it is a stranger, especially one who is superior. Women are more disturbed by invasion from the side, men by invasion from the front. This may be because women consider sideways invasion as a demand for affiliation, while men see a head-on invasion as threatening.

When a person's space is intruded, he will feel uncomfortable and may even display signs of annoyance—like rocking his chair, swing his legs, or tapping the table. All these non-verbally communicate the message: 'You are getting too close; your presence is making me uncomfortable.' There could be other sets of preliminary signals like closing of the eyes, drooping of the chin into the chest, and hunching the shoulders. All these make the same non-verbal appeal: 'I do not like your being here, go away.' If the intruder does not take the cue and depart, the person himself might leave the spot.

There could be strong sexual connotations in space invasion in body language. A woman moving into a man's territory encounters a different set of signals than a man moving into a woman's territory. Men are less likely to resent the invasion, since the woman herself takes the initiative, possibly indicating her acceptance of a flirtation and of a closer relationship. Women feel that they need to be on their guard.

The strong signal invariably sent by intruders is: 'You are a non-person, and therefore I can move in on you. You do not matter.'

In crowded places, there is a slightly different interpretation of the signals. There it is important that the individuals involved regard each other as non-persons to avoid awkwardness. An individual in a crowd expects to be treated as a non-person—an inanimate object—just as he treats others in that situation. This makes it possible for everyone to temporarily surrender their personal spaces, so as to make for easy mobility among them; for, an inanimate object does not 'own' its personal space.

There are several 'recognition ceremonies' of the way in which we recognize and react to invasion. In normal circumstances when we invade another's territory in, say, a library or a cafeteria, we send out a set of deferential signals. We apologize verbally and ask: 'Is this seat taken?' We lower our eyes when we sit down. When we take a seat in a crowded bus, the proper ceremony is to keep our eyes straight ahead of us and avoid looking at the person sitting next to us.

Intimate Zone Invasion

People tend to intrude the intimate zone either because of their closeness with the concerned individual, who may be a relative or friend, or for sexual reasons, or because they want to attack. Strangers are obviously prohibited entry into the intimate zone.

When we pat someone on the back or put an arm around the shoulder or waist, we are intruding upon his space. Depending on our relationship with him, we may rouse positive or negative feelings. A person who does not wish to offend the intruder may conceal negative feelings behind a false smile. Someone who is over-friendly and touches people indiscriminately at an early stage in the relationship, though seeming to be accepted, may be secretly disliked.

Dealing with Personal Space Violation

Unconscious Reactions

Everyone has automatic, unconscious reactions to violations of their personal space. These reactions happen so swiftly and so unconsciously that one would have difficulty in identifying them, because hardly anyone gives them a second thought, because their reactions are merely reflex actions. Some common reactions are listed below (see Amos, 2010).

Move away: When someone gets a bit too close, moving away is the most natural and automatic reaction. This may be accomplished with body movement, such as leaning back, or more pronounced movement, such as moving your chair away, sliding your entire body away, or, in extreme cases, even getting up and moving to a different location.

Put up a personal barrier: This is less complicated than building a wall. You may use things available around as barriers. For instance, you might rearrange your books or papers so they are between you and the other person; or, you might change arm position so that your arm is raised or manoeuvred into a position blocking the other person.

Body position: In most cases, this is a combination of moving away and putting up a barrier. For instance, you might turn slightly so your back is to the other person, effectively creating a barrier. Or, you might turn your head, avoid eye contact, raise your book or reading material, and so on.

Deliberate Reactions

Some people make quite deliberate decisions about how to deal with violations of their personal space. Their responses are often passive, but may also be quite active in some cases. Following are some common actions:

Spread out: This is very common in situations where you are sitting at a table that others might choose to sit at as well, such as at the library or in a cafeteria. As the other person approaches and begins to infringe upon your personal space, you spread out your belongings—books, purse, backpack, shopping bags, and jacket, anything—into the space around you. This visually communicates your boundaries and also works as a barrier between you and the other person.

Turn your back: This is another tactic to protect your personal space from another person. You might casually shift your position so your back is to the other person or even reposition your chair with your back acting as a barrier between the two of you.

Ask the other person to move: This is an active response typically used by people with a great deal of self-confidence and self-esteem. When a person begins to violate your personal space, you simply ask them to move away a bit. If you're not confident enough to be that bold, you might tell them you're expecting someone else to arrive soon and you'd like to keep the space available for that person.

Verbal warning: In cases where you feel particularly threatened, you might give the other person a verbal warning that you're uncomfortable and could they please move away. It might be something simply like 'please stop' or something more directive like 'you're sitting/standing too close to me, could you please move back'.

Most people focus more on passive measures than on active measures when their personal space is violated. It is simply too intimidating or uncomfortable to reclaim that space directly.

TOUCHING AND ZONES

Touches eliminate the space between people and can intensify experiences of intimacy in verbal communication or stand on their own as intimate behaviours.

Touching has to do with the intimate zones and personal space. Touch is probably the swiftest and most overt type of body language. By touching someone with the hand, or placing an arm around someone's shoulder, we can communicate more meaningfully and directly than with words. However, it must occur at the right moment and in the right context.

Touching, in itself, is a powerful signal. When a person touches inanimate objects, he signals in a loud and clear in non-verbal language that he is attached to them and wants to have them for his own always.

How we touch others is determined by how we feel about them. Full touch with the palm of the hand is warm and affectionate, while touching with the fingertips betrays less affection (Navarro and Poynter, 2010).

Other clues are: is a grip gentle or firm, and does one hold the other person on the back of the upper arm, on the shoulder, or in the middle of the back? Is the gesture a push or a tug? Is the touch closer to a pat, a rub, or a grabbing? People have different areas of personal intimacy, and this refers not only to the sexual dimension but also the dimension of self-control. Many adolescents are particularly sensitive to any touching that could be interpreted as patronizing or undue familiarity. Even the angle of one's holding another's hand might suggest a hurrying or coercive implicit attitude, or on the other hand, a respectful, gentle, permission-giving approach (Collett, 2003).

Touch can tell us something about respecting and trusting someone but also about power differentiations between people. Examples of differentiations in power as a message in the body language are:

- the friendly shoulder pat
- the stroke over the head
- the arm around someone's shoulder

Some people tend to be compulsive touchers, to the extent that they are totally insensitive to the feedback they get from friends. These are people who touch and fondle others even when the latter send non-verbal cues that the physical contact is not appreciated.

Varieties of Touching

Greetings and farewells: By far the most common touching gestures are used in greeting someone and when departing. Their actual forms, which include shaking hands, hugging, kissing, rubbing noses, and so on, differ from country to country and culture to culture.

Friends: Friends tend to greet each other with more intimate touching, such a hugging or even kissing (although this may vary with culture). Friendship touching will also vary with the intensity and type of friendship. Some people you just touch more and some do not like it. In a group of friends, one tactile person may convert the whole group to a more touchy culture.

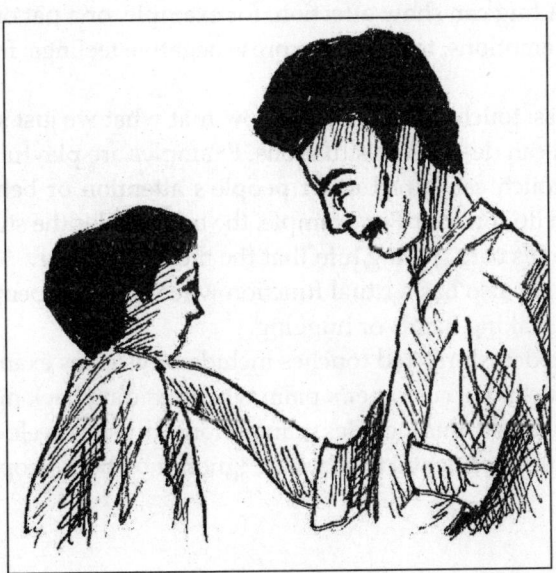

Families: Families touch one another more, in particular parents and children, where as well as sympathetic touching, there may be guidance and others forms of touch. As with friends (and lovers), families touch each other more partly because they trust one another and also to sustain bonding and trust.

Lovers: Partners and lovers touch each other a great deal. Intimacy does not have to be all sexual and is often just because it feels good. This may include holding hands, arms around each other, necking, nuzzling, and kissing.

Self-touch: When talking to someone in a position of authority, we tend to assume that our own actions, rather than those of the other person, are being judged, and this makes us feel self-conscious and insecure. There are several ways that we cope with these feelings. One is by engaging in auto-contact actions where we touch, hold, or stroke ourselves. These self-comforting gestures serve to reassure us—in the same manner when someone else touches, holds, or strokes us.

Touching Characteristics

Jones and Yarbrough (1985) have listed the different meanings related to touch:

- Positive emotions: touch can express affection, appreciation, support, trust, and sexual interest. A hug can show affection, for example, or a pat on the back shows support.
- Negative emotions: touch can express negative feelings, for example, by slapping or hitting.
- Playfulness: touch can let others know that what we just said is not to be taken seriously and can de-escalate situations. Examples are playful wrestling and tickling.
- Control: touch can direct other people's attention or behaviour and communicate status and dominance. For example, the boss guides the subordinate to the door with a hand on his back, telling him that the meeting is over.
- Ritual: touch also has a ritual function when greeting people or saying goodbye, for example, shaking hands or hugging.
- Task-related: task-related touches include physicians examining a patient, but also a cashier touching a customer's palm when handing back money.
- Accidental touch: this includes unintentional brushes in elevators or public transportation. Usually, accidental touches are ignored by both people.

Indian

In India, Muslims and Hindus typically do not touch with the left hand. To do so is a social insult. Left hand is for toilet functions. They also eat with right hand only, though in some parts of India one may use the left hand too if needed to break bread when one cannot mange it with a single hand.

It is also considered rather offensive to (even accidentally) step on someone. Basically, any action that involves ones foot and someone else's body is offensive. Apologies should be made immediately. Often, a simple statement of 'sorry' will not suffice. When a person steps on another' toes, literally, he may tap the offended person briefly with the tips of his fingers usually on the shoulder, and then in the same motion tap his own forehead. This is a form of apology, a way of seeking forgiveness for the action (Chandragiri, 2010).

CORPORATE ZONES AND SPACES

Body language is integral to success in the business world. From the way we interact with bosses, subordinates, and co-workers to our interaction with customers and beyond, our body language is one of the most powerful and influential communication tools at our disposal.

Business Meeting Dynamics

Your body language has a powerful influence on how you are perceived before, during, and after a meeting. Body language affects communication in meetings in several ways, such as: where you sit; whom you sit with or do not sit with; how you sit; whether you should even sit at all; what you do with your hands, your arms, your legs; eye contact; and overall body position.

Seating Arrangements

At a board meeting, the Chief Executive Officer usually sits at the head of the table, with those who are next in importance sitting closest to him. People who sit at the head of the table attract more attention than anyone else. They also do most of the talking and get deferred to more often.

People who are placed at the head of a rectangular table attract the most attention and do most of the talking. This is less evident with circular or square tables.

Rectangular and oval tables are fine for bilateral negotiations, where the two parties can occupy opposite and equivalent sides of the table. They are notoriously ill-suited for multi-party negotiations—one or more parties may threaten to walk out because they do not feel that the seats they are being offered reflect their importance in the negotiations.

In brief, a rectangular table usually acts as a barrier in conversation among people of equal status. In an office, it establishes the superior–subordinate distinction. A large table enhances the defensive and competitive attitudes of those who sit across it. A round table, on the contrary, gives the feeling of equality and tends to make people feel relaxed and informal.

Seating positions also influence relationships. Individuals sitting round a table are more likely to address their remarks to people sitting opposite them than to those sitting beside or at right angles to them. This may explain why, when they are seated with strangers, people usually choose to sit furthest from high-status and low-status individuals, and closest to those who have the same status as them.

When the leader is seated at the head of the table in a group meeting, there is a progression of perceived power that is related to how close each seat is to that of the leader's. The closer you sit to the leader, the more powerful and credible you are perceived to be. Some leaders make a conscious choice to sit along the side of the table rather than at the head of the table as a way to create a more relaxed atmosphere, but in general the seats closest to the leader are still perceived as being the most powerful.

Power Positions in a Meeting Room

The way meeting rooms are set-up can either inhibit or enhance participation and discussion.

- On rectangular tables, the short ends of the table (the heads) are decidedly more powerful than the sides. Even round tables will have similar location-associated power. Proximity and eye contact, all give strength to the viewer with respect to the dominant speaker's position.
- Prominent chairs (higher, more heavily padded, or chairs with a higher back or broader arm supports) give a 'throne' association and another subconscious advantage that connotes authority.
- Seats to the right of the most powerful people are next in the power hierarchy at tables with six or more seats — 'right hand man'.
- A wide table separates people very much, diminishes eye contact, hearing. Participants have to lean forward in a discussion. People at one end of a long table feel isolated. As a consequence, there could be 'side meetings' that put the main meeting off-track.
- At shorter tables (less than six seats), the eye contact of the seat opposite the dominant position gives that seat a 'second in command' connotation. Larger tables devalue that eye contact.
- Proximity to books on shelves connotes greater wisdom in the negotiation setting.
- The further from the door the seat is, the more powerful it is. Such seats provide the best view of the room entrance or exit and they project a powerful assumption

of permanence. Again, this seat should face the door it monitors. Your distance from that exit announces to all who enter that you are in no need of an exit and in no hurry to leave.

- A podium is a symbolic position of power. A portable or attached microphone also carries associated strength during a speaking engagement. These props reflect dominance. Always request them. They illustrate greater strength on your part if you can give them away as a gesture of intimacy in the presence of your audience. In situations where a microphone is absolutely necessary, movement with that microphone, away from your 'power base', will indicate strength. A dominant speaker is usually at a dais. As mentioned previously, the dais at a large meeting will be found at a location that is furthest from the door. The right over left rules dictates the power hierarchy at the dais.

Office Set-up

In an office set-up, one occupant may place his desk in a corner, so as to protect himself from intrusion from three sides; thus, he reinforces his sense of control. Another may place his desk so that his back is to the entrance. This is the most vulnerable position because he is exposed to whoever is approaching before he is aware of the visitor. A third occupant may so place his desk as to allow entry and have space at the front and on one side. This position is most comfortable, both for the occupant and the visitor. The occupant maintains control while at the same time sharing the maximum possible space with the other.

SUMMING UP

We all are aware of where the boundaries of our personal space are located, even though we may have never made any conscious effort to defining them. It is an innate sense which we develop throughout our lifetime in response to our personality, environment, and life experiences. We also learn how to communicate the location of those boundaries so that others can clearly know where they begin.

We generally communicate our need for personal space non-verbally. The methods we use for such communication are a combination of body language and other actions we take, consciously or unconsciously, to preserve our personal space.

Body language is perhaps the most powerful tool to communicate personal space. If it is used respectfully and responsibly, it becomes a very useful way of improving and influencing relationships.

Chapter 8

Traits and Attitudes

So far we have studied individual gestures and a variety of gestures and gesture cluster formations. The purpose was to facilitate the interpretation of body movements and behaviour. In this chapter we shall reverse the process. We shall single out certain traits and attitudes and study what form of gestures or gesture clusters communicate them.

Traits are often communicated in gesture clusters. It is rare for a person to be as alert as to take in all the gestures that form a cluster and to visualize the nuances in a cluster. However, being able to see even a few of the gestures in a cluster is good enough to make some judgement about the attitudes being communicated. Only, we must be aware that there is a fair amount of overlapping both in gesture formations and in attitudinal positions.

CONVERSATION TRAITS

A conversation is different from a speech. In conversations is unusual for more than one person to be speaking at a time, and when it does happen for any length of time, it is because the conversation has temporarily broken down. The most obvious thing about conversations is that people take turns. Psychologists have discovered that the time that elapses between one person completing their turn and the next person starting to talk can be so brief as to be almost non-existent—in some instances, it is less than fifty-thousandths of a second! These are called 'smooth transitions', because the switch between one speaker and the next is so seamless (Walker, 1982).

The universal rule of conversations is 'one person at a time', and although most conversations follow this rule, there are times when people speak at the same time and don't listen to each other. Some cases of 'overlap talk' arise because the listener is trying to interrupt in order to take over the speaker's role. However, other cases of overlap talk arise not through competition but purely because the listener wants to encourage the speaker.

Turn-taking is organized through a set of conventionalized signals that people produce while they are talking or listening (Beattie, 1983). By using turn-taking signals, the listener can indicate whether he wants to 'avoid' the speaker role or to 'take' it, and the speaker can signal whether he wants to 'hold' the floor or 'yield' the floor to the listener. 'Back-channel' signals (Yngve, 1970), that is, verbal responses like 'uh-huh', 'yes', and 'yeah', repetition of the speaker's words, nods, and brief smiles, indicate that the listener agrees with the speaker or understands what the speaker is saying. If the listener wants a turn to speak, he can produce an 'intention display', like leaning forward, lifting a finger, or opening your mouth slightly. He can also resort to 'alerting signals' like raising a hand or widening of eyes slightly to show the other person that one wants to speak. Or he can use expressions of 'back-calling' that call on the listener to provide backchannel and thus continue listening: like 'you see', 'don't you think', 'right?', 'OK', and 'know what I mean?' (Sebba and Tate, 1986).

When speakers want to give up the floor, they send 'turn-yielding signals' to the listener: shifting their gaze, a drop in vocal pitch, hand gestures, head-nods.

Repetitive nodding is an integral part of conversation. Listeners nod slowly while the other person is speaking to show that they are listening and to demonstrate that they do not want to take over the speaker's role. Fast nodding also shows that the listener understands the speaker, but it shows either that the listener supports the speaker wholeheartedly or that the listener wants to take over the speaker's role.

When a listener wants the speaker to continue, he adopts three behaviours. The first is producing an 'attentiveness display'; that is, remaining silent, orienting towards the speaker, and gazing intently at the speaker. The second is by producing an 'unintention display', like folding our arms, pressing our lips together, or placing a hand or a finger over our mouth. The third is by asking questions (Collett, 2003).

Speakers can discourage interruptions by being emphatic, by looking away from the listener, by keeping the hands in motion, by producing lists, and by talking in a way that minimizes the opportunities for listeners to start talking. When speakers are interrupted, there are several things they can do to hold or retrieve the floor. Talking louder is one option. Another strategy is to use what Albert Scheflen (1973) called a 'transfix'. A speaker who had his hand raised at the time of interruption will freeze it in mid-air, just as if he were playing a game of 'statues', and will continue to hold that position until he can regain the floor. By keeping his hand in this fixed position, he shows that he has not completed his turn and that he intends to stay that way until the speaking role returns to him. When he realizes that he is not going to get the turn back immediately, he is likely to lower his hand. In that way he can signal that he is abandoning his claim to the speaker role.

When people of different status are together, the most important person usually does most of the talking. This enables them to remind everyone else of their position. It also gives them a chance to hear the sound of their own voice and to listen to their own opinions rather than those of other people.

When groups of people meet for the first time, the order in which they speak provides a fairly good guide to who will dominate the proceedings afterwards. The first person to offer his or her opinion invariably assumes the role of leader; the last person to make a contribution tends to be the person who ends up taking orders.

TRAITS OF A LIAR

Much of what has been written about detection of lies appears facile. We must reconsider the conventional characteristics attributed to liars and focus on more reliable clues to lying. We will consider here the varied traits of lying.

Assumptions and Realties

Gaze Aversion

Most people believe that gaze aversion is a sign of lying. They assume that because liars feel guilty, embarrassed, and apprehensive, they find it difficult to look their victim in the eye, and they therefore look away. However, because gaze is fairly easy to control, liars can use their eyes to project an image of honesty. Knowing the assumption of people, many liars do the exact opposite; they deliberately increase their gaze to give the impression that they are telling the truth.

Hand Movements

People assume that liars become agitated and this gives rise to nervous hand movements like stroking one's hair, scratching one's head, or rubbing the hands together, or fidgeting. This tends to happen when the stakes are high or when the liar is not very good at deception. Generally, the exact opposite happens. Seasoned liars control their habitual gestures so as not to reveal themselves. Thus, they are likely to become more frozen, not more animated!

Movements of the hands and eyes tend to be under conscious control, so they are not reliable sources of information about lying. When people are asked to tell a lie, they tend to produce more signs of deception in the lower part than in the upper part of their body (Ekman and Friesen, 1969). Liars focus their efforts at concealment on their hands, arms, and face, because they know these are under scrutiny. Often, it is the tiny adjustments of the legs and feet that betray them.

Deception Cues

Mouth Cover

One gesture that reveals a lie is the 'mouth-cover'. They assume that if other people cannot see their mouth then they will not know where the lie has come from. Mouth-covering actions can range from full-blown versions where the hand completely covers the mouth to gestures where the hand supports the chin and a finger surreptitiously touches the corner of the mouth.

Nose Touch

As a substitute for touching the mouth, a liar touches his nose and experiences the momentary comfort of covering his mouth, without any risk of drawing attention to what he is really doing. It looks as if he is scratching his nose, but his real intention is to cover his mouth. Some researchers assume that nose-touching is a sign of deceit, quite separate from anything to do with the mouth. Hirsch and Wolf (1999) called this the 'Pinocchio syndrome', after the famous character whose wooden nose becomes longer every time he tells a lie. Hirsch suggested that when people lie, their nose becomes engorged with blood and that this produces a sensation that is alleviated by touching or rubbing the nose.

Birdwhistell (1955) however has a different interpretation of the gesture. He considered that when one person rubs his nose in the presence of another, it reveals the first person's dislike of the second. The nose-rub is also a gesture indicating an unconscious form of rejection (Collett, 2003).

Negative Emotions

Liars have to hide two things: first, the truth, and second, any emotions (like guilt, or the fear of being found out) that might arise out of their attempts at concealment. But liars can also experience the thrill of pulling the wool over other people's eyes—what Ekman (2001) has called 'duping delight'. A negative emotion can be concealed by turning away the head, by covering the face with the hands, or by masking it with a neutral or a positive emotion. The first two strategies do not always work because they tend to draw attention to what the liar is trying to conceal. Masking, on the other hand, enables liars to present an exterior that isn't necessarily connected with lying. The most commonly used masks are the 'straight face' and the smile.

However, contrary to the common assumptions, habitual liars smile less than those who are telling the truth. That is, because liars occasionally adjust their behaviour so that it is the opposite to what everyone expects of people who are telling a lie. And when they do smile, theirs is a counterfeit smile.

Micro-expressions

When people lie, they sometimes produce micro-expressions, which are completely involuntary, that reveal their true feelings. These provide valuable clues in the detection of deceit.

The way that people react when they are no longer required to convince others that they are telling the truth can also provide subtle clues to deceit.

Speech Clues

Most people believe that liars give themselves away by what they do rather than what they say or how they say it. In fact, it is the other way round—the best indicators of lying are to be found in people's speech rather than in their behaviour. Liars often beat about the bush, giving long-winded explanations with lots of digressions to short-answer questions. Liars avoid specifics of time, place, and persons. Liars often produce answers that are designed to confuse—they sound as if they make sense, but they do not. Liars make fewer references to themselves; they use words like 'I', 'me', and 'mine' less frequently than people who are telling the truth. Liars also tend to generalize by making frequent use of words like 'always', 'never', 'nobody', and 'everyone', thereby mentally distancing themselves from the lie. Liars are more likely to use disclaimers such as: 'You won't believe this'; 'I know this sounds strange, but'; and 'Let me assure you'. Disclaimers like these are designed to acknowledge any suspicion the other person may feel in order to discount it. Liars also produce more pauses between their words and sentences, and some of these pauses are filled with speech disfluencies like 'urn' and 'er'. Without realizing it, liars have a tendency to increase the psychological distance between themselves and the event they are describing (Collett, 2003).

Clusters

There are lists galore posted on the internet on how to identify through verbal and body language clues. However, no single clue can provide proofs that are convincing, since most gestures can have various interpretations. Besides, there are habitual liars who are experts at masking themselves so that they appear truthful. In case you do suspect someone is lying, and confront the person, you must observe if one or other of the following traits are present in the liar.

- It is a stated fact that lawyers avoid eye contact. Seasoned liars, as we have seen above, may overcompensate to the other extreme when trying to hide the lies by having prolonged eye contact.
- Liars often subconsciously seek a symbolic protective buffer between themselves and their accuser. Liars absent-mindedly use some object as a shield.
- Liars adopt defensive body positions, like crossing their arms or legs or taking a small step or two backwards.

- Liars resort to evasive answers and statements or raise questions as to why they should resort to doing the things they are accused of.
- When lying, a person may feel his mouth going dry, and so will lick his lips, swallow spittle, or sip from a glass.
- Liars feel uncomfortable with silences, since it gives space for the accuser to review what has been said and detect flaws. Liars therefore try to fill all pauses with pointless or odd conversation and unconnected ideas.
- A liar will usually be deliberate about gestures and expressions in an attempt to make the lies come across as believable, including fake smiles.
- As we have seen with eye movement, when someone is trying to recall something that happened, he will usually gaze upward; conversely, when someone is *pretending* to recall something, he will usually gaze downward.
- A person tends to sweat when lying, particularly on the forehead and palms. Liars betray themselves by wiping their brow or drying their hands on their clothes.
- In order to divert attention from his dishonest words and his face, a liar resorts to excessive gesturing in the hope of increasing his credibility.
- Fidgeting, drumming fingers, biting or picking at fingernails, biting lips, twirling hair, and picking at or adjusting clothing are some of the body language signs of lying.

MIRROR-IMAGING TRAITS

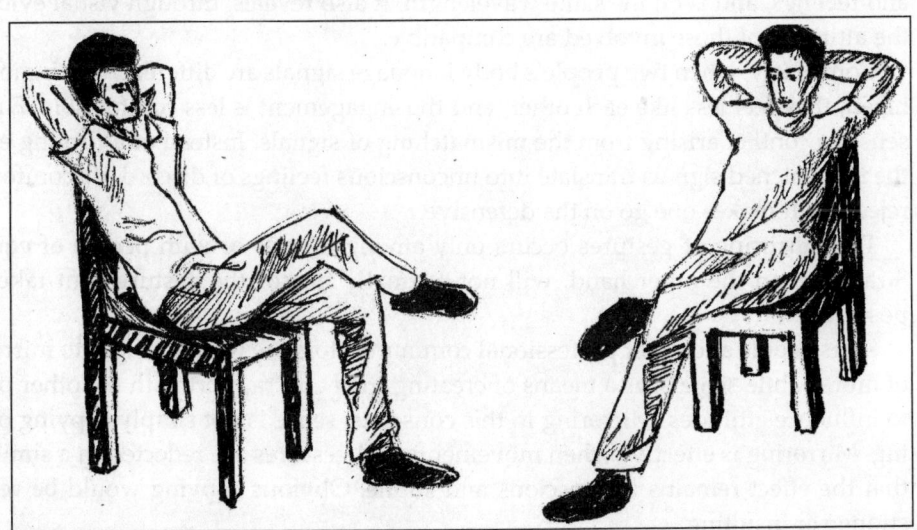

A trait of body language is commonly referred to as 'mirroring', where people 'mirror' or 'reflect' the gestures, body positions, or speech characteristics of the persons they are in contact with in a given situation. The term 'synchronized' is arguably a more accurate techni-cal term for this trait because mirroring implies visual signals only, when the principles of matching body language extend to audible signals also—notably speech pace, pitch, tone, and so on (Businessballs, 2011).

Mirroring is behaviour that copies someone else during communication with them—in displaying similar postures, gestures, or tone of voice. It may include imitating gestures, movements, body language, muscle tensions, expressions, tones, eye movements, breathing, pace of delivery, accent, attitude, choice of words, metaphors, or other features apparent in an interpersonal exchange.

When body language and speech characteristics are mirrored or synchronized between people, this tends to assist the process of creating and keeping rapport (a mutual feeling of empathy, understanding, trust), because it generates unconscious feelings of affirma-tion. When another person displays similar body language to our own, this makes us react unconsciously to feel that that person likes us and agrees with the way we are. In turn, we like that person because of our mutual similarity, and because we feel liked.

Mirroring happens very naturally when people are speaking. A listener will typically smile or frown or nod their head along with the speaker. In ordinary relationships, people naturally match each other's body language. When another person leans forward towards us at a table, we often mirror and do likewise. When they lean back and relax, we do the same. Its importance lies in the fact that such mirroring communicates to the one whose gesture is being copied that the respondent agrees with his or her ideas, attitudes, thoughts, and feelings, and is on the same wavelength. It also reveals, through visual evidence, that the attitudes of those involved are compatible.

Conversely, when two people's body language signals are different, that is, not synchro-nized, they feel less like each other, and the engagement is less comfortable. Each person senses a conflict arising from the mismatching of signals. Instead of affirming each other, the mismatched signals translate into unconscious feelings of discord, discomfort, or even rejection. It makes one go on the defensive.

The mirroring of gestures occurs only among friends or with people of equal status. Strangers, on the other hand, will not normally mirror the gestures but take up other postures.

Sales people and other professional communicators are widely taught to mirror all sorts of more subtle signals, as a means of creating trust and rapport with the other person and to influence attitudes. Mirroring in this conscious sense is not simply copying or mimick-ing. Mirroring is effective when movements and gestures are reflected in a similar way so that the effect remains unconscious and subtle. Obvious copying would be regarded as strange or insulting.

When we notice others mirroring us, we can safely conclude that they agree with us and have accepted us. To mirror the body language of another person is a good technique for making the other feel comfortable. However, this must not appear obvious. Also, only positive gestures must be mirrored, not negative ones. For example, if the defensive position of a person is mirrored, it will only add to his defensiveness.

Mirroring is easily observable in group situations. For instance, at a conference or a meeting when people take a break between sessions, it is interesting to note how mirroring takes place. We may observe two people informally chatting, both having similar gestures. If one person uncrosses his legs or arms, or balances his weight on one foot with the other crossed, his partner will follow suit. The particular gesture will continue for as long as they are in agreement regarding their 'transaction' of ideas or feelings. According to research findings, in a group situation, the members sometimes 'play' 'follow the leader', where mirroring is concerned. Either deliberately or unconsciously, they copy certain gestures and body positions of their 'leader'; for instance, if the leader folds his arms, they will follow suit. This, in turn, influences their attitude, and they will tend to share the views of the leader or ape his behaviour.

Mirroring is done deliberately when we want to send out a non-verbal message of agreement or acceptance to the other person. It could also be used to change the attitude of people. For instance, when people who seem indifferent to us have their gestures mirrored, they may change their attitudes and become more relaxed and receptive.

As in other aspects of body language, mirroring too must be done with discretion and prudence. Subordinates or students should not mirror the gestures of their seniors—like managers or principals—because that may be interpreted as a sign of intimidation or even insult. Nevertheless, mirroring could be effectively used to disarm those who 'act' superior or who try to take control and reverse the power structure. When their gestures are mirrored, they will abandon their 'superior' attitude and relate more on a more equal basis.

Mirroring also happens when people impulsively imitate the behaviour of others, like standing and clapping by members of an audience; wearing the same kind of clothing, shoes, ornaments; adopting the beliefs, customs, and mannerisms of people we admire. People who 'mirror' a friends by wearing lookalike T-shirts or caps may suggest a strong bonding with that friend and similar thinking or feeling. The reason for mirroring could be because it is 'safe' to do so or because one needs to be accepted by a group (Givens, 1999).

TRAITS OF A COMMANDING PERSON

Standing Tall

One need not be physically tall or built like a professional athlete to have a commanding and powerful presence. 'Power comes from within, and is primarily a matter of attitude' (Van Fleet, 1984).

Nevertheless, there are certain body language signals that can be cultivated in order to enhance the personality. Some physical characteristics that can be developed are: 'A strong

unflinching gaze, a tone of voice that implies complete self-confidence and commands immediate obedience, and above all, a solid presence that lets people know you are exactly what you ought to be' (Van Fleet, 1984).

To present yourself as a confidence person, your behaviour and physical appearance and manner must depict a confidence sometimes even beyond what you might actually feel. You must control your voice and gesture, be calm and have presence of mind in a tough situation, and make others feel that things are under control.

To convey positive messages:

- avoid closed gestures
- avoid fidgeting or letting your eyes wander
- maintain eye contact
- maintain good posture
- nod agreement and occasionally express it verbally to reinforce the nods
- smile

Superior–Subordinate Relations

Superiority can be established in the initial handshake. As we have seen, when someone grabs the other's hand firmly and turns it over so that his palm is directly on top of the other's, he is attempting a form of physical domination. A person who offers his hand with the palm up is showing a willingness to accept the subordinate role.

When a person stands beside one who is seated, he non-verbally communicates a sense of superiority. He seems to tower over, to dominate the seated person, who may feel vulnerable. If the standing person happens to be his boss, he will feel great pressure psychologically. Should the boss move to the back of the chair, the seated person will feel even more defenceless and threatened.

The person standing can ease the situation somewhat by adopting a relaxed posture; for instance, he can put his hand casually in his pocket with the thumb sticking out.

The feet-on-desk gesture signifies self-importance—sending out negative messages. This gesture, however, is often overlooked by subordinates.

Some signs of superior behaviour are: raised eyebrows, the light twisting of the head, the look of doubt revealing non-acceptance, and leaning back in a chair with hands clasped behind the head. What gives added authority to what one is saying palm-down gestures, squaring of shoulders, lifting of the face and chin, and visibly standing tall.

Sometimes a superior has to resort to several cues to indicate that his meeting with the subordinate is over, especially if the subordinate is insensitive to signals. One of the first non-verbal cues the boss gives him that the meeting is terminated is to stop looking at him. He either looks down or at some papers. If the hint is not taken by his subordinate, the boss goes to the next stage, that is, shifting his weight; he may give a long sigh and deliberately glance at his watch. If the subordinate still misses the cue, then he goes to the third stage: he may stand up or pick up his papers as if to put them away, and then ask whether the subordinate does not have another business to attend to or diplomatically (yet bluntly) asks him to leave. Bluntness can cause loss of respect for both parties. The superior wonders how dense his employee must be not to recognize such clearly sent gestures, while the subordinate leaves with a feeling of having been made a fool of by his boss and yet angry with himself for not having recognized the signals and thus having overstayed his welcome.

Behaviour

Assertive Behaviour

Lange and Jakubowski (1976) have made some remarks on the non-verbal components of assertive behaviour. Among the non-verbal indicators that might prove important in establishing assertion are the duration of looking at the other person, duration and loudness of speech, and affectation and an overload in speech.

In non-verbal behaviour, the non-verbal messages are congruent with the verbal ones and add support, strength, and emphasis to what is being said verbally.

In assertive behaviour, the voice is inappropriately loud for the situation, eye contact is firm but not a stare-down, body gestures that denote strength are used, and the speech pattern is fluent—without awkward hesitancies—expressive and clear, with due emphasis on keywords.

Non-assertive Behaviour

In non-assertive behaviour, the non-verbal behaviour includes avoidance of eye contact and body gestures such as wringing the hands, clutching the other person, stepping back from the other person while making an assertive remark, hunching the shoulders, and covering the mouth with a hand, nervous gestures which distract the listener from what the speaker is saying, and a wooden body posture. The tone of voice may be a sing-song or overly soft, and the speech pattern hesitant and filled with pauses. The throat may be cleared frequently. Facial gestures may include laughs, blinking while expressing anger, and raised eyebrows.

Aggressive Behaviour

In aggressive behaviour, the non-verbal behaviour is the one which dominates or demeans the other person. This behaviour includes eye contact and tries to stare down and dominate the other person, a high-pitched voice—not called for in the situation—a sarcastic or condescending tone of voice, and gestures typical of a parent admonishing a child, such as excessive finger pointing.

Inner Conflicts

There is a common and easily recognizable sequence of behaviour that indicates inner conflicts. An angry person, unable to express his feelings directly, scratches his head or rubs the back of his neck in frustration. Then he adopts a posture of threat, like taking a step forward but remaining frozen in that hostile pose.

Such persons may, in a redirected response, vent their feelings on a substitute target, like banging a table with their fists or kicking a door.

Good Listening

Van Fleet (1984) gives seven tips on how to 'listen' to an employee by observing his body language. These tips can be adapted to a variety of situations and interactions.

Eyes: The eyes reveal what he is really thinking, no matter what he says in words. You can know that he is pleased and feels good about a remark you have made if his pupils dilate. Conversely, if his pupils contract, it means he dislikes what he has heard. If his eyes narrow, it is an indication he does not believe what you have said, so he feels he has reason to not trust you or what you say.

Eyebrows: The lifting of one eyebrow indicates that he does not believe what you have said or thinks it is impossible. If he lifts both eyebrows, it means that he is surprised.

Nose and Ears: If he rubs his nose or tugs at his ear while saying he understands, it means that he is puzzled by what you are saying and probably does not know at all what you want him to do.

Forehead: Wrinkling the forehead downwards in a frown indicates that he is puzzled or is not pleased with your remark. If he wrinkles his forehead upwards, it reveals that he is surprised at what he has heard.

Shoulders: Shrugging the shoulders usually mean that he is completely indifferent. He does not care in the least what you are saying or demanding.

Fingers: When he drums or taps his fingers on the arm of the chair or the top of the desk, it means he is either nervous or impatient.

Arms: When he folds or crosses his arms across his chest, it usually means that he is isolating himself or creating a barrier from others, or is actually afraid of you and is trying to defend himself.

SUMMING UP

We would do well to bear in mind the suggestions of Van Fleet (1984) on how to project the power of our personality through body language.

Do not smile unless you are genuinely happy. This does not imply that you have to move around with a frown on your face as if you are bearing the burden of the whole world on your shoulders. Rather, it means your smile must come out spontaneously from the heart. The best way to control negative feelings and emotions is to have a neutral facial expression.

Do not allow other people to interrupt you. If you are interrupted while speaking, even by your superior, simply say, 'I'm sorry, but I have not finished yet', and then resume speaking at once where you were cut off. Thus, you will be able to have your full say on the given issue.

Do not restrain your body gestures. If you need to use your hands or arms to make a point, do so, but avoid pointing an accusing finger at anyone.

Look people straight in the eye. To avoid a staring down battle, it is best to look at a spot on the person's forehead till he averts his gaze. The trick is to pick a spot in the middle of the other's forehead, just above the level of his eyebrows. If you keep your eyes fixed on that particular spot, you cannot be stared down. Eventually, the other person will be forced to lower his gaze, in an act of submission, thus giving you a feeling of confidence and control.

Be completely relaxed. This does not imply that you be sloppy in the way you dress or careless about your appearance. Self-confidence is the key to real relaxation. Make sure that you know your job and will perform it sincerely. This will help you remain relaxed and enjoy your work.

Chapter 9

Body Language in Practice

STEPS TO SUCCESS

Your body language impacts your success in life. Whatever be your 'profession', it inadvertently has to do, by and large, with social interactions and personal encounters. The success of any encounter begins the moment someone lays eyes on you. One of the first things they notice about you is your aura, that distinctive atmosphere that surrounds you. You create it, and you are responsible for what it says about you and whom it attracts. Your aura enters with you and starts speaking long before your open your mouth. Since body language conveys more than half of any message in any face-to-face encounter, how you act is vital to your aura.

Edberg (2008) offers some pointer for improving body language in order to enhance ones appeal. Following is a summary:

- To change your body language, you must be aware of your body language. Notice how you sit, how you stand, how you use you hands and legs, what you do while talking to someone.
- Practice in front of a mirror; or, close your eyes and visualize how you would stand and sit to feel confident, open, and relaxed or whatever you want to communicate.
- Feelings work backwards too. If you smile a bit more, you will feel happier. If you sit up straight, you will feel more energetic and in control. If you slow down your movements, you will feel calmer. Your feelings will actually reinforce your new behaviour and feelings of weirdness will dissipate.
- Have eye contact, but do not stare. Keeping too much eye contact might creep people out. Giving no eye contact might make you seem insecure.
- Relax your shoulders. When you feel tense, it easily winds up as tension in your shoulders.
- Nod when they are talking.
- Lean, but not too much—if you want to show that you are interested in what someone is saying, lean towards the person talking. If you want to show that you're confident in yourself and relaxed, lean back a bit. But don't lean in too much or you might seem

needy and desperate for some approval. Or lean back too much or you might seem arrogant and distant.

- Smile and laugh when someone says something funny. People will be a lot more inclined to listen to you if you seem to be a positive person. But do not be the first to laugh at your own jokes, it makes you seem nervous and needy.
- Use your hands more confidently—instead of fidgeting with your hands and scratching your face, use them to communicate what you are trying to say.

PITFALLS

Some gestures project a very positive message, while others do nothing but set a negative tone. Most people are totally oblivious to their own body language, so the discipline of controlling these gestures can be quite challenging. Most of them are reflexive in nature, automatically matching up to what our minds are thinking at any given moment. Nevertheless, with the right information and a little practice, we can train ourselves to overcome most of our negative body language habits.

Hack and Hack (2008) give us a comprehensive list of negative gestures to avoid. The following has been adapted:

- Holding objects in front of your body: a coffee cup, notebook, handbag, and so on. It indicates shyness and resistance, such that you are hiding behind the objects in an effort to separate yourself from others. Instead, carry objects at your side whenever possible.
- Checking the time or inspecting your fingernails: a strong sign of boredom.
- Picking lint off of your clothes: if you do, most people will assume that you disapprove of their ideas and/or feel uneasy about giving them an honest opinion.
- Stroking your chin while looking at someone: 'I'm judging you!' People may assume that you're making a judgemental decision about them.
- Narrowing your eyes: it gives someone the impression that you do not like them (or their ideas).
- Standing too close: this just makes people feel uncomfortable. Most people consider the 4 square feet of space immediately surrounding their body to be personal space. Cross this invisible boundary with good friends and intimate mates only.
- Looking down while in the presence of others usually indicates disinterest. Sometimes it is even interpreted as a casual sign of arrogance. Always look straight ahead and make eye contact when you see someone you know.
- Touching your face during a conversation: face touching, especially on the nose, is commonly interpreted as an indication of deception. Also, covering up the mouth is

a common gesture people make when they are lying. Always keep your hands away from your face when you are speaking.

- Faking a smile: Another sign of deception commonly seen on the face of a fraud. Do not force yourself to smile.
- Leaning away from someone you like: a sign of being bored and disinterested. Some people may also interpret it to mean: 'I don't like you.' People typically lean towards people they like and away from people they dislike.
- Resting hands behind the head or on the hips: usually interpreted as a sign of superiority or bigheadedness. Only use these gestures when you are in the presence of close friends.
- Not directly facing the person you're speaking to: this indicates a certain level of discomfort or a lack of interest. Face directly forward during a conversation to give off the impression that you are truly interested in what the other person is saying.
- Crossing your arms: a sign of defensive resistance. Some people may also interpret it as a sign of egotism. Always try to keep your arms open and at your sides.
- Displaying a sluggish posture: when you are in an environment bustling with people, your posture becomes an immediate tell-tale sign of your confidence and composure. Your stance literally makes a stand for you, delivering a clear message about how you should be treated. It can make a huge difference in the way strangers respond to you. Place your feet a comfortable distance apart, keep your shoulders pulled back, head up, and greet people with direct eye contact and a firm handshake.
- Scratching at the backside of your head and neck: a typical sign of doubt and uncertainty. It can also be interpreted as an indication of lying. Try to keep your hands away from your head when you're communicating with others.
- Messing with the collar of your shirt: it screams: 'I feel horribly uncomfortable and/or nervous!' Once again, keep track of your hands. Don't fidget.
- Increasing your rate of blinking: a clear sign of anxiety. Be cognizant of your blinking habits when you are nervous, especially if someone is looking at you from a close proximity.
- Slouching your shoulders indicates low self-esteem. People associate perked up shoulders with strong self-confidence. Always pull your shoulders back. Not only will you look more confident, you will feel more confident as well.
- Standing with your hands crossed over our genitals: this casual posture almost guarantees that you'll lose a little respect before you even have the chance to speak a single word. People feeling nervous or unsure of themselves will unconsciously take a guarded stance. This stance pushes your shoulders forward and makes your entire body look smaller and weaker.
- Propping up your head with your hands: 'I'm getting bored!' Never prop up your head with your elbows and hands during a conversation.

- Wiping sweaty hands onto your clothes: a sign of frantic nervousness. If your hands are sweating, just let them sweat. Take a few deep breaths and try to relax.
- Sitting on the edge of your chair: a clear indication of being mentally and physically uncomfortable. It is apprehensive stances that will make others around you feel uncomfortable as well. Keep your rear end firmly planted on the surface of the seat. When you lean forward, use your back without moving your bottom.
- Foot and finger tapping usually indicates stress, impatience, or boredom. Monitor your habits and practice keeping your limbs at rest.
- Using your hands to fidget with small objects: a pen, paper ball, and so on. This is another sign of anxiety. It can also be interpreted as a lack of preparedness. It is always best to keep your hands comfortably at rest when you're in the presence of others.
- Repeatedly shifting body weight from foot to foot: this is another gesture that usually indicates mental and physical discomfort. People may also see this and assume that you are ready to abandon the conversation, especially if you are not directly facing them.

VIBRATIONS

Positive Vibes

- Head up and looking straight suggests a confident and positive approach.
- Sitting straight yet comfortably implies an attentive and self-assured personality.
- Looking straight without glaring or staring shows you are serious and attentive.
- Straight shoulders, arms resting on sides or on your thighs, legs uncrossed, pointing at the speaker show energy attentiveness and confidence.
- Well-combed hair, if long tied or combed neatly, implies neatness and a tidy approach.

Negative Vibes

- Feet dragging implies lazy attitude, unlikely to impress.
- Head down suggests timidity, again not a positive impression.
- Drooping shoulders could imply lethargy and weariness.
- Clumsy posture implies one is unfit for the important jobs.
- Weak handshake (in context) implies meek and ineffectual personality.
- Shifty eyes suggest nervousness or dishonesty.
- Arms crossed on chest suggest a defensive stance.

- Feet crossed while standing: concealing something or defensive.
- Fidgeting implies nervousness or lack of interest.
- Hands in pockets imply you have something to hide.

INTERACTING WITH DIFFICULT PEOPLE

Every now and then we come across people whom we find difficult to deal with because heir attitudes, actions, non-verbal behaviours are in conflict with our own attitudes, actions, and non-verbal behaviours. For example:

- Those who are dominant
- Those who are submissive
- Those who are angry
- Those who are confused or indecisive

Amos (2010) offers the following ways to use body language when interacting with difficult people:

Those who are dominant: Avoid body language that is directly confrontational, such as facing off against each other, extended eye contact, abrupt or aggressive gestures, or crossing personal boundaries of space. These are only likely to make the other person feel challenged and lead to more behaviour that is dominant. This does not mean you should become submissive and give in to the dominance; rather, it means you should assert your own position in a way that is calm, rational, and confident.

Those who are submissive: Avoid body language that is overtly dominant, such as crossing into their personal space, standing over them, or otherwise taking a body position that puts them in an inferior position. A better approach is to remain assertive but not overpowering, using a neutral facial expression and open body position to encourage the other person to participate more fully. If, however, the other person is using submissive behaviour in a way that's deliberately manipulative, don't let yourself fall into the trap of 'rescuing' him or her. Maintain your sense of calm and keep your non-verbal cues neutral.

Those who are angry: Avoid body language that might aggravate the other person, such as pointing, clenching your jaw or fists, shaking your head, or the like. Most of the time the best approach is to let the person express the initial burst of anger, keeping a neutral facial expression and body position. After the initial burst, paraphrase the information you heard and work through the issue, all the while maintaining a calm and confident position.

However, if at any point you feel threatened or that you might be in personal danger, you should always take immediate and appropriate action to protect yourself and maintain your personal safety.

Those who are confused or indecisive: Avoid body language that appears impatient or pushy, such as extended eye contact, leaning in close, gestures that indicate frustration, and so on. These kinds of non-verbal cues are likely to create even more confusion or indecisiveness in the other person. If you truly need to conclude the interaction, try using an open body position and hand gestures to present two or three distinct choices and then ask for a decision. However, if you find yourself in a situation where the person's confusion or indecision presents a safety risk or other potential danger to you or anyone else, take decisive action to prevent injury or harm.

Remember, these are general guidelines for dealing with difficult people. You should always use your best judgement based on whatever specific situations you encounter.

ELEVATOR (LIFT) ETIQUETTE

A ride in an elevator ('lift' in India) usually lasts less than 30 seconds. Often it is the body language and etiquette of fellow passengers that can really push people's buttons, so to speak. For some, it is just a quick lift, but on some level, many people find the elevator to be one awkward and uncomfortable place—and not just claustrophobics. Driver (2007) highlights some areas where people breach the unwritten rules of elevator etiquette. Below is a summary.

Even on elevators, there are invisible physical boundaries to observe. Just like a head-nod, a smile, and a wave hello, space 'speaks'. The study of 'perception and use of space' with humans is called proxemics and it applies to us everywhere, especially in tight spaces—like in an elevator!

Upon entering the elevator, you should stand as close to a wall or corner as possible; this will help you and others distance yourselves from one another with a hearty buffer zone. When it comes to body language, you can reduce a spatial invasion if you eliminate large body movements, decrease eye contact, and lower your tone and pitch of voice.

The more people that enter the elevator, the more your body language should get smaller. If you are going to a high floor, it will save everyone from sighing and bumping into each other if you just stand in the back. And if you are on one of the lower floors, please stand towards the front.

If there are four people, each person should take a corner. If there are five or more people, each must face the door, get taller and thinner, let hands, pocketbooks, brief cases hang down in front of the body, and do not touch people unless overcrowding forces shoulders and upper arms to touch.

Generally, most people on an elevator are in self-talk mode; thinking about their day or perhaps planning for tomorrow. They tend to gaze at the ground, the button panel, the closed doors, or they may quietly look at something they are holding in their hands.

While avoiding visual contact is a means of avoiding interactions, women and men approach the issue of eye contact in this 4×4 boxed-in space differently. Men prefer to have no eye contact with anyone inside the elevator, while the ladies need to know who they will be sharing this small space with, so they'll give a quick glance and maybe even flash the giant of all gestures—a smile.

Also, the most common facial expression seen in an elevator is the 'non-expression', which is used by most of us to keep strangers at a distance. The blank stare is probably the only tool we have to maintain our 'private space'—it sends the message, 'Do Not Disturb'. For the most part, conversations in the elevator are generally not recommended. But if you are the type of person that likes to talk to strangers, then keep the topic simple and light.

PRESENTATION GESTURES

Kuhnke (2010) summarizes body language traits in the acronym PLATE, in the context of a presentation.

As food is delivered on 'plates', so is the attitude we project to our listener.

P – Posture. How we hold our bodies reflects our state of being. Our state will influence how the audience reacts to us. To create a strong, confident, and accessible presence, stretch with your hands pointed towards the ceiling. Hold this position for 10 seconds to lengthen your spine. Then stand with your feet hip-width apart and your weight equally balanced on each foot. You will now send out a visual image of confidence and authority.

L – Legs. Move with purpose. Bobbers and bouncers convey an image of uncertainty and look uncomfortable. Random movements distract from the message. Breathe into your abdomen and claim your space. You are speaking to your audience because you are the person best suited to do the job.

A – Arms. Gestures are a physical means of telling your story. They help both you and your audience remember your message. They add interest and variety to what you are saying and support the voice, helping to keep it lively and full of energy. Make sure your gestures are specific and illustrative.

T – Tension. It is common for a speaker to feel tense. Use that tension productively, as a means of extra energy. If you show your audience that you are feeling tense, they will feel tense too. To get rid of tension from your body, tighten each muscle group in your body, starting at your toes. Tighten, tighten, tighten! Then release. This exercise will calm your body and focus your voice.

E – Eyes. The eyes are the mirror of the soul. If you look at your audience, they will look at you. Maintain eye contact for approximately 60 per cent of your speaking time.

S – Smile. Smiling is inborn, instinctive, and universal. A natural, spontaneous smile elicits a smile in response. A fake smile is easy to spot and will be perceived as untrustworthy and false. It is not natural to smile all the time, so don't feel compelled to do so! There are times when smiling is inappropriate and a stern or solemn is more appropriate and effective. As long as your smile is genuine, it is a good device to use at the beginning and end of your meeting or presentation.

CONCLUDING TEST

Provided below are several situations in which one has to deal with different people. What 'statement' do you think they are making through their non-verbal behaviour? There is a choice of four statements. Pick out the one that identifies the particular behaviour. (Answers are provided at the end.)

1. During a lecture period, the teacher has asked you to read out the assignment you have prepared. While you are speaking, you notice one of your classmates is busy reading a letter, ignoring your presentation.

    (a) I am a competitive person.
    (b) I think I am better than you.
    (c) I am a victim.
    (d) I have more important things to do than listen to you.

2. You have just paid for some purchases at a shop, and the cashier throws your change on the counter without looking at you.

    (a) I have a lot of emotional problems.
    (b) I have the upper hand in this situation.
    (c) I could never possibly have anything in common with you.
    (d) I do not trust you at all.

3. You have applied for a course in a large institution. As you are about to be interviewed by the organizer, he closes his office door, clears his desk, and shuts off his phone.

(a) I am a considerate, thoughtful person who believes people deserve my respect.

(b) I am a very special person.

(c) I do not like anybody.

(d) I like people and I am very curious about their attitudes.

4. You are sitting at a table with a friend who periodically takes a deep sigh and then commences to tap the fingers of his left hand on the table without ever saying a word.

(a) I am so depressed because everything in life is so routine.

(b) I am going to show you how powerful I am.

(c) I am nice to people if I have time.

(d) I am a very special person.

5. You have moved to a new residence. Often, when you walk out of your building you pass someone whom you do not know but have seen several times in the past month. You look at the person directly and smile with your lips closed to appear friendly and non-threatening. The person immediately looks away from you.

(a) I have low self-esteem.

(b) I am miserable and want you to know how miserable I am.

(c) I am very aggressive in all that I do.

(d) I think there is no point in being polite and courteous.

6. You are at an important meeting and the person sitting next to you continually taps his pen on the table at which you are seated.

(a) I will listen to your complaint, but do not expect me to fix anything.

(b) I consider such meetings beneath me.

(c) I have a chip on my shoulder.

(d) I do not like people to waste my time.

7. You are at a conference in which about 50 people are present. However, the speaker rarely looks at the left side of the room, where 25 people are seated, during his 15-minute speech.

(a) I am used to be treated like dirt, so do not waste your time on me.

(b) I dare you to call attention to my rude behaviour.

(c) I do not pay much attention to responding to the feelings of everyone I meet.

(b) I have a chip on my shoulder.

8. You are at a travel agent's office booking counter for an air ticket for your mother who is entitled to the senior citizen's concession. You mother, who is quite an alert and responsive person, is there beside you, but the ticket agent directs all questions about your mother's flight to you; she never once acknowledges your mother with eye contact.

    (a) I am very aggressive in all that I do.

    (b) I am nice to people if I have time.

    (c) I have the upper hand in this situation.

    (d) I do not pay much attention to responding to the feelings of everyone I meet.

9. You go to the boss' office where you have an appointment. The receptionist is busy typing. She does not say anything to you for over a minute. Then, without looking up at you, she simply says, 'Yes?'

    (a) I am miserable and want you to know how miserable I am.

    (b) I am going to show you how powerful I am.

    (c) I think there is no point in being polite and courteous.

    (d) I am a competitive person.

ANSWERS

1. d, 2. a, 3. a, 4. a, 5. a, 6. d, 7. c, 8. d, 9. b.

References

Amos, J. A. (2010). 'Violation of Your Personal Space', http://www.bodylanguageexpert.co.uk/Violation OfPersonalSpace.html (accessed on 1 July 2010).

Anderson, P. (1997). 'Cue of Culture: The Basics of Intercultural Differences in Nonverbal Communications', in Larry A. Samovar and Richard E. Porter (eds), *Intercultural Communication: A Reader*, 8th edn, Wadworth, USA.

Andersen, P. A., Hecht, M. L., Hoobler, G. D., and Smallwood, M. (2002). 'Nonverbal Communication across Cultures', in W. B. Gundykunst and B. Moody (eds), *Handbook of International and Intercultural Communication*, SAGE Publications, Thousand Oaks, CA.

APA (American Psychological Association). (1996). *Journal of Personality and Social Psychology*, Vol. 70, No. 2, pp. 205–18, American Psychological Association, Inc.

Argyle, M. (1967). *Bodily Communications*, Methuen, New York.

——. (1975). *Bodily Communications*, 2nd ed., Methuen, New York.

——. (1983). *The Psychology of Interpersonal Behaviour*, Pelican, New York.

——. (1988). *Bodily Communication*, 2nd ed., Methuen, New York.

——. (1992). *The Social Psychology of Everyday Life*, Routledge, London.

Armstrong, N. and Wagner, M. (2003). *Field Guide to Gestures: How to Identify and Interpret Virtually Every Gesture Known to Man*, Quirk Books, Philadelphia.

Athos, A. G. (1969). *Communication: The Use of Time, Space, and Things*, Harvard Business School, Boston.

Bacon, A. M. (1875). *A Manual of Gestures*, Griggs, Chicago.

Bacri, E. (1992). 'A Laughing Matter', *Reader's Digest*, September.

Bandler, R. and Grinder, J. (1979). *Frogs into Princes*, Real People Press, Moab, Utah.

Beattie, G. (1983). *Talk: An Analysis of Speech and Non-verbal Behaviour in Conversation*, Open University Press, Milton Keynes.

Beier, E. G. (1974). *Psychology Today*, October.

Birdwhistell, R. L. (1952). *Introduction to Kinesics*, Foreign Service Institute, Louisville, KY.

——. (1955). 'Do Gestures Speak Louder than Words?', *Collier's*, 4 March, pp. 56–57.

——. (1971). *Kinesics and Context*, Allen Lane, London.

Bjorseth, L. D. (2007). 'Show Confidence Through Your Walk and Posture', *Communicate and Network Your Way to More Success!*, Vol. 4, No. 5, November, Duoforce Enterprise, Inc, Lisle, IL.

——. (2010). 'Test Your People-reading Skills', in the blog Lillian Communicates, posted on 22 August 2010, http://www.lilliancommunicates.com/?tag=body-language

Brannigan, C. and Humphries, D. (1972). 'Human Non-verbal Behaviour, A Means of Communication', in N. G. Blurton-Jones (ed.), *Ethological Studies of Child Behaviour*, Cambridge University Press, Cambridge.

Brown, P. and Levinson, S. (1987). *Politeness: Some Universals in Language Usage*, Cambridge University Press, Cambridge.

British Broadcasting Corporation (BBC). (2003). 'Sleep Position Gives Personality Clue', http://news.bbc.co.uk/2/hi/health/3112170.stm (accessed on 14 February 2011).

British Broadcasting Corporation (BBC). (2010a). 'Edited Guide Entry, Body Language', created: 29 September 2010, http://www.bbc.co.uk/dna/h2g2/A427277 (accessed on 14 February 2011).

——. (2010b). 'Science and the Human Mind: Spot The Fake Smile', http://www.bbc.co.uk/science/humanbody/mind/surveys/smiles/ (accessed on 14 February 2011).

Brown, N. W. (2006). *Coping With Infuriating, Mean, Critical People—The Destructive Narcissistic Pattern*, Praeger, Westport, Conn.

Bulwer, John. (2003). *Chirologia or the Natural Language of the Hand*, Kessinger Publishing, Kila, MT.

Businessballs. (2011). http://www.businessballs.com/body-language.htm (accessed on 22 February 2011).

Chandragiri, J. (2010). 'Worldsmart: Gestures around the World', Geoleadership, www.globalbusinessleadership.com (accessed on 17 January 2011).

Chapman, A. (2010). 'Body Language', http://www.businessballs.com/body-language.htm (accessed on 23 February 2011).

Collett, P. (2003). *The Book of Tells: From the Bedroom to the Boardroom—How to Read Other People*, HarperCollins, Ltd, Ontario.

Condon, W. and Ogston, W. (1966). 'Sound Film Analysis of Normal and Pathological Behavior Patterns', *Journal of Nervous and Mental Disease*, Vol. 143, No. 4.

Cooke, J. (1959). 'A Few Gestures Encountered in a Virtually Gestureless Society', *Western Folklore*, Vol. 18, No. 3, pp. 233–37. doi:10.2307/1497708.Jean. (July 1959).

Darwin, C. (1965). *The Expression of Emotions in Man and Animals*, University of Chicago Press, Chicago.

Deasey, L. (2006). 'Night Moves', *The Sunday Telegraph*, 29 October, Australia.

Driver, J., (2007). *'The Unwritten Rules of Elevator Etiquette'*, TODAY.com, http://today.msnbc.msn.com/id/20335786/ns/today-relationships/t/unwritten-rules-elevator-etiquette/ (accessed on 18 August 2007).

Dyer, R. (1992). 'Don't Look Now: The Male Pin-up', in Caughie et al. (eds), *The Sexual Subject: A Screen Reader in Sexuality*, Routledge, London.

Eakins, B. W. and Eakins, R. G. (1978). *Sex Differences in Human Communication*, Houghton Mifflin, Boston.

Edberg, Henrik. (2008). 'Improve Your Body Language to Improve Your Likeability', http://www.isnare.com/?aid=128567&ca=Self+Help (accessed on 20 June 2010).

Eibl-Eibesfeldt, I. (1970). *Ethology: The Biology of Behavior*, Holt, Rinehart, and Winston, San Francisco.

——. (1973). 'The Expressive Behaviour of the Deaf-and-Blind-Born', in Mario von Cranach and Ian Vine (eds), *Social Communication and Movement*, European Monographs in Social Psychology 4, Academic Press, New York.

——. (1989). *Human Ethology*, Aldine de Gruyter, New York.

Ekman, P. (1979). 'About Brows—Emotional and Conversational Signals', in M. von Cranach, K. Foppa, W. Lepenies, and D. Ploog (eds), *Human Ethology*, Cambridge: Cambridge University Press, pp. 169–248.

——. (1982). *Emotion in the Human Face*, 2nd ed., Cambridge University Press, Cambridge.

——. (1994). *The Nature of Emotion: Fundamental Questions*, Oxford University Press, New York.

——. (2001). *Telling Lies*, W. W. Norton, New York.

——. (2010). Wikipedia, the free encyclopedia, Paul Ekman, http://en.wikipedia.org/wiki/Paul_Ekman (accessed on 29 June 2010).

Ekman, P. and Friesen, W. (1969). 'Nonverbal Leakage and Clues to Deception'. *Psychiatry*, Vol. 32.

———. (1971). 'Constants across Cultures in the Face and Emotion', *Journal of Personality and Social Psychology*, Vol. 17, No. 2, pp. 124–29.

———. (1975). *Unmasking the Face: A Guide to Recognizing Emotions From Facial Expressions*, Prentice-Hall, New York.

Ekman, P., Friesen, W., and Ellsworth P. (1972). *Emotions in the Human Face: Guidelines for Research and an Integration of Findings*, Pergamon Press, New York.

Ekman, P., Friesen, W., and Tomkins, S. (1971). 'Facial Affect Scoring Technique: A First Validity Study', *Semiotica*, Vol. 3.

Emerson, R. W. (1860). *The Conduct of Life, A Collection of Essays*. http://www.emersoncentral.com/conduct. htm

Fast, J. (1970). *Body Language*, M. Evan & Co., Philadelphia.

Feldman, S. (1969). *Mannerisms of Speech and Gestures in Everyday Life*, International Universities Press, New York.

Foot, H. (1986). 'Humor and Laughter', in O. Hargie (ed.), *The Handbook of Communication Skills* (2nd ed.), Routledge, London.

Fridlund, A. (1994). *Human Facial Expression, An Evolutionary View*, Academic Press, San Diego.

Givens, D. (1999). *The Nonverbal Dictionary of Gestures, Signs, and Body Language Cues*, Center for Nonverbal studies, Spokane, CA.

Goffman, E. (1969). *Behavior in Public Places: Notes on the Social Organization of Gatherings*, The Free Press, New York.

Haas, H. (1970). *The Human Animal*, G. P. Putnam and Sons, New York.

Hack, M. and Hack, A. (2008). '25 Acts of Body Language to Avoid', in the Marc and Angel Hack blog, posted on 7 July 2008, http://www.marcandangel.com/2008/07/07/25-acts-of-body-language-to-avoid/ (accessed on 27 May 2010).

Haggard, E. A. and Isaacs, K. S. (1966). 'Micromomentary Facial Expressions as Indicators of Ego Mechanisms in Psychotherapy', in L. A. Cottschalk and A. H. Auerbach (eds), *Methods of Research in Psychotherapy*. Appleton-Century-Crofts, New York.

Haidt, J. and Keltner D. (1999). 'Culture and Facial Expression: Open-ended Methods Find More Expressions and a Gradient of Recognition, Cognition and Emotion', *Journal of Social Psychology* (Psychology Press Ltd, Berkley), Vol. 13, No. 3, pp. 225–66.

Hall, E. (1959). *The Silent Language*, Doubleday and Co., New York.

———. (1969). *The Hidden Dimension*, Doubleday and Co., New York.

———. (1979). 'Learning the Arabs' Silent Language', an interview, *Psychology Today*, August.

Hall, E. and Hall, M. (1990). *Understanding Cultural Differences: Germans, French and Americans*. Intercultural Press, Yarmouth, ME.

Hartland, D. and Tosh, C. (2001). *Guide to Body Language*, Caxton Publishing Ltd, London.

Haviland, J. B. (2005). 'Gesture as Cultural and Linguistic Practice', in A. Sujoldzic (ed.), *Linguistic Anthropology, Encyclopaedia of Life Support Systems* (EOLSS), EOLSS Publishers, Oxford.

Hess, E. (1975). *The Tell-Tale Eye*, Van Nostrand R., New York.

Hill, J. H. (1977). 'Apes, Wolves, Birds, and Humans: Toward a Comparative Foundation for a Functional Theory of Language Evolution', *Sign Language Studies*, Vol. 14, pp. 21–58.

Hirsch, A. R. and Wolf, C. J. (1999). 'A Case Example Utilizing Practical Methods for Detecting Mendacity'. AMA Annual Meeting, Washington, DC, NR505: 208.

Honey, P. (1988). *Face To Face*, Gower Pub. Co., England.

Izard, C. (1994). 'Innate and Universal Facial Expressions: Evidence from Developmental and Cross-cultural Research', *Psychological Bulletin*, Vol. 115, pp. 288–99.

Izard, C. and Haynes, E. (1988). 'On the Form and Universality of the Contempt Expression', *Motivation and Emotion*, Vol. 12, No. 1, pp. 1–16.

James, J. (2009). *The Body Language Rules*, Sourcebooks Inc., Illinois.

James, W. (1890). *The Principles of Psychology*, H. Holt and Company, New York.

Jones, E. L. and Gerard, H. B. (1967). *Foundations of Social Psychology*, John Wiley, New York.

Jones, E. L. and Yarbrough, E. A. (1985). 'A Naturalistic Study of the Meanings of Touch', *Communication Monographs*, Vol. 52, pp. 19–56.

Kendon, A. (1983). 'Gesture and Speech: How They Interact', in J. M. Wiemann and R. P. Harrison (eds), *Nonverbal Interaction*, SAGE Publications, California.

Knapp, M. L. (1972). *Nonverbal Communication in Human Interaction*, Reinhart and Winston Inc., New York.

Knapp, M. L. and Hall, J. A. (2002). *Nonverbal Communication in Human Interaction*, Thomson Learning Communication, Crawfordsville, IN.

Kuhnke, E. (2010). *Body Language for Dummies*, Kuhnke Communications, Oxon, UK.

Lange, A. J. and Jakubowski, P. (1976). *Responsible Assertive Behaviour*, Research Press, USA.

Lewis, B. and Pucelik, F. (1990). *Magic of NLP Demystified*, Metamorphous Press, Oregon.

Marcos, L. R. (1973). 'The Emotional Correlates of Smiling and Laughter', *The American Journal of Psychoanalysis*, Vol. 36, No. 1.

Malandro, L. A., Barker, L. L., and Barker, D. A. (1989). *Nonverbal Communication*, 2nd ed., Addison-Wesley, Reading, MA.

Masson, J. L. and Patwardhan, M. V. (1970). 2 Vols, 'Aesthetic Rapture: The Rasaadhyaya of the Natya Shastra', Deccan College, Post Graduate and Research Institute, Poona.

McGrain, C. R. (1999). 'What Does Your Body Say When You Are Negotiating?', *Insight Magazine* (December 1998–January 1999), CPA Society, Illinois.

McGrew, W. C. (1972). 'Aspects of Social Development in Nursery School Children with Emphasis on Introduction to the Group', in N. G. Blurton Jones (ed.), *Ethological Studies of Child Behaviour*, pp. 129–56, University Press, Cambridge.

McNeill, D. (1992). *Hand and Mind: What Gestures Reveal About Thought*, University of Chicago Press, Chicago.

Mehrabian, A. (1968). 'Communication without Words', *Psychology Today*, Vol. 2, No. 4.

——. (1971). *Silent Messages: Implicit Communication of Emotions and Attributes*, 2nd ed., Wadsworth, Belmont, CA.

Menon, U. and Shweder, R. A. (1994). 'Kali's Tongue: Cultural Psychology, Cultural Consensus and the Meaning of 'shame' in Orissa, India', in H. Markus and S. Kitayama (eds), *Culture and the Emotions*, American Psychological Association, Washington DC.

Meyrowitz, J. (1985). *No sense of place: The Impact of Electronic Media on Social Behavior*, Oxford University Press, New York.

Morris, D. (1967). *The Naked Ape*, Cape, London.

——. (1977). *Manwatching: A Field Guide to Human Behaviour*, Triad/Panther, St Albans.

Morris, D. (1994). *Bodytalk: The Meaning of Human Gestures*, Crown Publishers, New York.

Nambiar, A. K. (1979). *NAMASTE its Philosophy and Significance in Indian Culture*, Spiritual India Publishing House, New Delhi.

Navarro, J. (2008). *What Every Body is Saying: An Ex-FBI Agent's Guide to Speed—Reading People*, HarperCollins, New York.

Navarro, J. and Poynter, T. S. (2010). *Louder Than Words*, HarperCollins, New York.

Nielsen, G. (1968). *Studies in Self Confrontation*, Howard Allan, USA.

Nierenberg, G. and Calero, H. (1975). *How to Read a Person like a Book*, Pocket Books, New York.

Ortega y Gasset. (1957). *Man and People*, W.W. Norton and Co., New York.

O'Sullivan, T., Hartley, J., Saunders, D., Montgomery, M., and Fiske, J. (1994). *Key Concepts in Communication and Cultural Studies*, Routledge, London.

Papousek, H. and Papousek, M. (1977). 'Mothering and the Cognitive Head Start: Psychobiological Considerations', in H. R. Schaffer (ed.), *Studies in Mother Infant Interaction*, Academic Press, London.

Paumgarten, N. (2005). 'Whatever', *New Yorker*, retrieved 16 March 2010, http://www.newyorker.com/archive/2005/07/11/050711ta_talk_paumgarten

Pease, A. (1993). *Body Language*, Sudha Publications, New Delhi.

Rank, J. (2011). 'Science Clarified, Real-Life Biology, Vol 3—Earth Science Vol 1, Behavior—How It Works', http://www.scienceclarified.com/everyday/Real-Life-Biology-Vol-3-Earth-Science-Vol-1/Behavior-How-it-works.html#ixzz17E2WWVsJ (downloaded on 18 May 2012).

Reiman, T. (2010). *The Yes Factor: Get What You Want. Say What You Mean, The Secrets of Persuasive Communication*, Penguin Group, Hudson Street Press, USA.

Roberts, A. (2007). *Helping Children to be Competent Learners*, Routledge, London.

Roberts, G. D. (2004). *Shantaram*, Little, Brown and Co., Great Britain.

Rozelle, R. M., Druckmann, D., and Baxter, J. C. (1986). 'Communication Skills', in O. Hargie (ed.), *A Handbook of Communication Skills*, Croom Helm, London.

Russell, J. A. (1994). 'Is There Universal Recognition of Emotion from Facial Expression? A Review of the Cross-cultural Studies', *Psychological Bulletin*, Vol. 115, pp. 102–41.

Scheflen, A. (1972). *Body Language and the Social Order*, Prentice-Hall, New Jersey.

———. (1973). *How Behavior Means*, Gordon and Breach, New York.

Schutz, W. C. (1958). *A Three-Dimensional Theory of Interpersonal Behaviour*, Holt, Rinehart & Winston, New York.

Sebba, M. and Tate, S. (1986). 'You Know What I Mean? Agreement Marking in British Black English', *Journal of Pragmatics*, Vol. 10, No. 16, pp. 3–72.

Shweder, R. A. (1993). 'The Cultural Psychology of the Emotions', in M. Lewis and J. Haviland (eds), *Handbook of Emotions*, pp. 417–31, Guilford Press, New York.

Siddons, H. (1822, reissued 1968). *Practical Illustration of Rhetorical Gestures and Action*, Benjamin Blom, Inc., New York.

Stern, D. and Bender, E. (1974). 'An Ethological Study of Children Approaching a Strange Adult: Sex Differences', in R. Friedman, R. Richart, and R. Vande Wiele (eds), *Sex Differences in Behavior*, pp. 233–58, John Wiley & Sons, NY.

Sussman, L. and Deep, S. (1989). *Comex, The Communication Experience in Human Relations*, S-W. Publ., USA. http://www.cultsock.org/index.php?page=nvc/nvc3.html (accessed on 20 June 2008).

Underwood, M. (2000). 'Facial Expressions', retrieved 16 January 2009 from http://www.cultsock.org/index. php?page=nvc/nvc3.html

Van Fleet, J. K. (1984). *Lifetime Conversation Guide*, Prentice-Hall Inc., New York.

Walker, M. (1982). 'Smooth Transitions in Conversational Turn-taking: Implications for Theory', *Journal of Psychology*, Vol. 110, pp. 31–37.

Walton, D. (1989). *Are You Communicating?*, McGraw-Hill, New York.

Watson, O. M. (1970). *Proxemic Behavior: A Cross Cultural Study*, Mouton, The Hague.

Westside Toastmasters. (n.d.). 'For Public Speaking and Leadership Education', *The Secret Signals of Cigarettes, Glasses and Make-Up, Book of Body Language*, Chapter 13, Santa Monica, California, http://westsidetoastmasters. com/resources/book_of_body_language/chap13.html (accessed on 18 May 2012).

Whiteside, R. L. (1975). *Face Language*, Pocket Books, New York.

Wikipedia (2011). 'Facepalm', retrieved 20 February 2011 from http://en.wikipedia.org/wiki/Facepalm

Wood, P. (2011). 'Sleep On It: What Your Sleep Positions Say about You', http://www.pattiwood.net/uploads/ sleep_position-%20individual.pdf (accessed on 17 March 2011).

Yngve, V. J. (1970). 'On Getting a Word in Edgewise', Papers from the 6th Regional Meeting of the Chicago Linguistic Society, Chicago Linguistic Society, Chicago.

Index

accompany and support speech, 4
Adam's apple jump, 65
adaptors, 14
anger, 40
anxiety, 17, 40, 4 1
anxiety laughter, 49
apologetic laughter, 49
arm positions, while sleeping, 119–122
arms, crossed or folded, 112–113
  gestures associated with
    reinforced arm-cross, 115–116
    standard arm-cross, 114–115
  interpretations of
    general observations, 113–114
    research, 113
  position of
    arm gripping, 117
    arms behind the back, 117–118
    one crossed arm, 116
    subtle arm crosses, 117

Bacon, Francis, 20
bedroom eyes, 80–81
behaviour, 17–18
Beier, E. G., 18–19
Birdwhistell, Ray, xiii, 6, 13
biting, 55
blank face, 51–52
blinking, 82–83
blushing, 13, 41–42
body language
  advantages of learning, 31–32
  approaches to the interpretation of
    congruence, 27
    context, 25–26

faking, 29
  inconsistency, 28–29
  micro-momentary signals, 29–30
  negative aspects of, 24–25
  over-congruence, 28
  positive aspects of, 25
dimensions of
  cultural variations, 23
  evolution, 20
  inborn, inherited, learned, 21–22
  status and age, 23
  universality, 22–23
functioning procedure, 4
main aspects of
  behaviour, 17–18
  body movements, 13–15
  emotions, 15–16
  gesture, 12–13
  moods, 18–19
  predictive, 19–20
  vibrations, 18
meaning of, 1–2
and paralanguage, 6–7
pitfalls of, 216–218
relation with paralinguistics, 7–8
similarities with verbal language, 6
as steps to success, 215–216
understanding of, 2–3
body movements, 13–15
  kinds of, 14
boredom, 40

calm, facial signal, 41
cheeks, body language related to, 60
  colour, 61

231

About the Author

Hedwig Lewis is an educationist and writer and has served as a lecturer and principal. He received the Rev T. A. Mathias Award for Innovative College Teachers from All India Association for Christian Higher Education (AIACHE), New Delhi, in 1993.

He has authored 30 books and his publications are on wide-ranging subjects that fall under several categories: spirituality, prayer, skill-building, biographies, inspirational, history, festive, and e-book. Some of his most noticeable works are *At Home With God* (1991), *Happiness Manufacturers* (2001), *Mirrors of Life* (1998), *Once Upon A Time* (2010), *Fun With Words* (1983), and *Gujarat Jesuits Remembered* (2002). Several of his books have been translated into Spanish and Lithuanian; some have been translated into different regional languages, including the previous edition of *Body Language*, which was translated into Malayalam.

Father Lewis is a Jesuit priest and can be reached at St Xavier's College, Ahmedabad (Gujarat, India). His website is http://joygift.tripod.com